D0540439

WAINWRIGHT'S
LAKELAND

Also by A. Wainwright and Derry Brabbs

FELLWALKING WITH WAINWRIGHT
WAINWRIGHT ON THE PENNINE WAY
WAINWRIGHT'S COAST TO COAST WALK
WAINWRIGHT IN SCOTLAND
WAINWRIGHT ON THE LAKELAND MOUNTAIN PASSES
WAINWRIGHT'S FAVOURITE LAKELAND MOUNTAINS
WAINWRIGHT IN THE VALLEYS OF LAKELAND

By A. Wainwright and Ed Geldard

WAINWRIGHT IN THE LIMESTONE DALES
WAINWRIGHT'S TOUR IN THE LAKE DISTRICT

Pictorial Guides to the Lakeland Fells

BOOK ONE: THE EASTERN FELLS
published 1955
BOOK TWO: THE FAR EASTERN FELLS
published 1957
BOOK THREE: THE CENTRAL FELLS
published 1958
BOOK FOUR: THE SOUTHERN FELLS
published 1960
BOOK FIVE: THE NORTHERN FELLS
published 1962
BOOK SIX: THE NORTH WESTERN FELLS
published 1964
BOOK SEVEN: THE WESTERN FELLS
published 1966

WAINWRIGHT'S LAKELAND

COMPRISING

FELLWALKING WITH WAINWRIGHT &
WAINWRIGHT ON THE LAKELAND MOUNTAIN PASSES

WITH PHOTOGRAPHS BY
DERRY BRABBS

MICHAEL JOSEPH
LONDON

This edition printed for Premier Books, Metnor Business Park, Hadrian Road,
Wallsend, Tyne and Wear, NE28 6HH
1995

Penguin Books Ltd, Registered Offices: Harmondsworth, Middlesex, England

Fellwalking with Wainwright first published by Michael Joseph 1984
Text and new line drawings © The Estate of the late A. Wainwright 1984
Original line drawings © Michael Joseph 1992
Photographs © Derry Brabbs 1984

Wainwright on the Lakeland Mountain Passes first published by Michael Joseph 1989
Text © The Estate of the late A. Wainwright 1989
Photographs © Derry Brabbs 1989
Maps © Michael Joseph 1989

First published in one volume as *Wainwright's Lakeland* 1994
© Michael Joseph 1994

All rights reserved.
Without limiting the rights under copyright
reserved above, no part of this publication may be
reproduced, stored in or introduced into a retrieval system,
or transmitted, in any form or by any means (electronic, mechanical,
photocopying, recording or otherwise) without the prior
written permission of both the copyright owner and
the above publisher of this book.

Printed and bound in Italy by L.E.G.O., Vicenza

A CIP catalogue record for this book is available from the British Library

ISBN 0 1408 7328 7

The moral right of the author has been asserted

FELLWALKING

WITH

WAINWRIGHT

18 of the author's favourite walks in Lakeland

CONTENTS

half-title page: *The Helvellyn Range from Fairfield*
page 5: *The North Western Fells from Hindscarth*
pages 6–7: *Derwentwater from Maiden Moor*

1 HIGH STREET AND HARTER FELL
FROM MARDALE HEAD   (7 MILES)

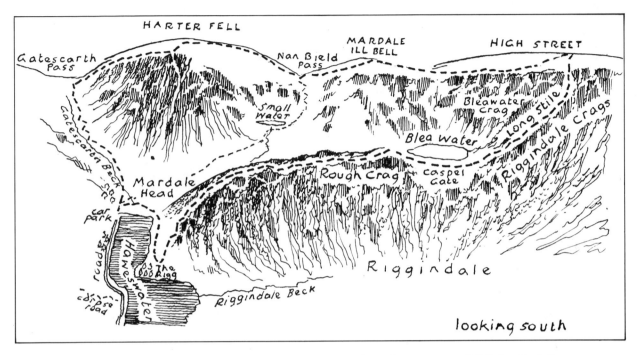

High Street, a fell named after a Roman road, is the culmination, at 2718 ft, of a lofty range rising from the valleys east of Windermere and extending for many miles at an elevation everywhere in excess of 2000 ft before finally descending to lower levels near the foot of Ullswater. This range forms a spine along the eastern fringe of Lakeland, providing a splendid full-day's march at a consistently high altitude, but is distant from the areas most favoured by fellwalkers and is comparatively unfrequented, appealing mainly to lovers of mountain solitude. Often I have been quite alone on High Street and seen no other person.

The late M. J. B. Baddeley, whose guidebook to the Lake District I revered more than the Bible in my early wanderings, described High Street as 'one of the least interesting of the Lake mountains'. One does not lightly question the judgment of so eminent an authority, but with this opinion I profoundly disagree.

High Street's few visitors are usually engaged on a traverse of the range and they find its broad summit merely a long grassy promenade with little of interest except the view westward. But if approached from Mardale Head, as described in this chapter, the ascent lacks nothing in beauty and exhilaration, the route following a rocky ridge, straight as an arrow, that leads directly to the top of the fell amidst mountain scenery of a very high order. I rate this a classic climb, a connoisseur's way to the summit.

(Opposite) Harter Fell from the old corpse road

I never go to Mardale Head now without thinking of a summer's day more than forty years ago when I walked over Gatescarth Pass and saw the valley of Mardale for the first time. It was a lovely vista. The floor of the dale was a fresh green strath shadowed by fine trees and deeply inurned between shaggy heights; beyond, receding in the distance, was Haweswater, then a natural lake. It was a peaceful scene, the seclusion of the valley being emphasised by its surround of rough mountains. Mardale was a bright jewel in a dark crown . . . I remember that day so well. Many early memories have faded, but not this one. Down in the valley, I went along the lane to the Dun Bull between walls splashed with lichens and draped with ivy. There was no welcome for me at the inn, which for centuries had been a meeting place of farmers and shepherds and the scene of many a festive occasion. It was empty, unoccupied. Around the corner was the small church amongst fine yews: it was a ghostly shell, the interior having been dismantled and the bodies in the graveyard exhumed for reburial elsewhere. The nearby vicarage and a few cottages were deserted and abandoned. This was the hamlet of Mardale Green, delightfully situated in the lee of a wooded hill, but now under sentence of death. Birds twittered in the trees and my footsteps echoed as I walked along the lane but there was no other sound, no sign of life. Even the sheep had gone. There were wild roses in fragrant hedgerows, foxgloves and harebells and wood anemones and primroses in the fields and under the trees, all cheerfully enjoying the warmth and sunshine; but there would be no other summers for them: they were doomed . . . Manchester Corporation had taken over the valley and built a great dam. The lake would be submerged beneath a new water level a hundred feet above. Already the impounded waters were creeping up the valley. Soon the hamlet of Mardale Green would be drowned: the church, the inn, the cottages, and the flowers, would all disappear, sunk without trace, and its history and traditions be forgotten. The flood was coming and it would fill the valley. Nature's plan for Mardale was being over-ruled. Manchester had another plan, to transform Mardale into a great Haweswater Reservoir. And no doubt be very proud of their achievement . . . I climbed out of the valley to Kidsty Pike. Looking back at Mardale Green from a distance, its buildings no longer seeming forlorn but cosily encompassed by trees and its silent pastures dappled by sunlight, I thought I had never seen a more beautiful picture. Nor a sadder one.

Haweswater today

When Manchester Corporation destroyed the sylvan beauty of Mardale by drowning it beneath the waters of a huge reservoir, they made a slight penance for their sins by constructing a tarmac road alongside to the head of the dale and providing space for cars to park at its terminus, a concession appreciated by fellwalking motorists who can thereby be quickly transported to the heart of a scene of mountain grandeur unsurpassed in the district. Harter Fell's wall of crags is dominant and seen intimately; High Street's wild recesses are more distant to the right and partly hidden by the ridge along which the ascent is to be made. Yes, there is an awesome grandeur hereabouts. Once there was a foreground of pastoral loveliness and shy charm, too, but that has gone, lost forever.

A much-trodden path leaves the car park but soon bifurcates at a wall corner, the left branch leading to Gatescarth Pass and the other heading half-right for Nan Bield, both popular walkers' routes. In fact, the path may be said to trifurcate; a third track, the one to be used for the ascent of High Street, goes sharp right around the head of the reservoir and crossing Mardale Beck. At this point, although early detours are generally not advisable when a long day's march lies ahead, a visit to the charming waterfall of Dodderwick Force can be made by walking upstream for a few minutes. Returning, the path is resumed alongside the reservoir and rises to a grassy col above the wooded promontory known as The Rigg.

Originally it was planned to build a rest-house or small hotel here to replace the Dun Bull, served by a new road along the west side of Haweswater, and the site would have been ideal for walkers coming down from the mountains, but other opinions prevailed and in the event the road was made along the east side and the new hotel sited midway, which is inconvenient for walkers who have to travel a further two miles on tarmac to reach it.

(Right) Dodderwick Force

From the col, the path doubles back at a higher level, climbing gradually, at first on grass and then amongst rocky outcrops, with a sharp zigzag to reach a wall on the crest of the ridge. Looking over the wall there is a splendid full-length view of Riggindale, now without a habitation, the former farm buildings at the mouth of this wild recess having also been casualties of the flood. From this viewpoint, the rocky escarpment of Rough Crag, above which the route continues, can be seen extending into the distance; around the head of the dale is a rim of crags, and on the far side rises the peaked summit of Kidsty Pike in profile.

Looking back over The Rigg and the reservoir to the fellside beyond, the zigzags of the old corpse road can be discerned, this being the way along which the dead of Mardale Green were carried, strapped to the backs of horses, for interment at Shap, eight hilly miles distant. This practice ceased in 1729 with the building of Mardale Church and the granting of a right of burial in a graveyard adjoining.

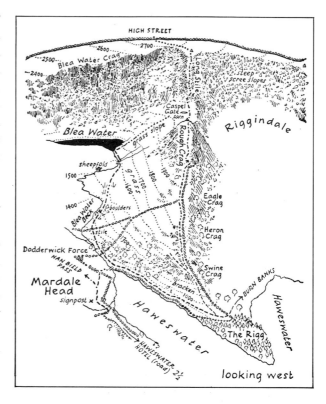

Riggindale

The path, still climbing, soon attains the top of the narrowing ridge and discloses a view to the south of the wild basin of Small Water below Nan Bield. Now at an easier gradient, it threads a way amongst outcrops, the scenery becoming more impressive as height is gained, and so reaches the summit cairn of Rough Crag where the route ahead is suddenly revealed. This is a place to halt and look around. Directly in front is the last stage of the ascent: across a grassy depression the rocky stairway of Long Stile rises steeply, leading unerringly up to the great curve of the skyline of High Street. To the left of Long Stile is the forbidding declivity of Bleawater Crag, the scene of a recent accident when a schoolboy fell to his death, and below it are the dark waters of Blea Water, better seen by a short stroll southwards. Behind is the imposing mass of Harter Fell, and to the immediate right the great gulf of Riggindale: from the edge of its cliffs an aerial view is obtained of this wild and lonely valley, now a sanctuary and grazing ground for deer and fell ponies.

I was standing here a few years ago, looking down into Riggindale, when a huge bird took off from the crags below and with two lazy flaps of its wings soared effortlessly across the valley and alighted on the topmost rocks of Kidsty Pike opposite, a flight accomplished in a few seconds only. There was no doubting its identity. It was a golden eagle . . . A decade ago, a pair of these magnificent birds made the crags around Mardale Head their home. Not for 150 years had the species been seen in Lakeland, but now they have returned, to the excited delight of ornithologists and all privileged to witness their soaring flight. To prevent disturbance, wardens of the Royal Society for the Protection of Birds kept a day and night guard within sight of the first nesting-places and the exact location was kept secret, their surveillance being relaxed as the birds became established in the district. There are many Eagle Crags in Lakeland, one of the buttresses of Rough Crag being so named, the inference being that in past centuries the district was a favourite habitat of eagles. It is a testimony to the wild seclusion of Mardale that it was chosen by the birds for their return. They are welcome. In a world fast becoming mainly concerned with material advantage, it is reassuring to have this evidence that nature conducts its affairs unchanged. The eagles are back, and it is the best thing that has happened to Mardale in the past fifty years.

High Street and Blea Water from Rough Crag

Long Stile and High Street from Rough Crag

Beyond the summit of Rough Crag, the ridge descends to a depression known as Caspel Gate. There is no gate, the name signifying a pass, but there is no pass either: a simple descent, left, on grass, leads down to Blea Water, but there is no way down into Riggindale on the right for ordinary walkers.

Ahead is Long Stile, a steep rocky spur of intimidating aspect, but there are no difficulties in its ascent and a final scree path emerges suddenly and abruptly on the plateau of High Street at a large cairn erected for the guidance of walkers descending by this route. The transition in scenery is immediate and complete: all is grass, there is not a rock in sight, and an easy five-minute perambulation brings one to a triangulation column alongside a crumbled wall.

This is the summit of High Street.

Although lacking in natural features of interest and having nothing to explore, the summit of High Street offers a splendid opportunity for rest, relaxation and quiet and undisturbed meditation: all is peaceful, and if the larks are singing overhead it is a blessed experience to be up here above the world and its worries. But only visitors of lively imagination will fully appreciate their surroundings. Any person so favoured may recline on the grass and witness, in his mind's eye, a pageant of history, for he has been preceded here by the ancient Britons who built their huts in the valleys around, by the Roman legions who marched across the top of the fell, by the Scots invaders who were repulsed on the Troutbeck slopes, and later by the dalesfolk who gathered on this lofty height for annual meetings and festivities.

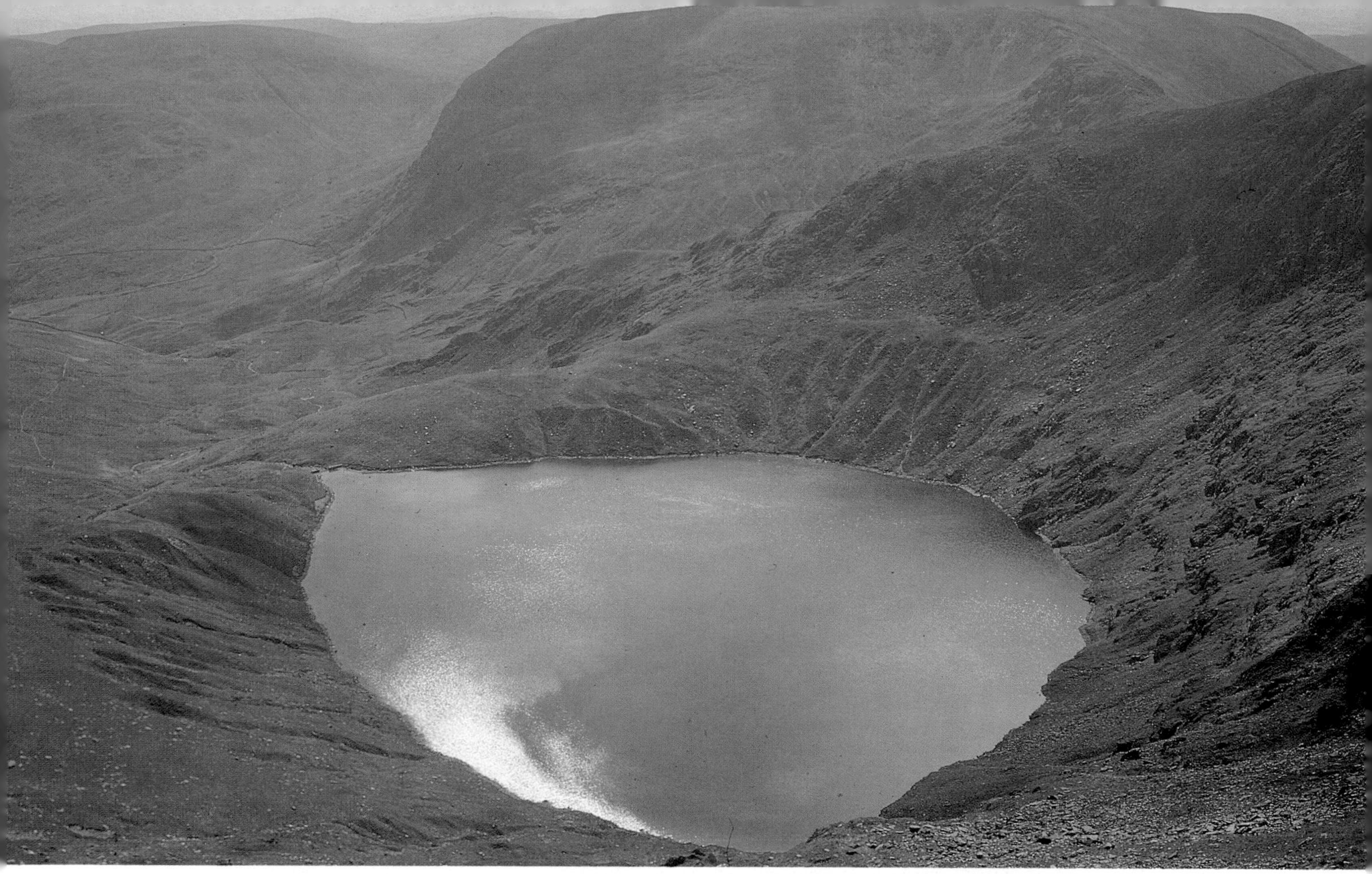

Harter Fell and Blea Water from High Street

If visibility is clear there is a wonderful panorama westwards where the mountains of Lakeland are seen arrayed in a tumult of peaks on the distant horizon.

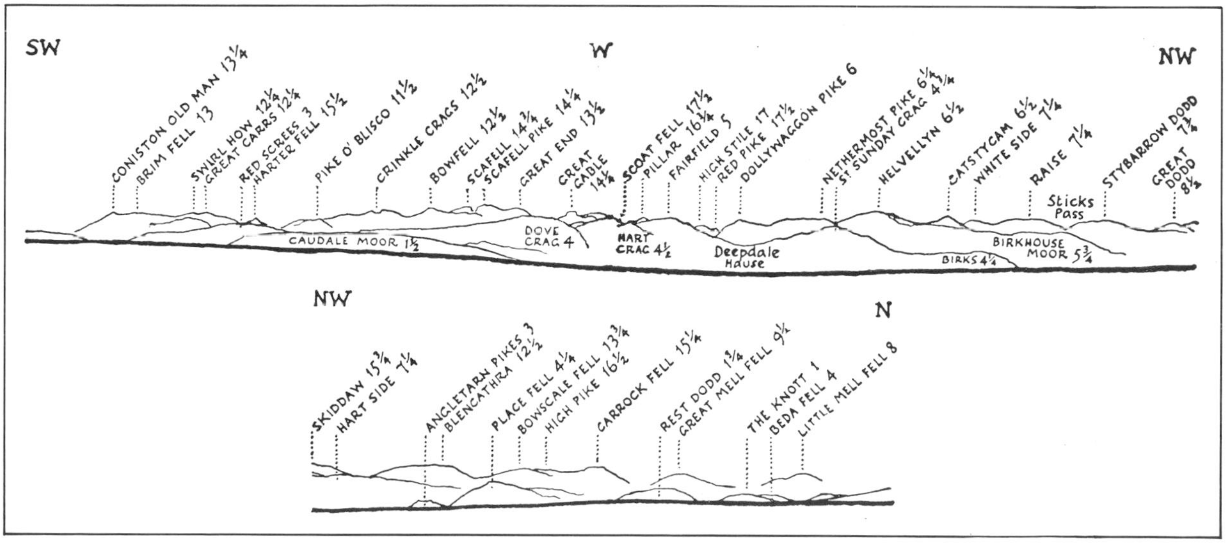

SW
W
NW
CONISTON OLD MAN 13¼
BRIM FELL 13
SWIRL HOW 12¼
GREAT CARRS 12¼
RED SCREES 3
HARTER FELL 15½
PIKE O' BLISCO 11½
CRINKLE CRAGS 12½
BOWFELL 12½
SCAFELL 14¾
SCAFELL PIKE 14¼
GREAT END 13½
GREAT GABLE 14¼
SCOAT FELL 17½
PILLAR 16¼
FAIRFIELD 5
HIGH STILE 17
RED PIKE 17½
DOLLYWAGGON PIKE 6
NETHERMOST PIKE 6¼
ST SUNDAY CRAG 4¾
HELVELLYN 6½
CATSTYCAM 6½
WHITE SIDE 7¼
RAISE 7¼
STYBARROW DODD 7¾
GREAT DODD 8½
Sticks Pass
CAUDALE MOOR 1½
DOVE CRAG 4
HART CRAG 4½
Deepdale Hause
BIRKS 4¼
BIRKHOUSE MOOR 5¾
NW
N
SKIDDAW 15¾
HART SIDE 7¼
ANGLETARN PIKES 3
BLENCATHRA 12½
PLACE FELL 4¼
BOWSCALE FELL 13¾
HIGH PIKE 16½
CARROCK FELL 15¼
REST DODD 1¾
GREAT MELL FELL 9½
THE KNOTT 1
BEDA FELL 4
LITTLE MELL FELL 8

By crossing the tumbled wall on the top of High Street and strolling westwards for a couple of minutes the Roman road is reached. This remarkable highway, still distinct and used as a footpath, is, at 2700 ft, the highest Roman road in the country. It linked the fort of Galava (Ambleside) and the fort of Brovacum (Brougham): a long day's march high above the valleys, its course being very direct, almost a beeline, proving the topographical knowledge of the surveyors and the ability of the engineers to master rough terrain – and the stamina and endurance of the legions who tramped this mountainous twenty-mile marathon.

The flat top of High Street is a smooth plateau of grass, a quiet and lonely wilderness, but in days gone by it was the venue of an annual meet of dalesfolk, always a great occasion of revelry and merriment, with horse-racing and wrestling and other sporting events, barrels of beer and hampers of food being carried up to provide an ample and memorable feast.

The Roman road on High Street

The tale is told that on one such occasion a dedicated hunter of foxes, a man named Dixon, upon seeing a fox run along the top and disappear over the edge of Bleawater Crag chased after it full tilt and fell hundreds of feet over the escarpment, coming to rest on the screes far below, where he raised himself, pointed in the direction the fox had gone and shouted excitedly to the horrified onlookers on the cliff top 'It's gone o'er theer, it's gone o'er theer!', and then dropped dead from his injuries, a victim of fanatical enthusiasm.

In those days the fell was better known as Racecourse Hill and appeared as such, in large lettering, on early Ordnance Survey maps. The name has been retained and still features on recent issues but in a much smaller type.

In early Victorian times the annual meet was transferred to the Dun Bull at Mardale Green, where the festivities continued apace on a day in the third week in November until brought to an end by the closure of the inn a hundred years later.

Blea Water

The next objective is the stony summit of Mardale Ill Bell, a mile south-east, and the walk to it, descending slightly across a pathless upland prairie, is easy and pleasant but featureless. A better plan is to go straight to the rim of Bleawater Crag and by following it along enjoy striking aerial views of Blea Water a thousand feet below, backed by Rough Crag and with the heights around Mardale in the further distance. Blea Water is large and circular and the deepest tarn in the district, reputedly occupying the crater of an extinct volcano although more likely to be of glacial origin.

At the wide depression between High Street and Mardale Ill Bell, a path will be found leading to the latter summit where there are two cairns, the southern one having a good view of the upper Kentmere valley. There is nothing here to suggest the presence of a line of crags nearby to the north, a fine vantage point for an appraisal of the topography of Mardale and its surroundings.

Haweswater and Small Water from Mardale Ill Bell

From the top of Mardale Ill Bell, at 2496 ft, a distinct and stony path goes down to Nan Bield Pass. I remember this as a thin and sketchy track, but obviously it has suffered much foot-traffic in recent years. On the descent, there occurs a glorious prospect of Haweswater and Small Water, in line one above the other: a picture no walkers with cameras can resist. Then, quite suddenly, after rounding a small hillock with striated rocks, Nan Bield is reached.

In my opinion, Nan Bield is the grandest of all Lakeland passes, being a narrow and steep-sided col, the climb to its top at 2100 ft being immediately followed by a sharp descent. There is a substantial wall-shelter on the summit. The pass was a trade route in the days of packhorses and down on the shore of Small Water are three stone refuges, roofed with slabs, built for the benefit of travellers overtaken by storms or darkness: these are low and entered by crawling, to the consternation of the many resident spiders.

The path on both sides of the pass is a series of zigzags to aid progress over the steep ground, but on the Mardale side it has become a river of stones, tiresome to descend, where thousands of impatient boots have scoured away the original well-graded path.

A descent to Mardale Head may be made from Nan Bield if time is pressing or the steep slope of Harter Fell directly opposite seems too much for tired limbs: the climb, however, is less formidable than it appears, the gradient soon easing into a gentle rise to the summit of Harter Fell.

Nan Bield Pass

The topmost cairn on Harter Fell, at 2539 ft, bristles with discarded iron fenceposts, forming a weird superstructure to the stones.

Every step now is downhill to Mardale Head and the path turns in that direction only to be halted on the edge of a tremendous crag. Here is disclosed the full length of Haweswater two thousand feet below: a most impressive view and the highlight of the whole journey.

(Right) The summit of Harter Fell

(Below) Haweswater from Harter Fell

There is palpably no way down the crag other than by falling over it, and the path turns sharply away south-east to skirt the declivity until advantage can be taken of a rock-free descent to the top of Gatescarth Pass in view below.

The path coming over Gatescarth Pass from Longsleddale is a joy to descend. This was also a trade route in days gone by, and the zigzags made centuries ago to ease the passage of laden ponies and driven sheep over steep ground have survived intact, unlike those on the Mardale side of Nan Bield and, having a grassy surface, are a pleasure to walk upon. I am a great enthusiast for zigzag paths: they have been engineered with care, always following the easiest line of ascent or descent. Habitual beeliners who cannot be bothered to go left and then right and left and right and commit the sacrilege of cutting corners, have not been active here and the path remains unspoilt. It is a lovely way down to Mardale Head and has the added bonus of a stream alongside, the first running water encountered since leaving Mardale Beck and a source of refreshment for thirsty throats and aching feet.

The descent of Gatescarth Pass

On the descent, the view forward opens up to reveal High Street and Rough Crag framed between the towering cliffs of Harter Fell, where the eagles on their return to Lakeland unsuccessfully established their first eyrie and then abandoned it for other sites, and the steep rise of Branstree on the right. After the last zigzag, a leisurely saunter down a gentle grass slope leads to Mardale Head and the waiting car.

2 THE KENTMERE ROUND
FROM KENTMERE VILLAGE (12 MILES)

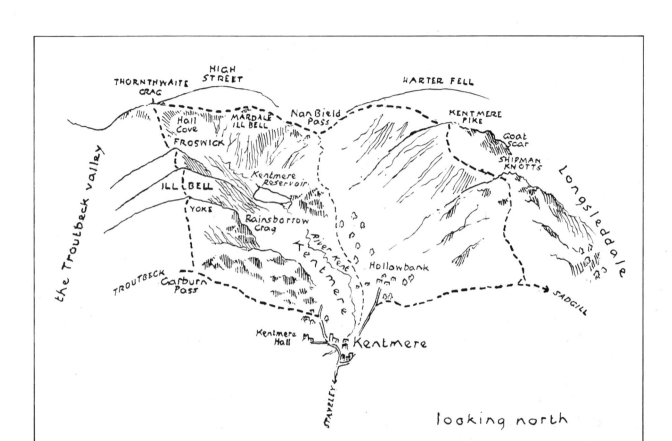

Many motorists approaching from the south regard their sighting of Windermere as the beginning of the Lake District and head eagerly along the A591 until it comes into view, unheeding or unaware of a side road signposted 'Kentmere' as they pass through the village of Staveley en route.

By doing so, they miss the loveliest of the lesser-known Lakeland valleys. Kentmere is delightful in all seasons, the lower reaches alongside the River Kent being especially charming. After three miles along its tree-lined road, in more open country, Kentmere Church is seen ahead on a small elevation. Only a few dwellings cluster round the church, but populated outposts nearby help to earn for Kentmere the status of a village although there is neither an inn nor a shop. The narrow road does not invite the parking of cars, but outside the church it widens to cater for the cars of worshippers and is taken advantage of by those who come to worship on the fells. This is the place, the only place, to leave a car.

(Opposite) The head of Kentmere

A short lane opposite the church leads to Kentmere Hall, the most interesting residence in the valley, with a ruinous 14th-century pele tower of four storeys linked by a staircase, and a vaulted cellar. The adjoining manor house, of rather later date, was originally the seat of the Gilpin family; a notable member was Bernard Gilpin, born here in 1517, who had a distinguished career in the Church and became known as 'The Apostle of the North'. The building is now occupied as a farmhouse.

Kentmere Hall

The first objective of the walk is Garburn Pass, to gain a foothold on the Ill Bell ridge, an imposing and effective barrier between the valleys of Troutbeck and Upper Kentmere. I have a long affection for this lofty ridge: it is in view from the windows of my home ten miles away, sometimes bathed in sunlight, sometimes sombre, often beheaded by low clouds and seemingly doubling its stature under a mantle of snow. It is a good barometer too, for when its outline dissolves in mist there will be rain in Kendal within an hour. Ill Bell is the dominant height on the ridge and has two satellites, Yoke and Froswick: all have very steep slopes above the Troutbeck Valley but these are bland and rock-free except where pierced by abandoned quarries. On the Kentmere side, the declivity is even steeper and breaks into precipitous crags. Travel along the crest, however, is simple and free from hazard; mist has no terrors but robs the walker of a superb view of Windermere and the western fells. A clear day is preferable for this expedition.

The walk starts from the church and goes along the road beyond until abreast of a cluster of houses and farm buildings on the left. The Garburn path passes between these and emerges into open pastures. In the first field on the left, and seen by looking over a wall, is a huge rock, apparently a craggy outcrop but in fact a tremendous boulder that has fallen from the heights above; it is one of the largest in the district. It is known as Badger Rock, or Brock Stone, and is a well-known local landmark although having little fame outside the valley. There are rock climbs of varying difficulty on its steep face.

(Right) Badger Rock
(Below) The new Kent Mere

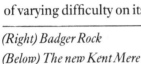

A little further along the path there is a downward view of Kentmere Hall amongst trees and, beyond it, a mile down the valley, is the unexpected sight of Kentmere's new lake. Until 1840 there had always been a shallow natural lake on the flat strath south of the church. It was known as Kent Mere and gave its name to the valley, but in that year it was drained to provide more land for cultivation: a purpose not entirely achieved, much of the reclaimed ground remaining too marshy for the plough and even for grazing. Analysis of the former bed of the lake in the present century revealed the presence of diatomaceous earth which, when extracted and processed, proved a valuable insulation material and led to the establishment of a works near the site. The draining of the lake was probably a factor in the erratic flow of the Kent thereafter, causing the promotion of an Act of Parliament authorising the construction of a reservoir at Kentmere Head to ensure regular supplies of water to the many woollen and corn mills down the river. In recent years, the supply of the diatomaceous earth became exhausted and the works closed; following the cessation of operations, a new lake, narrow but half a mile in length, came into being. This is now privately owned and intended as a nature reserve.

The path, everywhere pleasant, steepens as the top of Garburn Pass is approached below a line of crags up on the right, through which an adventurous scrambler may force a passage to gain the ridge above more directly – a deviation not worth the extra effort.

I once saw an adder basking in the sunshine on a large flat stone at the side of the path hereabouts, one of only two I have ever seen in the district, the other being near Tarn Hows. There was no ill feeling; indeed the beautiful creature winked at me as I passed. The day was peaceful, the sun warm, the stone comfortable. All was well with the world and life was good; besides, the prey didn't seem too wholesome, so why bother to attack? The adder resumed its siesta and I went on my way.

Garburn Pass is thought to be a section of an old road that cut across the south-eastern fringe of Lakeland, the path being of cart width, and this theory is supported by its naming as Garburn Road on the Troutbeck side, where it is a lane between walls, and by its obvious continuation as a broad track, crossing the low fells from Kentmere to Longsleddale, whence presumably it traversed Mosedale and descended Wet Sleddale to Shap.

The summit of Yoke looking towards Ill Bell

When the top of Garburn Pass is reached, a splendid prospect of the western fells unfolds suddenly and to good effect after the limited confines of the climb to it. Here the walk parts company with the path which continues down to Troutbeck, and turns sharp right along a rising moorland, marshy in places, and narrowing as height is gained. The first summit reached is Yoke, with a cairn at 2309 ft but little else of immediate interest: the ground eastwards, however, soon breaks into the tremendous Rainsborrow Crag, which falls precipitously into the depths of upper Kentmere, a refuge for foxes and a resort of rock-climbers, and the most imposing natural feature in the valley. The presence of this fearful crag is not suspected from the summit of Yoke, and attention is mainly focussed on the graceful cone of Ill Bell further along the ridge.

The summit of Ill Bell, 2476 ft, can be bypassed from Yoke along a level track across the western flank, but is of unusual interest and commands such fine views that it should certainly be visited. A multiplicity of cairns, three of long-standing, augmented by others that have sprouted in recent years, crowd the small top and suggest that the summit has some great significance in mountaineering history or is the apex of a major rock climb, but in fact has no such distinctions. Nevertheless, it is a splendid airy perch, and with the ground falling away out of sight all round, gives the impression of an island in the sky. It is a rough and stony top, with cairn-building material in profuse supply. Its special joy is a superb full-length view of Windermere.

From the northern edge, there is a graphic picture of the continuation of the route, looking over the next summit on the ridge, Froswick, to its culmination beyond at Thornthwaite Crag. It will be seen that the walk lies along the crest of a profound drop into the head of Kentmere far below, the effects of erosion and landslips being much in evidence, the eastern slope of Froswick in particular being a chaos of tumbled rocks and scree.

The summit of Ill Bell

A rough descent from the top of Ill Bell is followed by a gentle rise to the summit of Froswick, 2359 ft, which from some directions appears as a minor replica of Ill Bell. Froswick was the first mountain I saw at close quarters: I was toiling up Scots Rake out of upper Troutbeck, head down and watching where I was putting my feet, when I halted to look up and saw the peaked summit of Froswick overtopping the slope, much higher than I expected and seeming almost unattainable. The sight was quite awesome, even frightening: I had little appreciation of scale and perspective in those days. Upon ultimately gaining the ridge and looking back along it, Froswick was seen as an insignificant height dwarfed by Ill Bell behind it.

The obelisk on Thornthwaite Crag

From Froswick's small and neat summit there is a simple descent to a small depression on the ridge and a long rise to Thornthwaite Crag, the path being joined in the later stages of the climb by the Roman road coming up Scots Rake.

Thornthwaite Crag is easily identifiable from afar by its tall obelisk, a conspicuous landmark. This is a pillar of stones 14 ft high and commanding a view of four valleys, beautifully constructed and a fine monument to the skill of its unknown builder.

(Opposite) Thornthwaite Crag and Froswick from Ill Bell; (below) Looking back to Rainsborrow Crag

From the top of Thornthwaite Crag, 2569 ft, the walk changes direction, turning east and abandoning the Roman road which heads for High Street, now in full view, and following the edge of an escarpment with the wild amphitheatre of Hall Cove far below. Marshy patches along here are the source of the River Kent, developing into trickles that combine to form a well-defined stream, seen far below as it winds down the valley to Kentmere Reservoir. This considerable sheet of water will have been glimpsed from the Ill Bell ridge, but is here seen in full dimension.

In the mid-19th century, no fewer than fifteen mills on the banks of the Kent were drawing water from the river for driving their machinery, this being their only source of power, and often in times of drought production was halted or restricted. To avert this occasional failure of supplies, an Act of Parliament authorised the construction of reservoirs in the valleys of the Kent and its tributaries, the Sprint and the Mint, to be administered by commissioners (the mill owners) for the purpose of impounding water that could be released when needed to maintain an adequate flow in the rivers. Five reservoirs were proposed but only one was made: Kentmere Head Reservoir, as it was then named, completed in 1848. The others were never proceeded with because the cost proved greatly in excess of the estimate, and an alternative source of power – coal – became readily available as means of transport improved. The industrial use of the reservoir has ceased but, surprisingly, it has never been adapted to serve domestic needs.

The head of Kentmere from below Ill Bell

Kentmere from above Hall Cove

The walk continues eastwards to the top of Mardale Ill Bell, 2496 ft, the prefix being added to the name to distinguish it from the better known and more imposing fell of Ill Bell visited earlier in the walk. From the rugged outcrops south of the summit, there is a splendid retrospect of the whole ridge traversed from Garburn Pass, Rainsborrow Crag now being seen in profile and the steep and scarred declivities of Ill Bell and especially Froswick well displayed.

From Mardale Ill Bell, the route coincides for a time with that of Walk 1, a distinct path going down to Nan Bield Pass and affording views of Small Water and Haweswater. The good track crossing the pass, an old trade route, offers a quicker return to Kentmere if desired and is a delightful descent, at first down unspoilt zigzags and then across open moorland, reaching the valley by the side of a rocky bluff known as Tongue Scar, a long-established haunt of badgers, and proceeding thence to the village in charming surroundings. But for those determined to do the walk as planned, the steep-facing slope of Harter Fell must be tackled. The summit may be bypassed when easier ground is reached by heading south, contouring the fell until a ridge path is joined and the summit of Kentmere Pike reached.

The top of Kentmere Pike is uninteresting, the only feature being a triangulation column alongside a wall that continues without a break along a declining ridge to the Kentmere – Sadgill 'road' two miles south and is a perfect guide in misty conditions. Although the top of Kentmere Pike is merely a grassy sward, the ground eastwards soon drops away into the wild hollow of Settle Earth, an uncompromising downfall of crags and boulders and scree.

Alongside the wall, the path descends easily on grass. It was about here one Sunday midday that I came across a local shepherd and his dogs taking a rest. He seemed to want to talk and told me that he had spent the morning chasing foxes out of the Longsleddale crags and over into Mardale, his reason for this extraordinary behaviour being that he had heard of a fox-shoot planned to take place that afternoon around the head of Longsleddale. He was a supporter of fox-hunting with hounds which ensured a swift death for the foxes, but totally opposed to the shooting of them, this practice too often resulting only in wounding them, sometimes so badly that they could no longer search for food and died miserably from hunger and their injuries. A very ordinary man but with a concern for the welfare of wild creatures that raised him above most other men. 'They'll shoot nowt today!' he said with a satisfied smile.

(Above) Settle Earth from Goat Scar   *(Opposite) The valley of Longsleddale from Goat Scar*

Further down the ridge, Goat Scar juts out above Longsleddale and the short detour to its cairn is strongly recommended, this being a magnificent viewpoint. Longsleddale is seen aerially from the wild head of the valley to the lovely wooded lower reaches while, looking back, the grim fastnesses of Settle Earth can now be appreciated.

Now the ridge levels and there is a slight rise to the last summit of the day, Shipman Knotts, 1926 ft. This is a rocky upthrust of the ridge, with outcrops everywhere and very steep slopes falling to the woods of Sadgill. From its cairn, Goat Scar is seen in profile and across the deep trench of Longsleddale the cliffs of Buckbarrow Crag buttress the easy upper slopes of Tarn Crag where another obelisk stands on the skyline, this being a survey post built by Manchester Corporation when constructing a tunnel to convey their Haweswater aqueduct; when its purpose was served, it was left to rot and is already partially collapsed.

(Above) Tarn Crag from Shipman Knotts   *(Opposite) Kent Falls*

Leaving Shipman Knotts, it is necessary to continue down on the west side of the wall to avoid being trapped by an unclimbable wall lower down. The descent is without incident: there is little vestige of a path but by keeping in the company of the wall, the cart-track coming up from Kentmere and going over to Sadgill is reached near its highest point. About here, a little-used path branches off and descends directly to Green Quarter on the outskirts of Kentmere village, but it is much better to go along the cart-track and enjoy, when some small barns are reached, a classic view of the head of Kentmere around which the course of the day's march can be traced. Then a lane is entered, this joining the tarmac road to Hollowbank.

The last stage of the walk is down this road to the left, with a possible short detour when a signposted lane comes in on the right: by going a few paces along this and trespassing down a small field, Kent Falls may be seen in a charming setting.

It is well not to anticipate a drink or a meal in the village. For such deserved refreshment, after retrieving the parked car up the steep incline to the church, it will probably be necessary to travel down the valley to Staveley or Kendal. It should be in the nature of a celebration for the accomplishment of a memorable walk.

3 THE FAIRFIELD HORSESHOE
FROM AMBLESIDE   (11 MILES)

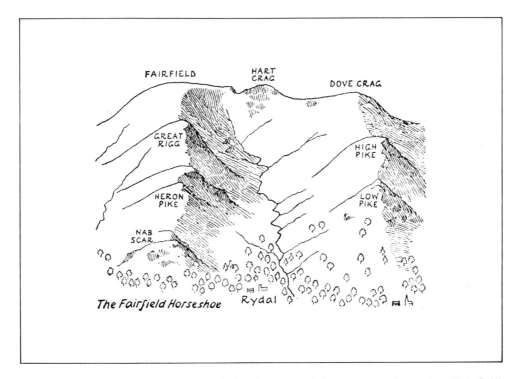

One of the best-known walks in Lakeland is around the great arc formed by Fairfield and its two southern ridges enclosing the deep valley of Rydal Beck. Four summits in excess of 2500 ft and four of lower altitude are visited during the course of the walk, the whole round being at a high level and providing a succession of contrasting views – grim mountain fastnesses seen intimately, and lovely lakes and valleys seen distantly. In recent years, this has become a very popular expedition and the full circuit is now the objective of an annual fell race. The whole course is known as the Fairfield Horseshoe and is sufficiently well defined to make any errors of route finding unlikely.

Fellrunners will complete the whole round in less than two hours without seeing anything other than the track before them. I admire those who can perform such feats. I envy their fitness but not their achievements; racers and record breakers seem to me to be out of place on the high fells. Mountains are there to be enjoyed, and enjoyed leisurely. I never could travel at speed on foot, nor have I ever wanted to. Sour grapes don't enter into it. My preference always is to walk slowly, halting often to look around and see what is to be seen.

Fairfield is too good to be treated merely as a checkpoint. The Horseshoe deserves a full day and is liberal in its rewards for those who linger and look.

(Opposite) The Fairfield Horseshoe from Todd Crag

The walk may be started along either of the two southern ridges. Although my natural inclination is to do a circular walk clockwise, I prefer in this instance to travel anti-clockwise, partly to avoid the steep initial climb to Nab Scar, partly to take advantage of easier gradients in ascent, but especially to enjoy the morning approach to High Sweden Bridge, always a delightful start to a day on the fells.

A purist determined to do the ridge, the whole ridge and nothing but the ridge, will leave Ambleside by way of Low Sweden Bridge, reach the ridge wall as it emerges from the valley trees and follow it upwards without deviation.

Non-purists like myself, out for pleasure, will leave Ambleside along the steep Kirkstone road and turn off at Sweden Bridge Lane to a gate at the end of the tarmac. I was once standing here when a fox came running down the rough lane beyond, squeezed through the bars of the gate and disappeared into a private garden nearby, completely ignoring my presence. It was followed a minute later by a straggling pack of hounds. Fox-hunters say that a fox enjoys the excitement of being chased and has no sense of fear until it is actually caught. I'm afraid I don't believe a word of it. The fox I saw was terrified: it was running for its life, and knew it.

Beyond the gate, Sweden Bridge Lane is delightful, rising between walls with a glorious view of the Vale of Rydal deep in a mountain surround. Further on, the lane enters a woodland, now having Scandale Beck tumbling down a ravine alongside, heard but not seen until the charming centuries-old High Sweden Bridge is reached.

Sweden Bridge Lane

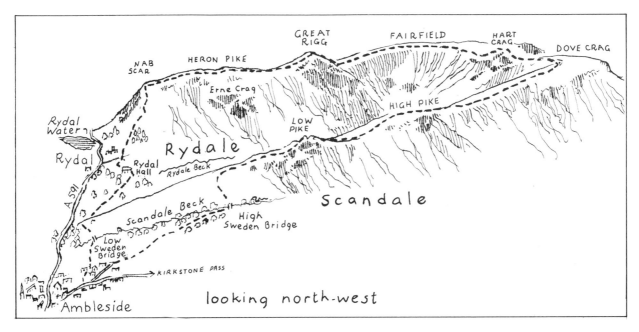

GREAT RIGG   FAIRFIELD   HART CRAG   DOVE CRAG

NAB SCAR   HERON PIKE

Erne Crag

HIGH PIKE

LOW PIKE

Rydal Water

Rydal

Rydale

Rydal Hall   Rydale Beck

A591

Scandale Beck

Scandale

High Sweden Bridge

Low Sweden Bridge

→ KIRKSTONE PASS

looking north-west

Ambleside

High Sweden Bridge

Scandale Beck, flowing under High Sweden Bridge, is the last running water encountered on the route until the return, some hours later, to valley level. After taking a photograph of the bridge, as every visitor does, and resisting the temptation to linger in this lovely spot, it is crossed and a grassy slope is climbed from it to the wall on the ridge between Scandale and Rydale, the latter here coming into view. This is the Horseshoe proper and from here on all walkers become purists without option. The wall is followed upwards, easily but with one awkward step to negotiate, to the rocky top of Low Pike, 1657 ft, the first summit on the ridge and scenically the best. Low Pike is the objective of the annual guides' race at Ambleside Sports. Although of modest altitude, it commands a splendid prospect of the other ridge of the Horseshoe with Fairfield dominant at the head of Rydale and of the woodlands of Rydal Park down below to the left. The lakes of Windermere, Esthwaite Water, Coniston Water and Rydal Water are all in view from this vantage point. Ahead, due north, is the next summit, High Pike.

There is a descent from Low Pike to a depression on the ridge and a steep climb follows to the top of High Pike alongside the wall, which hereabouts is worthy of notice: it is still in pristine condition despite nearly two centuries of storms and strong winds. Everywhere, even on the steepest ground, the stones are laid in persevering horizontal courses and with such skill in construction that they are securely wedged without the use of mortar. The men who built the stone walls that run for miles over the high fells of Lakeland were experts at their craft; they had to collect the stones from the ground nearby and cut them to shape on the site, they often spent the nights on the fells to save travelling and their reward was eight pence a day. They are forgotten. The walls they built so well are monuments to these unkown craftsmen. Other men have been knighted for less.

The wall

(Opposite) The summit of Low Pike   *(Above) High Pike and Bakestones*

The top of High Pike has nothing of interest to delay progress. It is flat and grassy, not at all the sharp peak suggested when seen from below. The summit cairn stands at 2155 ft on the edge of a decaying crag overlooking Scandale. The view westwards is obstructed by the high wall which, although still a work of art, is rather a nuisance to those who like to sit at ease and study panoramas.

Without any inducements to linger, the route is continued along the rising ridge to Dove Crag, which hitherto has been hidden by High Pike but is now revealed ahead and reached by a simple ascent in the company of the wall.

Walkers arriving at the top of Dove Crag on a first visit will be surprised to find no sign at all of any crag, the summit cairn at 2603 ft occupying a small rock platform on a broad and featureless plateau. But any disappointment is more than countered by the excellence of the panorama, the view over the gulf of Kirkstone to the far eastern fells, not yet seen during the walk, now being revealed.

Here the route turns north-west, still following the wall, which is now sadly crumbled and only a shadow of its former self, but walkers with a liking for exploration should continue due north down the slope to reach the brink of the crag that gives its name to the fell. Here one can look down Easy Gully, but the tremendous overhanging cliff can only be suspected by the great void below: a small wall marks the limit of exploration and is a warning that should be heeded, for the ground beyond breaks away in a fearful precipice. From a safe stance, however, the wild beauty of Dovedale, a tangle of knobbly hillocks and wooded slopes, can be seen far below descending to the Patterdale valley at Hartsop: a lovely picture enhanced by range after range of lofty fells in the background.

Dovedale from the top of Easy Gully

The ridge wall descends to a wide depression before the rise to the next summit, Hart Crag. In this hollow I was once joined by a wandering foxhound. It is not unusual to come across solitary hounds that have lost the scent or perhaps merely be out for exercise: they are always friendly. On another occasion a hound spent the day with me, joining me from the doorway of the Kirkstile Inn at Loweswater, climbing with me to the top of Hen Comb, patiently waiting for half an hour while I took photographs and made notes, and then returning with me to the valley where it disappeared into the inn without a word or sign of goodbye. It was nice to have company that needed no conversation.

(Top left) High Bakestones; (top right) The summit of Hart Crag; (above) Fairfield from Hart Crag

From the depression, it is possible to make a very steep and pathless way down into Rydale in emergency but the main route now climbs to the rocky top of Hart Crag, 2698 ft, which overlooks both Rydale and Dovedale's wilder and less attractive neighbouring valley of Deepdale. The summit is defended on both flanks by crags, those on the north side falling into the grim hollow of Link Cove. Fairfield is now directly ahead and reached by descending to a narrow col formerly known as The Step and encompassed by cliffs: an exciting situation. There is no hindrance to progress, however, and a steep pull up the facing slope leads to the long plateau of Fairfield.

The walk along the top of Fairfield to the summit cairn at 2863 ft is easy underfoot, on soft turf. Sensational views down into the wild upper reaches of Deepdale can be obtained by keeping close to the edge of the northern cliffs. There now no wall to act as guide in mist, and this is the one place on the route where there could be confusion in murky conditions, some of the many cairns not necessarily indicating lines of approach or descent and being dangerously misleading. In clear weather there are no problems and a fine panorama can be enjoyed.

(Right) Cofa Pike
(Opposite) Grasmere, Coniston Water and finally the sea

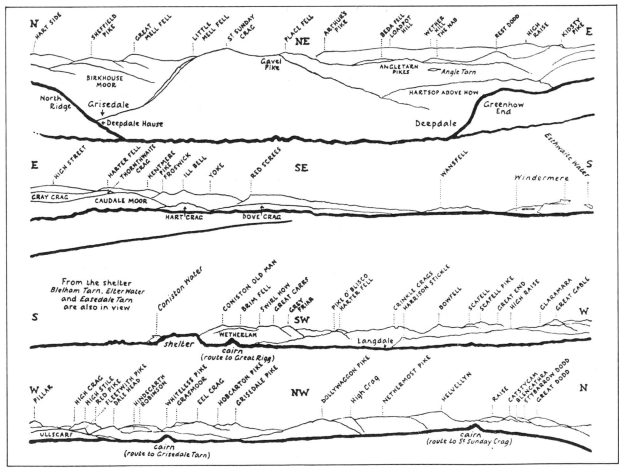

From the summit cairn of Fairfield a detour is recommended to the sharp peak of Cofa Pike, 300 yards along the ridge descending due north in the direction of St Sunday Crag. This is a neat rocky upthrust blessed with a most impressive view of the northern cliffs of Fairfield, the highlight of the expedition. Also well seen from this vantage point is the tremendous bulk of Helvellyn, towering into the sky across the deep trench of Grisedale, and the more shapely outline of St Sunday Crag rising beyond the depression of Deepdale Hause.

St Sunday Crag

Returning to the top of Fairfield, and with two-thirds of the walk now completed, the other leg of the Horseshoe has yet to be traversed, the route heading due south from the summit cairn along a narrowing ridge to the prominent dome of Great Rigg directly in front. This is the last fell of any significance; its summit, at 2513 ft, is attained by a short climb and has nothing of interest except a large cairn and a carpet of level turf that many a cricket ground would envy. The western slopes of Great Rigg are grassy, but the eastern side is a sharp declivity, rough and rocky, falling into the head of Rydale. Rydale, incidentally, is a name that does not appear on Ordnance maps but, as it contains Rydal Beck and ends at Rydal, the name is appropriate for this long valley.

(Opposite) The north face of Fairfield   *(Above) The summit of Great Rigg*

A long descent from Great Rigg leads to an undulating section of the ridge where two minor summits share the name of Heron Pike, the higher being 2003 ft. Neither deserves to be called a pike and there are no herons: the name is probably a corruption of Erne, a cliff on the Rydale flank having the name of Erne Crag. A lack of interesting features on the ridge hereabouts is compensated by the increasing beauty of the valleys ahead and now not far distant.

Next follows the last stage of the Horseshoe: an easy descent to Nab Scar, 1450 ft, directly overlooking Rydal Water, to which it falls in slopes so steep and craggy that even the most ardent purist will prefer to take the tourist path and turn away south-east. This path is steep and severely eroded, making the descent the roughest part of the whole journey. Some repairs have been effected by wardens of the National Park and steps constructed: a contentious improvement, many walkers feeling that steps are for going up to bed, not for climbing mountains. At the foot of the steepness, the path descends easier ground, passing a plantation and so reaching the lane that climbs into Rydale from the nearby A591.

Nab Scar from Rydal Water

Nab Scar is a very familiar object overlooking the A591 alongside Rydal Water and is invested with a certain romance because of its associations with the Lake Poets who lived at the base of its wooded slopes. It has a subterranean tunnel carrying the Thirlmere Aqueduct but there are no visible signs of it and nothing mars the attractiveness of this colourful height.

Scandale Beck at Low Sweden Bridge

The return to Ambleside may be made along the busy main road, but a much more pleasant alternative is available on public footpaths passing alongside Rydal Hall and through the grounds of Rydal Park to Low Sweden Bridge, where Scandale Beck comes tumbling down a wooded ravine in spectacular cascades. From a farm across the bridge, tarmac lanes lead into Ambleside.

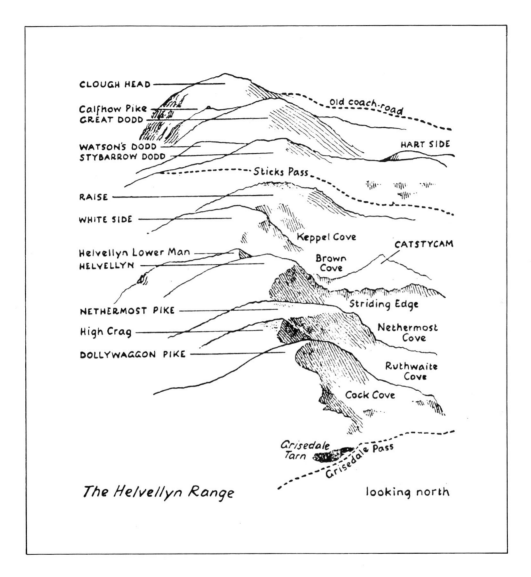

The Helvellyn Range   looking north

Helvellyn is the pivot of a long range of fells extending from Grisedale Tarn to
Thirlspot and forming a high barrier between the valleys of Thirlmere and Ullswater.
It is also, at 3118 ft, the dominant height, overtopping not only its satellites but all the
other fells in the district except the Scafells. The range is the most extensive
continuous area of high fell country in Lakeland and its complete traverse an obvious
challenge to active walkers. But the star attraction is Helvellyn itself.

(Opposite) Helvellyn from Cofa Pike

Helvellyn is climbed more often than any other mountain in Lakeland and, more than any other, it is the objective and ambition of tourists who do not normally climb. Thousands of people of all ages reach its top every year and there are very few days, if any at all, when no visitor calls at the wall-shelter on its summit. There are many reasons for its popularity: its lovely name is a magnet; legend and immortal poems are associated with it, conferring an aura of romance; the views are comprehensive and extend to far distances, making a fine panorama; the summit has a reputation as the best place to watch the sun rise; it overtops all else for miles around; no mountain is more accessible from a main road; and it has as its principal feature Striding Edge, the most exciting of all walkers' routes; and although it can be a grim place in wild weather, it is generally a very friendly giant, proud to have so much attention. There is some mystical quality about Helvellyn that inspires affection, and its devotees return often.

Helvellyn is a Jekyll and Hyde mountain. It is unfortunate that the ascent is usually made by well-trodden paths up the western slopes from the main road along its base, this flank, although benign and free from hazard, being dull and relatively uninteresting. Approached from the east, however, it presents a very different picture, the climb being exhilarating and in beautiful and impressive surroundings and the mountain revealing the other side of its character, a stern and forbidding appearance. This is the way to go for those who prefer a spice of adventure and sustained interest on their fellwalking expeditions.

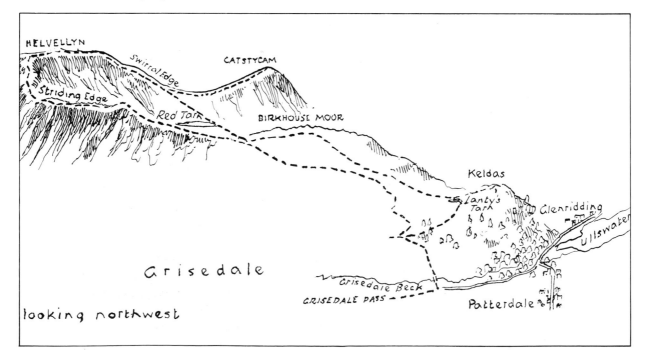

Grisedale

Just beyond Patterdale Church on the road to Glenridding, a side road branches off to the left and rises gradually into Grisedale. In a short mile, at the end of the tarmac (often cluttered with parked cars), a signposted path turns off at right angles. From this point, the greater part of the approach route to Helvellyn can be prospected: a conspicuous gap in a wall-corner at the top left end of a large enclosure is the next objective. This gap is a mile and a half distant and 1500 ft higher, and obviously will require much time and collar-work to attain. In fact, most of the climbing on the walk occurs within this steep enclosure on the flank of Birkhouse Moor, the unremitting ascent being compensated by impressive views throughout of the upper reaches of Grisedale deeply confined by St Sunday Crag and Dollywaggon Pike.

The signposted path crosses Grisedale Beck by a bridge and starts the steep ascent beyond. At a junction of paths, the route continues uphill half left to a zigzag, where it turns right: this is an old pony track and drove-road for sheep, well graded and a pleasure to walk upon. At the corner of the first zigzag, another track going off to the left is a post-war variation created by impatient walkers wanting a more direct line to the gap. For many years, this modern alternative was pounded by boots until it fell apart in a landslip of boulders and scree, loose and dangerous and making an ugly scar on the fellside; walkers are now requested not to use this newer track. The pony route fell into disuse during these years but is incomparably better underfoot than the short cuts adopted by clumsy walkers. The men who laid its course long ago knew what they were doing; there is a lesson here for the beeline walkers of today. The pony route continues to climb in gentle curves and then aims directly for the gap.

Excitement mounts as the gap in the wall is passed through: there is a feeling that great things are ahead although as yet not fully in view. Gradually the path rises along the crest of steepening cliffs on the left and reaches the foot of an abrupt tower of rock. This has the name of High Spying How but is rarely referred to as such: to walkers coming this way it is the start of Striding Edge.

High Spying How

On my first visit here, as a raw apprentice on the hills and never having climbed a mountain before, and with a cousin equally bereft of experience, an eerie happening gave us a bad fright. We had set forth from Patterdale determined to see Striding Edge, having read much about it. Driving rain started as we climbed out of Grisedale but we went on hoping it would abate, which it never did. Soon we were enveloped in thick mist and soaked to the skin; there were no weather-protective anoraks and over-trousers in those days. We found the gap and went on along the crest, seeing nothing but a few yards of ground at our feet. Then suddenly there was a window in the mist and before us loomed a giant apparition, black as night: the uppermost rocks of the tower, its base remaining hidden so that it appeared as some threatening monster in the sky. We summoned a shred of courage and went on, traversing Striding Edge without seeing it and in due course arrived at the wall-shelter on Helvellyn.

In clear weather, the dark tower of High Spying How, although still impressive, has no terrors, and a distinct path climbing round its flank brings Striding Edge underfoot and a thrilling prospect ahead.

Striding Edge was long regarded as a fearful place to be avoided and in icy conditions or gale force winds can be frightening indeed and quite dangerous. It is Helvellyn's most dramatic feature: a narrow ridge of naked rock, a succession of jagged fangs high above and between very steep and shattered cliffs. The traverse can be made difficult or easy according to choice: an experienced scrambler on rocks will prefer to make his way along the very crest, but ordinary walkers will use a simple path running alongside a few feet below. In calm weather, this is an exhilarating adventure with an awkward drop at the far end the only hazard. The Edge is about 300 yards in length and so fascinating that one is tempted to go back and do it again. In modern times, Striding Edge has become the highlight in the itineraries of countless walkers who, in summer, have to travel in procession along it; there are even reports of people having to queue to get on it. There is an iron monument on the Edge that may be passed unnoticed: this is the Dixon Memorial, erected in 1858 to mark the scene of a fatal fall during a fox-hunt. The Dixons of those days seem to have been accident-prone; another Dixon fell to his death from the rim of Bleawater Crag on High Street.

Striding Edge and Helvellyn

(Opposite) Looking down Striding Edge from Helvellyn; (above) The summit of Helvellyn

Having safely negotiated the awkward chimney that terminates Striding Edge, a steep climb on a badly eroded path leads to easy ground on Helvellyn's broad and grassy top, the point of arrival thereon being at Gough's Memorial, erected in 1890 to commemorate a fatal accident in 1803. Charles Gough was a Kendal man out for a walk with his dog when he was killed by a fall from Striding Edge. Three months went by before his body was found with his faithful dog standing guard by the side of his dead master. The incident was widely reported and both Wordsworth and Scott wrote poems about it, dwelling more on the fidelity of the dog than on poor Gough. It is testimony to the infrequency of mountain ascents in those early days that three months should elapse before the discovery of the corpse.

It is now merely a short stroll to a cross-wall built as a shelter from wind and the summit is a few steps beyond; it might have been expected that the highest point would accommodate a massive cairn, but such is not the case, due no doubt to the paucity of suitable stones lying around. There is another memorial nearby at the top of the Wythburn path, a small tablet recording the landing of an aeroplane on Helvellyn by Bert Hinkler in 1926.

From the summit a magnificent all-round panorama presents itself.

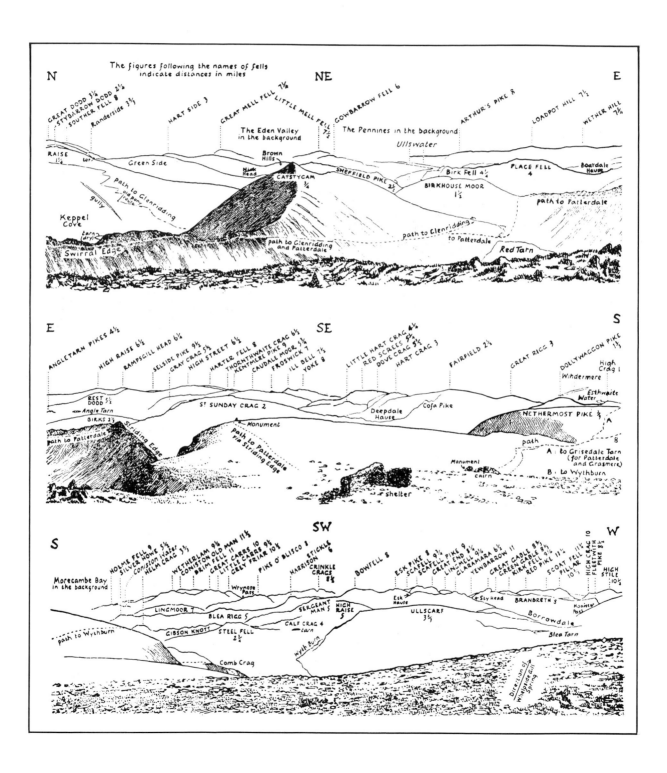

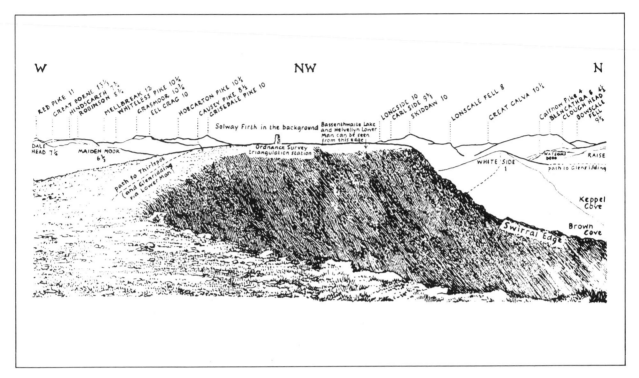

Continuing the story of my first visit with a cousin, Helvellyn now provided a mystery I was not to solve until the chance came for a second visit in the following year but which puzzled me greatly in the meantime. Our aim was Thirlspot, and both the Ordnance Survey and Bartholomew's maps showed only a pony route descending from Helvellyn's Lower Man and rising over the next fell, White Side, before finally coming down alongside Fisher Gill to Thirlspot. Still in pouring rain and with no visibility, we left the summit on a distinct and much-used path in the right direction, north, having no doubt that this was the promised pony route. Doubts began to arise, however, as our path continued to go down, directly and purposefully, with no sign of a rise to the top of White Side. Which path were we following, then, and where did it go? We were obviously off course, but went on, ever downwards, until emerging from the mist with Thirlspot below us.

On my second visit, in clear weather, I went up by the pony route charted on the maps, finding it difficult to trace, totally neglected, and intermittent over long distances. I came down by the blazed trail to Thirlspot as on the previous occasion. It was then clear to me that the pony route had been abandoned in favour of this newer and shorter way, which became known as the White Stones route. But not for many years thereafter was it acknowledged officially by inclusion on maps. To round off the story: we tramped to Keswick in sluicing rain and presented ourselves, two very sodden wretches, for a night's lodging at a boarding house. We were admitted by the lady of the house, each given a complete change of outfit from the husband's wardrobe, and royally fed, and in the morning our clothes were returned to us dry, warm and ironed. I mention this as an example of the concern and hospitality I was later to find typical of all the places, boarding houses, cottages and farms, where I had overnight stays in the district.

The next objective on the walk is Swirral Edge which, unlike Striding Edge, is steeply downhill. It is not seen from Helvellyn's summit and can be missed. To reach it, skirt the edge of the north-eastern cliffs where there is a sensational view of Red Tarn in a stony basin below, pass a triangulation column, and two minutes further, an obvious path descends a breach in the crags with the ground falling away sharply on both sides. This is Swirral Edge. The way down is eroded and slippery: two accidents have occurred here recently, one in snowy conditions and proving fatal.

At the foot of Swirral Edge, the path continues down to the outlet of Red Tarn, but straight ahead along a rising ridge is the shapely peak of Catstycam, 2917 ft, also known as Catchedicam and meaning Wild Cat's Hill, and a deviation to its small and neat summit is recommended before going down to the tarn. It is a wonderfully airy perch, the ground on three sides falling away out of sight almost at once, and has a retrospective view of the imposing cliffs of Helvellyn and the steep declivity of Swirral Edge. Then, returning down the ridge, the path down to Red Tarn can be resumed. The outlet is forded and the facing slope ascended to regain the gap in the wall used on the approach from Grisedale, thus completing the circuit of the Edges.

Catstycam from Swirral Edge

(Above) Helvellyn and Swirral Edge from Catstycam; (below) Helvellyn and Red Tarn

From the gap in the wall, the pony route may be used to reverse the line of ascent on the outward journey and is a very pleasant way down into Grisedale, but this means retracing steps for the last two miles. If time permits, a more interesting alternative, affording lovely views of Ullswater and involving little extra climbing, is available by following the top side of the wall across the higher reaches of Birkhouse Moor and then descending to a depression containing Lanty's Tarn in a beautiful setting amongst trees.

Lanty's Tarn

Ullswater from Keldas

A short rise beyond Lanty's Tarn leads to the cairn on an abrupt wooded height known as Keldas which, although of modest altitude, is one of the finest viewpoints in Lakeland, a place where artists and photographers suffer paroxysms of joy. The views of Ullswater, framed between lovely pines, are superb. Keldas is deservedly a very popular resort of sojourners at Patterdale and Glenridding, offering rewards out of all proportion to the ease of ascent.

Descent from Keldas on the side overlooking Ullswater is definitely out of bounds, the slope being very steep, craggy and densely wooded. It is necessary to return to Lanty's Tarn and from there take a grassy trod south to the junction of paths met on the outward journey, there going down to the bridge over Grisedale Beck and so happily back to Patterdale; a perfect end to a perfect day, with a memory of Striding Edge that will never fade.

5 BLENCATHRA
FROM THRELKELD   (6 MILES)

Blencathra from the east

A few decades ago, Blencathra seemed to be in danger of losing its lovely Celtic name in favour of the more prosaic Saddleback, which many writers who wrote about it (including Baddeley) and many walkers who walked on it appeared to prefer, their justification for doing so being the mountain's high skyline when seen from the east, a depression on the ridge between the summit and Foule Crag suggesting a saddle. The Ordnance Survey, to their credit, have not been influenced to abandon the old name but give both versions on their maps, naming the mountain as 'Saddleback or Blencathra'. I would be better pleased with 'Blencathra or Saddleback'. Happily the old name has been revived and is again in common use. There are many saddlebacks on the fells, named and unnamed. But only one Blencathra.

(Opposite) Blencathra from Castlerigg Stone Circle

Threlkeld is now bypassed by a broad highway, the revised A66, happily for the inhabitants although its planned continuation through the outskirts of Keswick aroused much abortive opposition from outdoor associations concerned that the gentle beauty of the Lake District should not be scarred by the works of man.

Hall's Fell, named after Threlkeld Hall in the valley below it, is reached by following the old road through the village eastwards and turning up a lane on the left to Gategill, once a centre of lead-mining activity and having the kennels of the Blencathra Foxhounds adjacent, but now a scene of devastation, the debris of the mine intermingling with stones fallen into the narrow confines of the gill from the towering slopes on both sides. When an intake wall turns away on the right, the open fell is reached above it and an enchanting track winds upwards through the heather, enchanting because it cannot be seen from below and is revealed ahead only a few yards at a time, beckoning irresistibly up the broad base of the fell to the exciting ridge above. As height is gained, the fell narrows to a crest known locally as Narrow Edge and with good reason, and from here onwards the walk is delectable, threading a way amongst low crags and rocky steps and gateways and towers. A thin track on grass avoids all difficulties, but this is no place for travelling at speed: care is needed especially at one awkward spot where a rockface has to be traversed along a horizontal crack. But it is all quite delightful and the views down into the deep ravines on both sides are sensational.

Then the ridge, still well defined, rises sharply to the top of the fell, arriving there precisely at a heap of stones marking the highest point of Blencathra, at 2847 ft. With labours over for the time being, a splendid panorama can be enjoyed, the view between south and west being particularly good and crowded with detail.

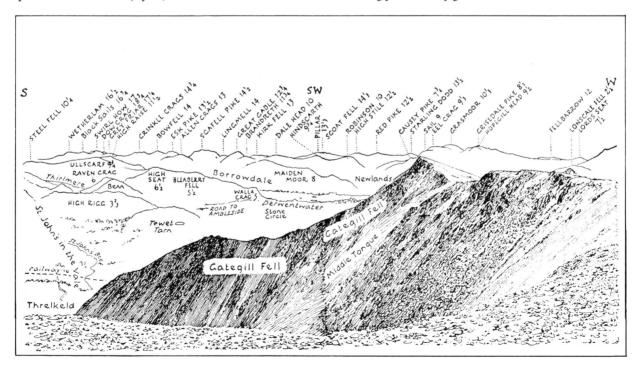

(Opposite) Narrow Edge looking up to Blencathra

The summit of Blencathra

Samuel T. Coleridge wrote of the summit:

On stern Blencathra's perilous height
The winds are tyrannous and strong . . .

but, although steep declivities fall away very sharply, there are no perils for those who walk circumspectly; and there are gentle breezes as well as strong winds, and soft couches for sunbathing. Blencathra isn't a monster.

The walk continues, now on excellent turf, in the direction of Foule Crag, seen due north, and descends easily to the saddle that inspired the naming of the mountain as Saddleback. Here in the depression is a landmark that has aroused the curiosity of visitors for many years: a collection of white crystallised stones of high quartz content laid on the ground in the form of a cross. This cross owes its existence to the industry of a Threlkeld man, Harold Robinson. Originally there was a very small cross of stones here (locally ascribed as a memorial to a walker who lost his life by a fall nearby), and Mr Robinson, an enthusiastic hill wanderer who has climbed his favourite mountain, Blencathra, hundreds of times, collected more stones (veins of quartzite occur in the native slate around) and extended the cross to its present size of 16 ft by 10 ft during a succession of visits from 1945 onwards. A much smaller but similar white cross on the southern slope of the saddle is more recent and the work of persons unknown.

(Below) The white cross   *(Opposite) Sharp Edge*

The next objective is Sharp Edge, which can be seen jutting from the steep slope on the right. A river of stones, formerly a path, leads steeply down to a narrow neck or col connecting the Edge with the mountain. Its aspect is intimidating; to the pioneer walkers of the last century, it was a place of terror. An early visitor, a Mr Green, described his passage along Sharp Edge as follows:

> We had not gone far before we were aware that our journey would be attended with perils; the passage gradually grew narrower and the declivity on each hand awfully precipitous. From walking erect we were reduced to the necessity either of bestriding the ridge or of moving on one of its sides with our hands lying over the top, as a security against falling into the tarn or into a frightful gully, both of immense depth. Sometimes we thought it prudent to return, but this seemed unmanly, and we proceeded, thinking with Shakespeare that 'dangers retreat when boldly they're confronted'.

Sharp Edge is even narrower than Striding Edge on Helvellyn, the crest in places being a razor-edge and the crags falling from it near vertical. But, like Striding Edge, a pedestrian path accompanies the crest a few feet below it on the north side and is without difficulty except for an initial problem where a sloping slab is negotiated by shuffling along it in a sitting position. Sharp Edge is much shorter than Striding Edge, and at the far end the path turns steeply down to the tarn mentioned by Mr Green, Scales Tarn, which is situated so far from Sharp Edge that he could not possibly have fallen into it.

Scales Tarn

Scales Tarn occupies a lonely basin shadowed by craggy heights. Sir Walter Scott refers to it thus in his *Bridal of Triermain:*

> Never sunbeam could discern
> The surface of that sable tarn,
> In whose black mirror you may spy
> The stars, while noontide lights the sky.

These words are well larded with poetic licence. I have sat in warm sunshine by Scales Tarn, and never have I seen stars reflected on the surface of the water in daylight. Of interest are lava deposits in the vicinity.

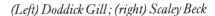

(Left) Doddick Gill ; (right) Scaley Beck

From the outlet of the tarn, a path descends into the valley of the River Glenderamackin and continues distinctly above the river until departing from it to climb over a low col into Mousthwaite Comb and so reach the hamlet of Scales, where there is an inn, the White Horse. Here the A66 can be joined for a quick return to Threlkeld; where the old road can be used, it should be: it is quiet, pleasant and tree-shaded. But to many fellwalkers, tramping on tarmac is anathema, and these may find a way back to Gategill on grass by keeping above the intake walls from Scales, this route giving intimate views of Scaley Beck and Doddick Gill in deep ravines, both crossed on the way.

Threlkeld offers rest and refreshment and those who do this walk will feel a need for both. But they will have had a grand day, and it is not unlikely that they will share my affection, not for Saddleback but for Blencathra.

6 SKIDDAW
FROM RAVENSTONE (6 MILES)

Skiddaw is the fourth highest mountain in Lakeland, one of the noblest in appearance, and the first to take shape when the landscape was being formed by convulsions of Nature.

It would be a gross exaggeration to say that Skiddaw is to Keswick what the Matterhorn is to Zermatt, but there is a certain affinity. Both are mountains of distinction, both are commanding heights dominating the valleys below, both are magnets that catch the eye whenever seen and draw the feet towards them, both are greatly loved by those who are privileged to live in their company. But there the analogy ends.

Skiddaw is not a detached peak soaring high into the sky; on the contrary, it is the centre-piece of a group, its summit magnificently buttressed by a circle of lesser heights, all of them proud members of the Skiddaw family, the whole forming a splendid and complete example of mountain structure especially well seen from all directions because of its isolation. Its outlines are smooth, its curves graceful, but because the slopes are steep everywhere, the quick build-up of the massif from valley levels to central summit is appreciated at a glance – and it should be an appreciative glance, for such massive strength and such beauty of outline rarely go together. Here, on Skiddaw, they do.

Skiddaw is the oldest of the Lakeland mountains according to the evidence of its rocks. It is apparent, even to unobservant walkers, that the stones covering the summit and exposed in eroded gullies and watercourses are very different in character from those seen in the central part of the Lake District: the latter are of volcanic origin, those on Skiddaw are marine deposits and consist in the main of soft shales and slate that splits readily into thin wafers and soon crumbles and decays when exposed to the atmosphere; hence it has no commercial value.

Skiddaw was formed long before the volcanos of central Lakeland became active; later it overlooked a vast glacier system, a world of ice. Some volcanic boulders are found along the lower southern slopes of the Skiddaw group: these rocks have been identified with those of the cliffs enclosing St John's Vale, having been carried along and deposited here when the glaciers retreated and scoured the flanks of Skiddaw on their way to the frozen sea.

Skiddaw is a giant in stature, but an affable and friendly giant. And a benevolent one. Keswick people have an inborn affection for Skiddaw, and it is well earned. The mountain makes a great contribution to the scenic beauty of the Vale of Keswick, shelters it from northerly gales, supplies it with pure water, feeds its sheep, and provides a recreation ground for its visitors. Throughout the centuries, Skiddaw's beacon has warned of impending troubles and alarms – 'the red glare on Skiddaw roused the burghers of Carlisle' – and today shares in Keswick's rejoicings.

Skiddaw and Keswick are inseparable.

(Opposite) Skiddaw from Ashness Bridge

Skiddaw from the boat landings on Derwentwater

Before the district was invaded by motor cars and the more remote mountains thus made more accessible, Skiddaw was the mountain most often climbed, Keswick then having a convenient railway service. The ascent of Skiddaw was the highlight of a visit to Keswick and almost a tradition. The top was regularly attained on the backs of ponies, refreshments being available at a hut midway. Not all who did the climb enjoyed the experience: there are reports of visitors being struck with horror at the sight of the steep declivities falling from their feet, of others wishing to lose blood and return to the safe ground below. But the ascent was the manly thing to do for sojourners at Keswick, an epic performance, and all went up the same way, on pony or on foot; a beaten track came into being designed to ease the passage of ponies. At that time, this was the only route to the summit and it is still today by far the most popular, often crowded with earnest pedestrians many of whom are unaware of any other.

All mountain climbs are worth the effort, but it must be admitted that the tourist path, starting from the back of Latrigg (Skiddaw's cub) is tedious and unexciting. Infinitely to be preferred is the route I like to follow, up and over the Ullock Pike ridge to the west, high above Bassenthwaite Lake: it is an exhilarating expedition, quiet and unfrequented, and has excellent views throughout.

The walk starts from the Ravenstone Hotel, between Little Crosthwaite and High Side on the Carlisle road out of Keswick, where a gated lane alongside the hotel grounds, with Dodd Wood on the right, leads steeply up to the open fell. Ullock Pike is now seen towering over rough, craggy and uninviting slopes that rule out a direct ascent. To circumvent this difficulty, turn left above an intake wall, away from Ullock Pike, and make a great loop to reach the ridge, known as the Edge, from which the summit springs. Already there is a pleasing prospect of Bassenthwaite Lake below the line of approach and an impressive view down into Southerndale on the east side. On the ridge below will be seen a strange group of boulders, Watches, which will be visited on the return journey. Now every step is a joy. The Edge rises ahead and is followed over minor undulations on a thin track amid heather, with sensational views into the depths of Southerndale as height is gained. The sharp peak of Ullock Pike, looking like a baby Matterhorn, soars ahead and is duly reached after passing over a false summit. The highest point, at 2230 ft, is a delectable spot, a place to linger amongst comfortable heather couches, and enjoy magnificent views. Skiddaw is now prominent and the route to it over the next summit, Long Side, can be traced, but it is Bassenthwaite Lake far below that most arrests the attention. The large scale Ordnance maps show a Hanging Stone on the nearby crags but this is not worth the search, being merely an unremarkable rock anchored to the lip of a small cliff. It is with reluctance that one leaves the airy perch of this lovely summit; it is the sort of place to make one wish it could be parcelled up and taken home for the back garden. It is delightful. All worldly troubles vanish on the top of Ullock Pike.

The Edge, Ullock Pike

Ullock Pike from Chapel hamlet

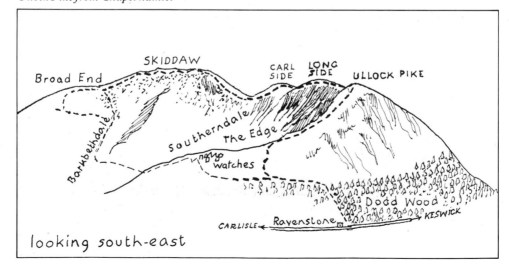

looking south-east

From Ullock Pike, the walk continues along the crest of a well-defined ridge named Longside Edge, with startling glimpses down the shattered cliffs falling into the depths of Southerndale. At one point, a cleft cuts into the ridge but there is no rock to handle and an easy rise leads to the top of Long Side, 2405 ft. This summit is also very pleasant, a carpet of dry moss, heather and bilberry tempting another halt. Strictly this summit is nameless, Long Side properly being the broad western flank, the lower slopes of which are densely afforested.

From the top of Long Side, a narrow trod descends to the depression before Carl Side, and a grassy beeline may be made for its summit at 2420 ft, or it may be bypassed by a more direct track to the tiny Carlside Tarn and the col that connects Carl Side to a broad shoulder of Skiddaw.

(Right, above) The summit of Ullock Pike, looking to Long Side; (right) The summit of Long Side, looking across to Ullock Pike; (below) From Carl Side, looking to Skiddaw

Carlside Col is a high neck of land, with Southerndale going steeply down on the left and a stony ravine descending on the right. There are interesting formations around where the slate bedrock breaks the surface. Rising ahead is a shoulder of Skiddaw, littered with loose shale and scree that makes the ascent arduous. Relief from effort is obtained on easier ground above where a cairn marks the south top of Skiddaw at an elevation of 3034 ft. Here the popular tourist path is joined and parties of human beings may be expected. The view south from this point is quite beautiful but better still is the comprehensive panorama seen from Skiddaw Little Man, prominent half a mile down the tourist path, where the outlook over Derwentwater and Borrowdale to the central heights of Lakeland is superb. I consider this viewpoint to be the finest in the district.

Long Side and Ullock Pike with Carlside Col in the foreground

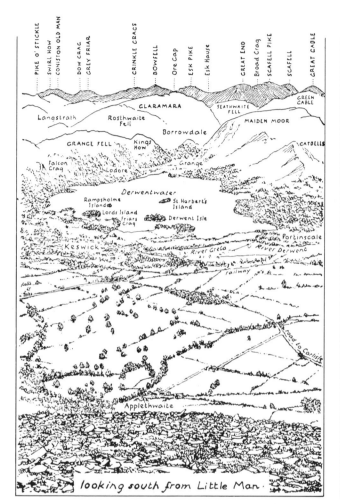

looking south from Little Man.

The summit of Skiddaw

The top of Skiddaw is in the form of an undulating ridge exceeding 3000 ft throughout its length of almost half a mile, providing an easy promenade and a rare feeling of freedom and escape from the world far below and, for a time, quite forgotten.

There is a south top and a north top, a middle top and a main top, all in a straight line and connected by stony pavements. In mist, it is not uncommon to assume that the middle top is the highest, there being a fall in the ground beyond, but the true summit, at 3054 ft, is further along and has a triangulation column.

Skiddaw is often described as 'merely a grassy hill', but its airy summit is the summit of a mountain. It commands a far-reaching view, north to the Solway Firth and the hills of Galloway, west to the sea, east to the Pennines and south to Lakeland, the principal fells being arrayed in a great arc between east and west. Walkers who have been to the Isle of Man will be pleased to see it again.

One evening during the early years of the war, I went up Skiddaw at dusk to spend the night on the summit, finding the blackness illumined by a strange red glow in the sky to the south; next day came the news that Liverpool had been bombed.

From the north top, and again out of sight and sound of other human beings, the walk goes on in the same direction, down the descending ridge to a col, with the profound hollow of Barkbethdale far below on the left, and a way down into that valley may be made from this point on a steep and stony slope. Or, alternatively, to avoid rough ground, the walk may be continued to Broad End, there descending grassy slopes on the left to reach a drove-road or sledgate that enters Barkbethdale at a lower level. This valley is quiet and unfrequented except by sheep, and almost unknown except to the shepherds of Barkbeth Farm. The sledgate leads distinctly to an intake wall and this should be followed to the left into the next valley, Southerndale, where the grimmer aspects of Ullock Pike and Long Side are revealed.

Barkbethdale

(Above) Southerndale; (below, right) Watches

Southerndale Beck is crossed by a footbridge and the facing slope climbed to renew acquaintance with the Edge at its lower part and here will be found the strange group of boulders known as Watches, huddled together as if assembled in conference and suggesting, at first sight, a Druids' Circle. The formation is natural, however, but unusual and, being in a vast expanse of grass, unexpected. The name of Watches given to it on large-scale Ordnance maps, is no less intriguing.

Without having solved the mystery of Watches, the intake wall followed in the early part of the walk is quickly reached down the west slope, and by turning left alongside it, the lane going down to Ravenstone returns the walker to the main Keswick–Carlisle road and his parked car; or, if without one, a regular bus service is available.

7 THE LANGDALE PIKES
FROM GREAT LANGDALE (6 MILES)

There are many mountains in Lakeland with such a distinctive outline that they are instantly identifiable on sight by most visitors to the district, but no mountain profile arrests and excites the attention more than that of the Langdale Pikes, nor is more well known by name, nor is more easily recognisable. To travellers on the road alongside Windermere, to those who sail on the waters of the lake or picnic on its shores, their abrupt outline has a dramatic appeal not shared by higher mountains within the range of view. Even visitors whose itineraries go no further than the pier at Waterhead, and the many who think that all mountains look alike, know the group by name and proudly and loudly announce it to their company. The Langdale Pikes cannot be ignored.

The distant view from Windermere is impressive, but when the Pikes are seen more intimately on the approach along the lovely valley of Great Langdale they become imposing indeed, even awesome, leaping from the flat pastures in a tremendous upsurge that stirs the imagination and even the emotions, and most especially whenever the towering peaks come into view suddenly and unexpectedly. The difference in altitude between top and base is little more than 2000 ft yet, because it occurs in a lateral distance of only three-quarters of a mile, it is enough to convey a remarkable impression of remoteness and inaccessibility to the craggy summits surmounting the rugged slopes.

(Opposite) Langdale Pikes from Lingmoor Fell

There are five summits in the group, extending in an arc and all overtopping the steep Langdale flank. In the order of their appearance from the west they are Pike o' Stickle, Loft Crag, Thorn Crag, Harrison Stickle and Pavey Ark.

Pike o' Stickle and Loft Crag

The usual route of ascent from Great Langdale is much trodden, and every turn and twist of the ingenious and circuitous path has been faithfully followed by generations of walkers. But it is unremittingly steep and on most days over-populated by the red and orange blobs of aspiring and perspiring climbers and littered by the recumbent bodies of those who have fallen by the wayside. Its one virtue is that it is as direct as the rough ground permits, but for walkers wishing to visit all five summits it has the disadvantage of arriving amongst them midway so that some untidy retracing of steps is necessary.

Whenever I have a choice between a steep path and an easy one I prefer the latter, and if it takes me on a roundabout course and is longer in distance so much the better: less effort will be entailed and more will be seen on the way.

For years I had walked along Mickleden from Great Langdale without ever being aware of a zigzag path up the west bank of Troughton Beck and in fact it cannot be traced from below. I am indebted to the Ordnance Survey for indicating this path on the 1901 edition of their six-inch map. It is an old drove-road, engineered for bringing sheep down to the valley, and is omitted from modern versions of their maps. I never saw anyone using it. This route is quiet, unencumbered with red and orange blobs, calls for less collar-work than the popular path, and has the advantage of arriving at one end of the five summits so that they can be visited one after another in a continuous traverse without deviations and back-tracking. This is the way I like to go.

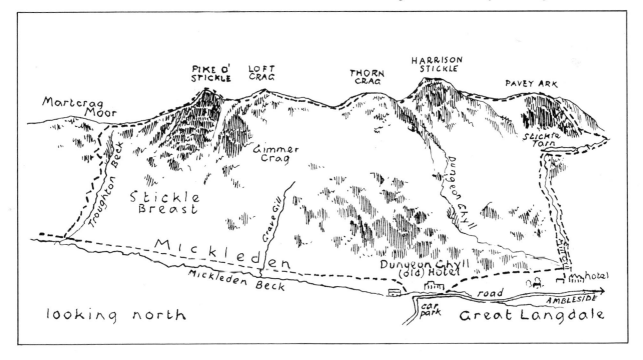

The walk starts from the old Dungeon Ghyll Hotel or the car park nearby, and proceeds along the side-valley of Mickleden as if bound for Rossett Gill or Stake Pass, passing along the base of Loft Crag, identifiable by the great buttress of Gimmer Crag, and then below the formidable acclivities of Stickle Breast, rising in tiered crags to the neat dome of Pike o' Stickle towering above. Beyond, the watercourse of Troughton Beck comes down on the right and, on its far bank, although not readily seen, rises the zigzag drove-road, not in evidence at first but becoming clear when the ground steepens. It is a long climb through 1400 ft of altitude, but relieved by the impressive sight of the wild upper parts of Pike o' Stickle. When the zigzags end, easier ground is ahead and the plateau of Martcrag Moor is reached. Here it will be seen, with surprise, that the Pikes do not fall away sharply on their north side as is suggested by their bold appearance from the valley; on the contrary, the summits rise but little above a sprawling and rather drab moorland. Turning right, and keeping close to the Mickleden edge, the thimble-shaped top of Pike o' Stickle is soon reached by a simple scramble, the summit cairn, at 2323 ft, having a fine view forward to the dominating height of Harrison Stickle, the highest of the group. There is little scope for exploration on the top of Pike o' Stickle, the ground falling away in precipices on three sides. Loft Crag, seen ahead, is the next objective but cannot be reached by a beeline, the short scramble to Pike o' Stickle's summit being reversed and a descent then made to the head of a wide scree gully, a place both of repute and ill-repute.

Pike o' Stickle from Troughton Beck

(Above) Harrison Stickle; (below) Loft Crag and Harrison Stickle from Pike o'Stickle

Until the Lake District was discovered in the early 19th century by discerning travellers who sang its praises in so fulsome a manner that they were followed by an ever-increasing flood of tourists, it was a land apart, reached only by a few turnpikes, aloof and unaffected by major national events and contributing nothing worthy of record in the history books. True, there had been a skirmish in Rannerdale between the natives and the Norman invaders, but that incident was almost forgotten. There were no famous battles here; civil wars, the rise and fall of Parliaments, the founding of the British Empire – these were matters that changed nothing here amongst the mountains. The Industrial Revolution meant nothing to the sheep, although they did hear talk of a railway reaching Keswick. Life went on undisturbed as it had done for centuries. There had been Celts and Vikings here and their place names lived on, but all that was ages ago. History had little to do with the Lake District.

But if Lakeland lacks an exciting history, a chance discovery a few decades ago established that it had an unsuspected and quite remarkable pre-history, evidenced by the stone-axe 'factories' of Neolithic man. The head of a stone axe, perfectly fashioned and obviously man-made, was found in a scree gully falling from Pike o' Stickle, and a search revealed more, some of them imperfect and obviously discarded, but many in good condition. Excitement ran high amongst local archaeologists; enthusiastic searchers scoured the loose scree of the gully and the fells in the vicinity, discovering other axes and chipping sites in many places around Langdale and always on the same high contour. Proof was positive. Thousands of years ago, there had been an industry here for the manufacture of stone axes, and on so active a scale that Langdale is now established as the most important of such sites in the country.

The intrusion of a narrow vein of a very hard and durable stone in the volcanic rocks of Great Langdale, emerging on the surface along a high-level contour around the head of the valley, provided the material from which the prehistoric natives of the district fashioned their axes. Working sites have been located from Martcrag Moor to Harrison Stickle, but the screes of Pike o' Stickle have yielded the most prolific discoveries. The really remarkable feature is not so much the presence of a particularly rich stratum in one of the gullies falling from Pike o' Stickle, nor the making of implements from it so long ago; the facts that most tax the imagination are, first, that the primitive inhabitants of Lakeland should have located such an insignificant geological fault and recognised its value and, second, that the plentiful evidences of their industry should have remained undisturbed and unnoticed throughout the ages until modern times.

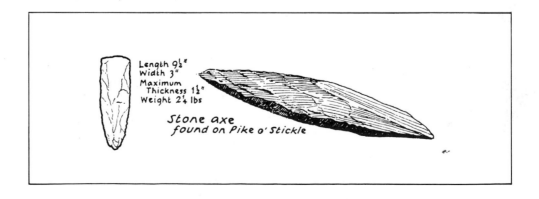

Length 9½"
Width 3"
Maximum Thickness 1½"
Weight 2¼ lbs

Stone axe found on Pike o' Stickle

The scree gully has been so badly eroded by eager searchers of stone axes that it has become slippery and even dangerous, and walkers have been asked by the local Mountain Rescue Association to regard it as out of bounds. Before passing on, however, a man-made cave in one of the walls of the gully is worthy of notice: its connection with stone-axe manufacture has not yet been accepted by learned archaeologists although the coincidence seems too great to be denied. It provides shelter for several persons.

Pike o' Stickle from Loft Crag

(Above) Langdale and Windermere from Harrison Stickle; (below) The upper ravine of Dungeon Ghyll

From the head of the gully there is a simple rise to the abrupt summit of Loft Crag, 2270 ft, an airy and pleasant top that has below it on the Langdale flank the imposing buttress of Gimmer Crag, a very popular resort of rock-climbers. The walk continues with an easy descent to another depression, this being crossed by the well-blazed tourist path. Rising beyond it is Thorn Crag, quickly ascended from this point and having nothing of special interest except an intimate view of the impending mass of Harrison Stickle, from which it is separated by a fearful chasm formed by the headwaters of Dungeon Ghyll. This hazard is avoided by descending the north slope of Thorn Crag rejoining the path for the final stiff pull up to Harrison Stickle.

I once spent an autumn night on this slope. I had walked up from the valley on a lovely evening and, having selected a bed in the heather, watched a fox on a grassy shelf below me, obviously enjoying life, playing and leaping and rolling like a ginger kitten, not knowing that he might be destined to be torn to pieces by dogs and that a brave hunter might cut off his tail for a trophy. Foxes, men say, are pests . . .

After darkness had fallen, a grey mist and a drizzling rain descended on the mountain. I had with me a khaki blanket, an Army reject, which served me well: there were posh sleeping bags in the shops but at a price beyond my pocket. In those days, I was rather addicted to spending nights out amongst the mountains. They were eerie vigils. The silence was absolute, the mountains were black silhouettes around me like crouching monsters. I was always too apprehensive to sleep and passed the long hours of darkness with a cigarette every thirty minutes. At sunrise, the mountains changed quickly from black to grey to rosy pink and welcomed me to their company. After my first such experience, I quite lost my fear of mountains; they became friends. The reason for this eccentric pastime, apart from wanting to feel myself part of the scene, was that it gave me a dawn start on the tops and a full day's walking and exploration ahead of me.

On this occasion when the first light of day filtered through the murk, I went up to the top of Harrison Stickle and quite suddenly and unexpectedly emerged from the mist and saw before me the summit rocks, stark and clear under a cloudless sky. I walked across to the Langdale cairn and was transfixed by the most beautiful scene I have ever witnessed. I was standing on an island in the midst of a sea of cotton wool that extended to the far horizon. Across the valley a few other peaks pierced the mist, also like islands rising from the sea, sharply defined but sullen in the half-light of dawn. I waited for the sun to rise. Gradually I felt the warmth of the first rays; the summit rocks became diffused with a soft pink glow and within minutes were bathed in sunshine and casting long shadows. There was a profound stillness in the air; down below the mist, I could hear a cock crowing at one of the Langdale farms, but there was no other sound, not even the whisper of a breeze. Then slowly the mist receded from the shoulders of the distant peaks and settled over the valleys. Langdale was completely filled by a white mist that extended from Rossett Pike at the dalehead and curved like an unbroken glacier, following the contours of the valley away into the distance over Elterwater and above the length of Windermere to the sea, a river of vapour, a mantle of unblemished purity. Alone I saw it; there were people down there in their beds who knew nothing of the glory of the morning. Still I waited. Very slowly the mist began to break, patches of green appeared, and within half an hour every vestige had dissipated, and I could see the fields of Langdale far below as on a map. The transformation was complete.

Harrison Stickle and Pavey Ark from across Langdale

The summit of Harrison Stickle, 2403 ft, takes the form of an elevated ridge supported by crags, the south side being precipitous. As befits the highest of the Pikes, the view commands the whole area and extends far into the distance. To the north is the last summit to be visited, Pavey Ark, the abrupt downfall of its great cliff being seen in profile.

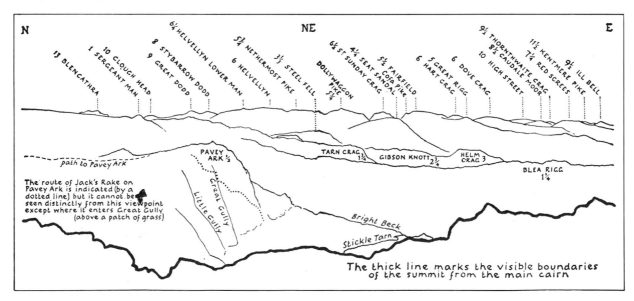

N — NE — E

13 BLENCATHRA
1 SERGEANT MAN
10 CLOUGH HEAD
8 STYBARROW DOD
9 GREAT DOD
6¼ HELVELLYN LOWER MAN
5¼ NETHERMOST PIKE
6 HELVELLYN
3½ STEEL FELL
3⅓
6½ ST SUNDAY CRAG
DOLLYWAGGON PIKE 5¼
4¼ SEAT SANDAL
5¼ FAIRFIELD
COFA PIKE
6 HART CRAG
5 GREAT RIGG
6 DOVE CRAG
10 HIGH STREET
9½ THORNTHWAITE CRAG
8½ CAUDALE MOOR
7¼ RED SCREES
11½ KENTMERE PIKE
9½ ILL BELL

path to Pavey Ark

PAVEY ARK ½

TARN CRAG 1¼

GIBSON KNOTT 2¼

HELM CRAG 3

BLEA RIGG 1¼

The route of Jack's Rake on Pavey Ark is indicated (by a dotted line) but it cannot be seen distinctly from this viewpoint except where it enters Great Gully (above a patch of grass)

Great Gully
Little Gully

Bright Beck

Stickle Tarn

The thick line marks the visible boundaries of the summit from the main cairn

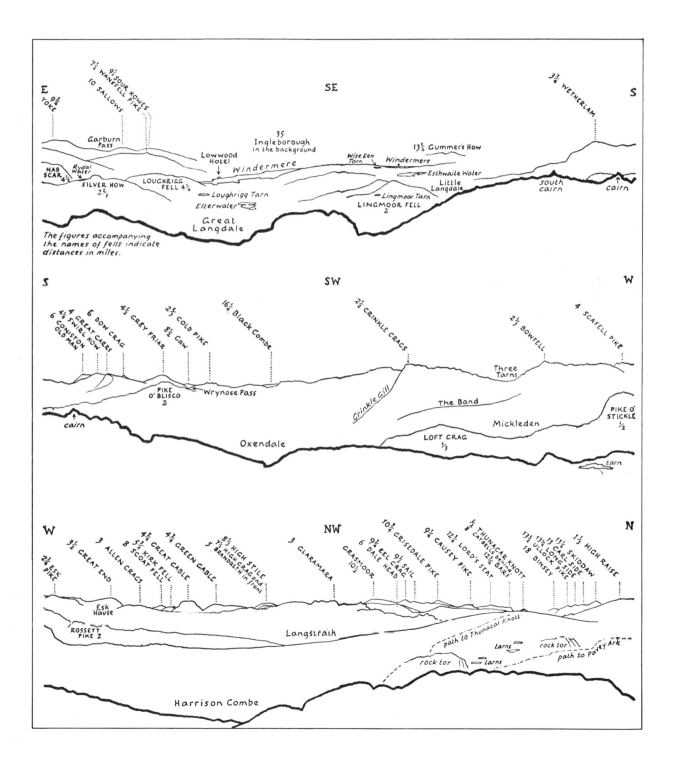

The way down from the summit of Harrison Stickle is initially rough and rocks have to be handled, but it is not difficult and soon reaches the grassy ridge leading up through outcrops to the top of Pavey Ark, 2288 ft. This is a delightful place: attractive grey rocks of a rough texture, not unlike the gabbro of Skye, are all around and interspersed with terraces of bilberry. Explorers should not wander too far from the cairn, the ground to the east falling in a tremendous plunge to the waters of Stickle Tarn far below: this is one of the greatest precipices in the district.

Pavey Ark from Harrison Stickle

Stickle Tarn is the next objective, but it is palpably obvious that there is no direct way down to it. The route continues beyond the cairn, keeping close to the edge of the crags until a wide grassy breach occurs on the right. This offers a remarkably simple escape from the fringe of rocks. I call it North Rake. As though cut out of the craggy surround by a knife, it leads straight down to the easy moorland below without hazards and with grass underfoot. An opening in the cliffs midway is better ignored: it leads into Easy Gully and debouches at the foot of the precipice but has a large chockstone which is awkward to negotiate.

At the lower end of North Rake, Bright Beck is crossed and followed downstream to its entry into Stickle Tarn, the walk continuing along the east bank of this large sheet of water. Now the cliffs of Pavey Ark are seen to great advantage, soaring into the sky in a broad and near-vertical wall of rock with channels of scree pouring from black clefts and gullies, the awesome grandeur of the scene enhanced by the dark waters of the tarn.

Pavey Ark from Stickle Tarn

Stickle Tarn has a dam, its waters formerly being impounded for the use of the gunpowder works at Elterwater, long gone. It is a popular excursion from Langdale, and from here down to the valley, parties of visitors must be expected. Issuing from the tarn is Mill Gill, in wet weather a cataract rather than a stream, and there are so-called paths on both banks going down to the valley; that on the west side is cut to ribbons of stones by over-use and that on the east side, once a thin track, suffers likewise by the pounding of boots. Both descend to the New Dungeon Ghyll Hotel and the valley road, but if the old hotel and the large car park is the destination, the intake wall can be followed to avoid almost a mile of road walking. Nobody ever climbs the Langdale Pikes without taking a last lingering look at them before leaving their magnificent presence.

8 CRINKLE CRAGS
FROM GREAT LANGDALE   (8 MILES)

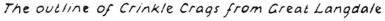

The outline of Crinkle Crags from Great Langdale

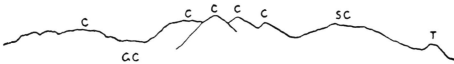

C : The five Crinkles   GC : Great Cove
T : Rock tower near Three Tarns   SC : Shelter Crags

The highest Crinkle (2816') is second from the left on the diagram.
When seen from the valley it does not appear to be the highest, as
it is set back a little from the line of the others.

A few of the fells of Lakeland have inherited their name from the Norse invaders of long ago, and these rough men must surely have had poetry in their souls for they have left us with Blencathra, Helvellyn, Glaramara and other romantic titles. Some fells have taken their names from communities in their vicinity, such as Coniston Old Man, Rosthwaite Fell and Glenridding Dodd. Some are named after the valleys from which they rise, Langdale Pikes, Bowscale Fell and Esk Pike being examples, and some, such as Watson's Dodd, Harrison Stickle and Robinson, owe their names to forgotten dalesmen. But most were named by the first settlers because of obvious physical characteristics, Great Gable, Red Pike, Steeple and Pillar amongst them.

In this latter category is the fell known as Crinkle Crags, so named by the early men of Langdale, an apt description for the serrated skyline seen from that valley: a succession of knobs and depressions distinguishing it from all others in the area. These undulations, seeming trivial at a distance, are revealed at close range as steep rocky buttresses and scree gullies above wild and arid slopes, the whole a scene of rugged grandeur.

Crinkle Crags has a special appeal for walkers who like rough ground underfoot without finding themselves in difficult situations. The full traverse of the five summits is an exciting adventure, a lofty promenade amidst rocky outcrops and boulders throughout, and with unsurpassed views down into Langdale and across to the Scafells and Bowfell. But in misty conditions it is easy to go astray, the path being intermittent in places and the terrain confusing. The company of Crinkle Crags should be sought only in clear and settled weather – then it is with reluctance that one says farewell at the end of an exhilarating day.

(Opposite) Crinkle Crags from Pike o'Blisco

Crinkle Crags and Bowfell from Red Tarn

A good path descends from Pike o' Blisco to Red Tarn. I never like losing height that I know must be regained, nor do most fellwalkers, but in this instance the traverse of the Pike will have been enjoyed so much that there will be few grumbles.

Red Tarn is an unattractive sheet of water but not without merit on a hot day. It is a walkers' crossroads, four paths converging near the outlet.

Gladstone's Finger

From a small patch of red scree 100 yards below the outlet of Red Tarn the continuation of the route to Crinkle Crags climbs the grass slope to the west and is fairly steep until a prominent crag on the right, Great Knott, is rounded, when the gradient eases and the path heads directly for the first Crinkle, now in sight ahead. Here a diversion from the path is recommended, crossing to the right to the edge of the crags of Great Knott and following a parallel course until, at the top of a short scree gully, the remarkable pinnacle known as Gladstone's Finger is disclosed, rising out of a choke of stones: a slender monolith that has survived ages of weathering while much around it has disintegrated. Beyond this gully, and keeping on the same course, a dramatic view of the second and third Crinkles is revealed across the profound hollow of Great Cove. Then the path is resumed for the traverse of the first Crinkle, 2733 ft. This takes the form of a ridge, rough and rocky with many cairns to keep walkers on the right track; sheer cliffs make an abrupt edge to the ridge and there are sensational views down two gullies. The second (and highest and biggest) Crinkle is now ahead, appearing as a huge rocky dome.

The second Crinkle, from the first

The first Crinkle is descended at its far end to a grassy depression and an obvious scree gully is seen leading upwards to the top of the second Crinkle. Things are not as they seem, however; the gully, when entered, is found to be not at all an obvious route. Here is the Bad Step, the most difficult obstacle on any pedestrian path in the district: two chockstones block the gully entirely, forming a rocky wall ten feet high and as near vertical as makes no difference, and quite beyond the powers of the average walker to scale. To avoid this problem, it is usual to turn left at the depression and climb a wide grassy rake that leads to the summit of the second Crinkle, 2816 ft, which is named Long Top because of a high lateral spur going off westwards. Here the Scafell range comes suddenly into view across upper Eskdale and Bowfell appears ahead over a very bouldery foreground.

The Bad Step from below

The Scafell range from Long Top

Bowfell from the third Crinkle

The next objective after Long Top is the third Crinkle, seen rising like a pyramid from a desert of stones. Walkers whose luck is in will find amongst the rocks on the initial stage of the descent from Long Top a most unexpected and welcome spring: it is the highest flow of water in the Lake District but only worth searching for after rain. A clear path goes down to the head of a wide scree gully known as Mickledore and then skirts the base of the third Crinkle, a pathless scramble over boulders being necessary to reach its neat summit at 2740 ft. This has a fine view of Bowfell, seen over the fourth and fifth Crinkles, but the gem is the prospect of the green fields of Great Langdale in sharp contrast to the wilderness of stones all around.

The fourth and fifth Crinkles, next to be visited, are replicas of the third but of descending height. The path skirts both summits on the west side, gradually declining amongst a desolation of boulders and scree; grass is at a premium hereabouts. The top of the fourth, at 2730 ft, is only a few yards from the path and quickly attained. The top of the fifth, at 2680 ft, which is named Gunson Knott, is 20 yards from the path and reached by a scramble. These two minor summits, although encompassed by very rough ground, should not be by-passed: both are small domes formed by piled rocks and both have superlative views of Great Langdale.

Beyond the fifth Crinkle, the stones are left behind and normal walking can be resumed as the path passes over the shoulder of Shelter Crags and descends to the wide grassy depression of Three Tarns (actually there are four), below the huge façade of Bowfell, riven by a dozen parallel gullies known as the Links of Bowfell.

(Above) Bowfell from one of the Three Tarns   *(Opposite) Hell Gill and Whorneyside Force*

Three Tarns is another walkers' crossroads and much visited, usually during the ascent of Bowfell, and is a popular crossing between Eskdale and Great Langdale. The latter valley can be reached directly from here by way of a long descending shoulder of Bowfell, The Band, which has a good path down to Stool End.

But Crinkle Crags has not yet exhausted its surprises, and instead of returning to Great Langdale immediately, a much more interesting route follows the stream taking shape on the right, Buscoe Sike, which soon enters the deep chasm of Hell Gill. The bed of the gill is impassable but there is no difficulty in descending along the edge of the ravine, which in its lower reaches displays the waterfall of Whorneyside Force.

(Above) Crinkle Gill ; (below) Browney Gill

At the foot of Hell Gill the scenery is most spectacular. Crinkle Gill and Browney Gill join forces here in typical Wild West country, a meeting place of gulches and canyons and tumbling waters in very rough terrain devastated by rockfalls and landslips. Escape is provided by a path alongside the combined streams, hereon called Oxendale Beck, and Stool End is reached without further excitement. But before arriving at the farm, a look back reveals again the five Crinkles, aloof and seemingly unattainable, that have given such an enjoyable adventure and made the day so memorable.

Crinkle Crags from Oxendale

9 BOWFELL AND ESK PIKE
FROM GREAT LANGDALE   (8 MILES)

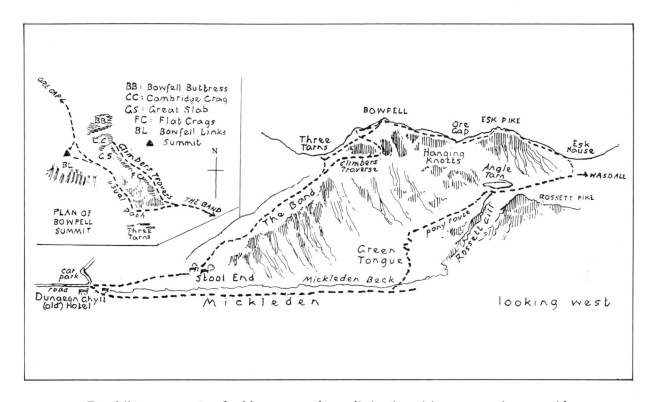

BB: Bowfell Buttress
CC: Cambridge Crag
GS: Great Slab
FC: Flat Crags
BL: Bowfell Links
▲ Summit

PLAN OF BOWFELL SUMMIT

BOWFELL

ESK PIKE

Three Tarns

Climbers Traverse

Hanging Knotts

Ore Gap

Esk Hause

Angle Tarn

WASDALL

ROSSETT PIKE

The Band

Green Tongue

pony route

Rossett Gill

Stool End

Mickleden Beck

car park

road

Dungeon Ghyll (old) Hotel

Mickleden

looking west

Bowfell is a mountain of noble aspect and rare distinction, rising as a massive pyramid at the head of three lovely valleys, Great Langdale, Eskdale and Langstrath, and commanding attention whenever it appears in a view. Shapeliness and sturdiness do not always go together but here on Bowfell they do. The higher the slopes rise from their sprawling base the rougher they become, finally rearing up steeply to form a broken wall of rock around the peaked summit and boulder-strewn top. These rocks display strange and unusual characteristics unlike others found elsewhere; they are not seen from the paths in regular use but merit a leisurely exploration. There is both grace and strength in the uppermost reaches of Bowfell.

Most visitors get their first view of Bowfell from Great Langdale where its dominating presence cannot be ignored: the lower slopes spring sharply from the flat valley pastures and provide an upward route so obvious and inviting that its ascent is almost inevitable. It is a challenge that cannot be denied. Moreover, the way to the summit is simple and straightforward with no problems of route finding, making it eminently suitable as an introduction to fellwalking. Bowfell is a popular climb and a great favourite. Deservedly so. It ranks amongst the best of the Lakeland fells.

(Opposite) Bowfell from Pike o' Blisco

Bowfell from Great Langdale

The walk starts from the car park at the head of Great Langdale with a level half-mile along the access road to Stool End Farm, where the ground immediately beyond rises as a broad grassy buttress between the side valleys of Oxendale, left, and Mickleden, right. This is The Band, a shoulder of Bowfell coming directly down from the summit pyramid and providing the ladder by which the climb is made. The boots of thousands of pilgrims every year have carved a distinct path, with initial variations, from the farm gate. The climb is continuous, without respite, and has little of interest in the vicinity of the path. The Oxendale flank is grassy but the Mickleden slope is craggy, falling away abruptly into shadowy depths occasionally glimpsed from the path. The best features of the rather tedious ascent are the views, as the elevation increases, of the mountains on both sides, Pike o' Blisco standing up grandly across Oxendale and Pike o' Stickle being a most imposing object towering over Mickleden.

(Above) Pike o' Stickle and Loft Crag from The Band; (below) Pike o' Blisco from The Band

When The Band steepens into the final rocky pyramid, the tourist path veers left to the wide depression of Three Tarns, from there reaching the summit by a steep scree path on the right. But to see the best of Bowfell and reach the top by a detour of sustained interest, walkers should keep to the Mickleden edge until a horizontal track turns off along the base of a line of cliffs, Flat Crags. This is the Climbers' Traverse and is a joy to follow. The track runs below the line of cliffs until confronted by a huge rock buttress, Cambridge Crag, which descends to the level of the traverse and, joy of joys, has a spout of clear cold water issuing from a crevice at its base. The situation here is awe-inspiring. Across a scree gully beyond Cambridge Crag rises Bowfell Buttress, a clean-cut tower of rock soaring majestically out of rivers of stones on both sides and affording popular rock-climbing routes: it was to provide easy access to the Buttress that the traverse was devised. Flat Crags and Cambridge Crag appear to be unassailable from this point, and below on the right steep slopes plunge down into the head of Mickleden. Having tasted the waterspout and found it to be nectar, a way of escape from what appears to be a dead end, an impasse, must be sought, and although grandmothers and infants may consider it prudent to turn back here, for active walkers there is hope of further progress upwards by a scramble up the pile of boulders and stones on the left side of Cambridge Crag, a hope soon to be fulfilled.

(Below) The Climbers' Traverse　　　　　　　　*(Opposite) Bowfell Buttress from the foot of Cambridge Crag*

In the course of the scramble up the edge of Cambridge Crag, an extraordinary scene unfolds: stretching away to the left is a vast slab of rock, naked except where vegetation has gained a roothold in the cracks and crevices. It is really the upper part of Flat Crags, tilted at an angle so easy that it can be walked upon. The top rim is seen to take the form of a low parapet, like a giant kerbstone. This unusual feature is unique and has no counterpart elsewhere in the district. I call it the Great Slab.

The Great Slab

The summit of Bowfell looking to the Scafell range

Easier ground is reached at the top of Cambridge Crag, but easier only in the sense that the gradient is less steep. It has, however, a covering of boulders and care should be exercised in crossing them towards the summit, which is now in view ahead.

I was once gingerly picking my way through these boulders when one heeled over and trapped my leg against another. Happily I was able to heave it back into its original socket and went on my way, only realising later that I might have been securely held and unable to free myself. This incident happened within shouting distance of the tourist path and no doubt I would have been rescued later in the day. But what an ignominy that would have been for an advocate of solitary fellwalking!

Before going up to the summit cairn, a detour half-left, crossing the well-trodden popular path, leads to the edge overlooking the Three Tarns depression and another of Bowfell's unusual formations is revealed. From the edge a dozen short scree gullies fall away steeply, one after another and all to a pattern, as though seamed by a giant comb. These are the Links of Bowfell.

Here ends an hour's exciting exploration of Bowfell's secret nooks and crannies and rock scenery, all unseen and unsuspected by walkers who adhere rigidly to the popular route of ascent. Now for the ultimate reward: the summit at 2960 ft.

A large cairn surmounts a chaotic upheaval of boulders in a surround of rocky outcrops and stones: here is nature in the raw. It is likely that the top will be populated by other walkers; if so it is to be hoped that they are quietly enjoying their achievement and not being too noisily exultant about it. I like to have mountain summits all to myself. They are the loneliest of places and are best appreciated in silence. Human discords, loud conversations, shouting, raucous laughter and the modern evil of transistor radios are totally out of place. If such distractions occur on Bowfell's summit they must be endured, for the all-round view should not be hurriedly dismissed but studied at all points of the compass; this is a panorama that many consider to be the finest in Lakeland.

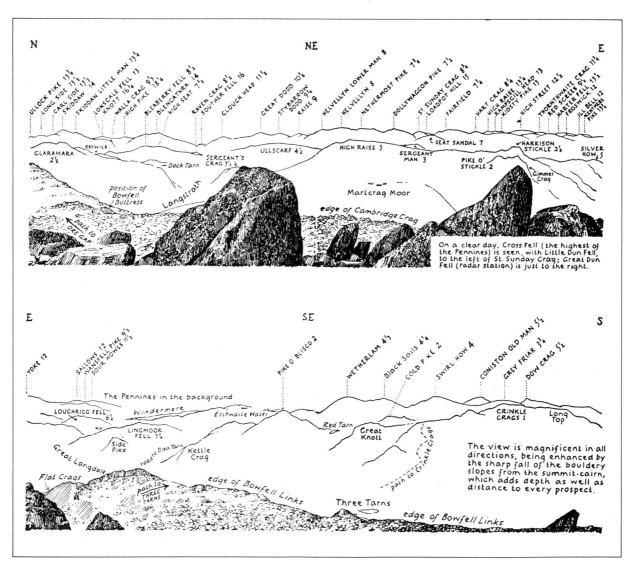

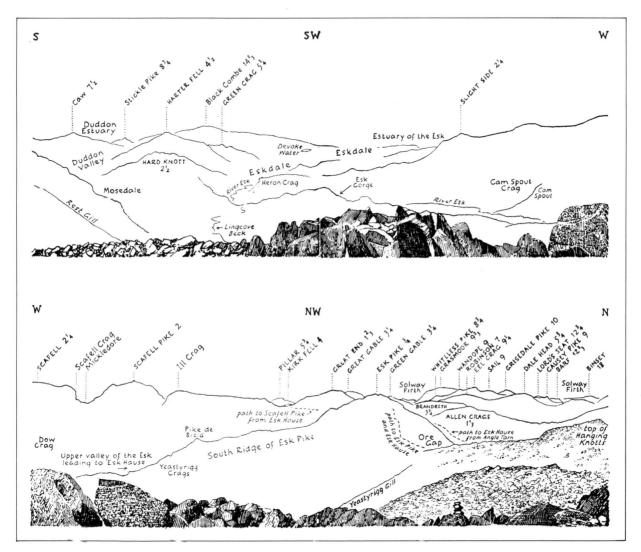

The neighbouring fell of Esk Pike is the next objective, and the path going up to its summit from the intermediate depression of Ore Gap can be seen from afar. Ore Gap is reached by a path along the top of Bowfell's north ridge, where a deviation to the right gives a downward view of the topmost rocks of Bowfell Buttress and, further, the crags of Hanging Knotts. The path is well cairned, now unnecessarily so because boots have scoured a blazed track that can be followed easily even in bad conditions. This over-abundance of cairns occurs on many mountain paths. Originally, when the paths were sketchy and intermittent, these piles of stones were useful in guiding walkers along the right tracks, especially in mist, but such is the recent popularity of fellwalking that most paths have become distinct and can be followed without the help of cairns, but they are still a reassuring comfort when visibility is restricted to a few yards.

Ore Gap, a narrow col, is also variously known as Ure Gap and Ewer Gap, but Ore is probably the correct spelling of the name and is certainly appropriate, for a pronounced vein of hematite passes through the depression, the evidence being plain to see in the red soil exposed along the path.

If it is desired to shorten the walk a quick descent can be made from Ore Gap to Angle Tarn and the Langdale path down on the right, but those more resolute will cross the gap and continue up the obvious path leading to the top of Esk Pike.

Esk Pike is a rare example of a fell given its name by walkers. It was nameless on maps until quite recently but was increasingly referred to as Esk Pike, appropriately because it stands at the head of Eskdale, and this name has now been adopted by the Ordnance Survey. The summit is notable for its colourful rocks which, unlike those on the other tops in this area of Borrowdale volcanics, are sharp and splintery, of natural hues of brown and white and splashed with green lichens. The highest point is a craggy outcrop, rising out of a debris of flaked and fragmented stones. In the lee of the summit crag, which is cut away vertically on the north side, is a shelter formed by substantial walls, a good refuge in storms and quite the most effective of all mountain shelters.

The walk continues in the same direction and a descent is made to the wide grassy depression of Esk Hause, with the massive bulk of Great End beyond and a view down to the left into the wild recesses of upper Eskdale.

Esk Hause

Esk Hause is the furthest point of the walk. The easy slope on the right is next descended to a very familiar landmark: a large wall shelter on the highest part of the popular pedestrian highway that links Great Langdale and Wasdale and is commonly but incorrectly referred to as Esk Hause. The true Esk Hause was left five minutes ago. Early photographs show a wooden signpost here, but this like many others has gone, probably to fuel camp fires.

The wall shelter on the Great Langdale – Wasdale path

The Langdale path is followed to the right down a long easy slope, with Langstrath opening up on the left, and arrives alongside Angle Tarn, a dark and sinister sheet of water in the shadow of the crags of Hanging Knotts but a welcome and refreshing halting place often frequented by naked bathers. Issuing from it, and crossed by the path, is Angletarn Gill, a feeder of Langstrath Beck.

Angle Tarn

Beyond Angle Tarn there is a short rise to Rossett Pass, the path then declining to the top of Rossett Gill, probably the best known and certainly the least liked and most abused walkers' route in the district. Thousands upon thousands of booted pedestrians every year have scraped away all vestiges of greenery and transformed a once-quiet watercourse into a wide channel of loose scree, toilsome to ascend and unpleasant to descend. Nobody has a good word to say about Rossett Gill. For years I toiled up and down this dusty ladder of stones without being aware of an alternative route, but a happy purchase of a set of the 1901 edition of the Ordnance Survey maps on the scale of six inches to a mile, and a study thereof, disclosed the existence of a pony route that had obviously fallen into disuse and been omitted from later maps; it was a route that avoided the gill completely and followed a circuitous course along the lower slopes of Bowfell. I went along to trace it and had little difficulty in doing so: it was intermittent in places but was gently graded and skilfully constructed to ease the passage of laden ponies. It was a pleasure to walk upon. Never again would I suffer the scourge of Rossett Gill.

I was able to obtain some information about this ancient track from a native of Langdale who had a knowledge of earlier days in the valley. It is believed that it had been used for the secret transport of goods smuggled into Ravenglass and carried over the hills by packhorses. My informant also told me of a packwoman's grave near the gill, out of the sight of passing walkers, and from his precise instructions I was able to locate it, finding it to be marked by stones laid on the ground in the form of a cross; the exact situation I have never disclosed to avoid disturbance. This is the grave of a woman who regularly called at Langdale farms carrying a pack of articles for sale and whose mortal remains were found and buried here 190 years ago. Another feature of the pony route is a hidden sheepfold, cleverly screened from the valley below and used by the dalesmen to conceal their sheep in the far-off days of border raids. Beyond the sheepfold, the path serves as a causeway to a small natural pool, and then turns down to Mickleden, still far below.

In the later stages of the pony route, a few ancient cairns act as guides down the grassy slopes of Green Tongue. This final section is not distinct underfoot (although, as is often the case, clearly discernible from a distance) but the descent on grass to the floor of the valley is simple. The point of the crossing of Mickleden Beck by the packhorses is obscure but the stream can conveniently be forded at several places to join the well-trodden path along Mickleden leading to Dungeon Ghyll and the car park. Few, having done this walk, will drive away without a long last look at Bowfell: a look not only of respect but probably even of affection born of their close and intimate acquaintance with this grand mountain.

Rossett Gill

10 THE CONISTON FELLS
FROM CONISTON   (10 MILES)

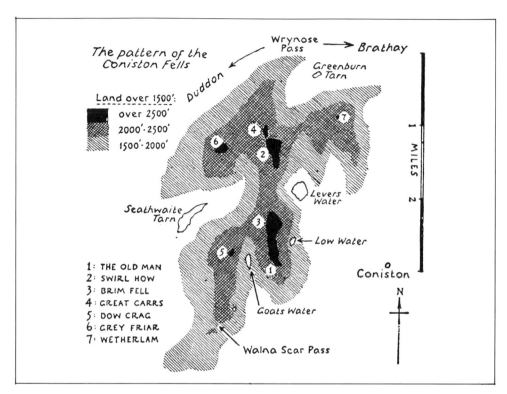

The pattern of the
Coniston Fells

Land over 1500':
- over 2500'
- 2000'-2500'
- 1500'-2000'

Wrynose Pass → Brathay

Duddon

Greenburn O Tarn

Levers Water

Seathwaite Tarn

Low Water

Coniston

1: THE OLD MAN
2: SWIRL HOW
3: BRIM FELL
4: GREAT CARRS
5: DOW CRAG
6: GREY FRIAR
7: WETHERLAM

Goats Water

Walna Scar Pass

N

The Coniston Fells are a separate geographical unit, almost entirely severed from the adjacent mountain areas of Lakeland by the Duddon and Brathay valleys which form clearly defined boundaries to the group, the only high link with neighbouring fells occurring at the watershed between the two river systems, Wrynose Pass. Until 1974, these natural boundaries were adopted for local government purposes, the Coniston Fells being wholly within the county of Lancashire; an anachronism, really, because in appearance and character and traditions they are an integral part of the Lake District, as much so as Cumberland and Westmorland which shared the other fell country in the region. In 1974, the Rivers Duddon and Brathay lost administrative significance, the Furness area of Lancashire including the Coniston Fells being merged with Cumberland and Westmorland in the new county of Cumbria, a reorganisation justified by geographical considerations. Lancashire thus lost its finest scenery, a favoured and favourite territory that the people of that county had been proud to claim as their own.

The high ground of the Coniston group takes the form of a semi-circle, with two major off-shoots, and comprises several named fells with distinctive summits. Of these, Coniston Old Man is the most popular objective of sojourners in the village of Coniston, its ascent being almost a ritual undertaken by visitors of all ages, from babies in rucksacks to senior citizens supported by sticks, all toiling upwards in a staggered and staggering procession. The Old Man is regarded as a shrine, and many are its pilgrims.

(Opposite) Coniston Old Man from Lad Stones

No mountain in Lakeland has been more cruelly exploited than Coniston Old Man. His breast is pierced by a labyrinth of the tunnels and shafts of abandoned copper mines, and great slices have been, and are being, cut away to produce a green slate internationally in demand for its beautiful colour, fine texture and durability. The eastern flank is an industrial mess of old workings and dusty access roads. Yet the Old Man remains a benevolent giant revered by generations of walkers and is held in high esteem by the inhabitants of the village he shelters, for he has contributed much to their prosperity. Despite all his ugly scars, the Old Man retains a proud and dignified bearing, shedding his tears quietly into a lovely tarn at the base of the summit escarpment. He has seen better days but, despite his mutilations, more people than ever come to pay their respects.

It is a common practice of active walkers after arriving at the summit of the Old Man to continue north over Brim Fell to Swirl How, there crossing to Wetherlam and returning to Coniston by the ridge of Lad Stones. This is a splendid high-level walk, usually referred to as the 'Coniston Round', nowhere difficult and on terrain that is kind to the feet. But it omits the grandest feature of the Coniston Fells, this highlight being the tremendous rock-face of Dow Crag, one of the greatest scenes in the district and for the past hundred years a Mecca for rock climbers. Dow Crag is too good to be left out of a walk on the Coniston Fells and can conveniently be included in the itinerary of the usual Coniston Round, having as a further advantage a quiet approach that avoids quarrying activity and the busy tourist path.

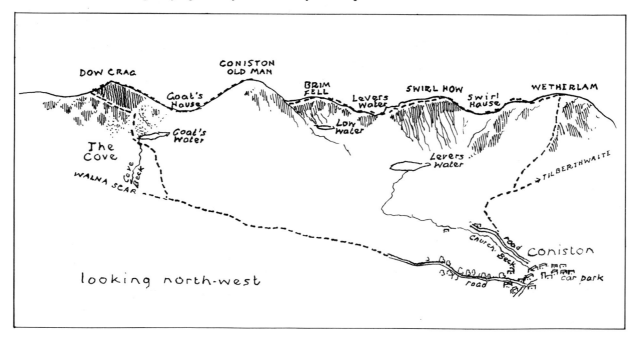

The approach to Dow Crag

Leave Coniston by the steep tarmac road leading up past the former railway station for three-quarters of a mile to the open fell and the Walna Scar path. Here at the end of the tarmac, a quarry road turns off to the right and there is parking space for cars. There is nothing to be gained by leaving a car here on this occasion, however, the return not being made to this point but directly to the village.

The Walna Scar path is followed along the base of the Old Man, the first section having been widened and roughly surfaced to serve a quarry, after which it continues distinctly and climbs gradually. The desolate moor declining on the left has a considerable antiquarian interest, having revealed evidences that it was the home of a Bronze Age population; in modern times, it achieved a fleeting national publicity when a young walker sighted a flying saucer close overhead and produced a convincing photograph to support his story. In the absence of any such distractions, the walk continues through a natural rock gateway and soon afterwards a cairned track branches to the right; this is followed into a mountain amphitheatre known as The Cove, where Dow Crag is revealed ahead.

The first glimpse of the crag is impressive and becomes more so with every step along the track, which leads eager walkers to the outlet of a large tarn, Goat's Water, deeply inurned in a wild setting with Dow Crag high above. Amongst the rocks of the issuing stream there was formerly a simple memorial stone inscribed 'Charmer 1911', Charmer being a foxhound killed in a fall from the crag. Charmer rests in peace but not so his memorial, which unkind hands have uprooted and cast aside: it is now difficult to find amongst the boulders of the stream bed. Poor Charmer: in life he was greatly loved, surely in death he deserved more respect?

Charmer's Grave

The outlet of Goat's Water is forded and a track rising across slopes of scree is followed to a pile of large boulders forming a cave below the lowest part of the crag, which now looks fearfully imposing and even intimidating as it soars above. The cliffs are palpably unassailable except by supermen; knees tremble at the thought of venturing upwards. However, by proceeding along the base of the buttresses on the left on a rising course and passing the gloomy cleft of Great Gully, a stony recess is reached where Easy Gully (so called) debouches in a chaotic welter of stones and boulders. Easy Gully offers a direct ascent to the ridge above for rock-climbers only, but for lesser mortals there is a line of escape to the left, where a stony rake, steep but crag-free, leads up to easier ground above: this I call South Rake. At the top, now again on welcome grass, a turn to the right and a final short scramble on rocks brings the summit of Dow Crag underfoot.

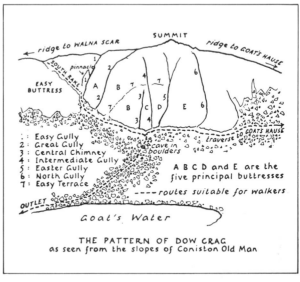

THE PATTERN OF DOW CRAG
as seen from the slopes of Coniston Old Man

1: Easy Gully
2: Great Gully
3: Central Chimney
4: Intermediate Gully
5: Easter Gully
6: North Gully
7: Easy Terrace

A B C D and E are the five principal buttresses

- - - - routes suitable for walkers

(Opposite) Dow Crag across Goat's Water; (below left) Looking down Dow Crag; (below right) Dow Crag from the path to the Old Man

(Left) The summit of Dow Crag; (right) Goat's Water from Goat's Hause

Dow Crag, 2555 ft, has one of the most delectable summits in the whole of Lakeland, taking the form of a small neat peak of piled rocks, an exquisite perch elevated above a frightful precipice and having a sensational view of Goat's Water nearly a thousand feet below. To attain it, even after cheating by using the easy South Rake, gives a satisfaction little less than would have been felt after a direct climb up the crag. This is the grandest spot on the walk and should be savoured to the full before departing.

Next there is a long and easy descent along the rim of the crags to Goat's Hause, a col linking Dow Crag with Coniston Old Man and having a full length view of Goat's Water, and then a steady climb inclining right to the top of the Old Man on ground broken by small outcrops of slate in unusual formations of vertical flakes. Human noise often indicates the position of the summit cairn before it can be seen.

There is a wide prospect of the Furness district and the waters of Morecambe Bay from the summit of the Old Man, and a strongly-built platform of slate on the highest point is, almost as a traditional custom, often occupied by parties of visitors obsessed in a search for Blackpool Tower on the far horizon. There has been some wavering by the Ordnance Survey about the height of the mountain, 2631 ft, 2633 ft and 2635 ft being variously quoted on their maps before resolving the doubt by switching to the new-fangled metres, a change deplored by all who take a pride in the hills. Now the Old Man has been demoted from 2631 ft or 2633 ft or 2635 ft to 803m which, after all he has suffered, is surely a case of adding insult to injury.

The next objective is the large cairn on Brim Fell, reached by a simple stroll along the edge of the cliffs plunging down on the right to Low Water. There is little cause for delay here and a long descent follows to the depression of Levers Hause, named after the large tarn of Levers Water seen down on the right; a dam constructed at its outflow ensured ample supplies of water for the copper mines.

(Above) The summit of Coniston Old Man; (below) Levers Water from Levers Hause

(Opposite) Brim Fell from Little How Crags   *(Above) Great Carrs from the summit of Swirl How*

Beyond Levers Hause, there is a steady climb to come alongside the upper fringe of Little How Crags and Great How Crags and then the gradient eases, levelling out to give a simple approach to the cairn on Swirl How, 2630 ft, which is found to stand on the verge of a profound abyss to the north, where the Greenburn valley lies far below a downfall of crags and scree.

Swirl How is the hub of the Coniston Fells, having an altitude only inches lower than that of the Old Man, and being the pivot of three important ridges. The views, too, are more embracing; of the nearer surroundings, Great Carrs most catches the eye, its east face an unbroken tumble of crags and screes into Greenburn. Great Carrs was the scene of a wartime aeroplane crash, its top still having parts of the undercarriage scattered around and the wrecked fuselage visible in a gully below.

The summit of Swirl How is very pleasant on the right sort of day, a place to linger and enjoy a wonderful panorama. It is, moreover, relatively unfrequented, quiet and uncluttered by babies and senior citizens, a place for undisturbed meditation and appreciation of the gift of legs and these friendly fells on which to exercise them, a place to count blessings.

Prison Band from the lower slopes of Black Sails

The walk now turns east, sharply descending the rocky ridge of Prison Band and so reaching Swirl Hause, a pass between the Greenburn valley on the left and Coniston via Levers Water on the right. Beyond the hause, a further climb leads to the subsidiary top of Black Sails and forward to the stony summit of Wetherlam and a fine prospect over Little Langdale and Windermere to the distant Pennines.

The summit of Wetherlam

Wetherlam, like the Old Man, has an eastern flank pock-marked with the relics of disused workings and the shafts and tunnels of old mines. In lengthy explorations here I have counted a hundred man-made openings in the ground, many of them without protection and very dangerous. Wander not on Wetherlam after dark!

All that remains to be done to complete the walk is to proceed along the declining south ridge of Wetherlam (no path and no difficulties). Lower down, the ridge is known as Lad Stones, and here by veering down the slope on the left a good path coming from Tilberthwaite is joined; this descends to a road in Coppermines Valley that goes down alongside Church Beck and an attractive waterfall to enter the main street of Coniston.

Waterfall, Church Beck

11 THE NEWLANDS ROUND
FROM LITTLE TOWN   (9 MILES)

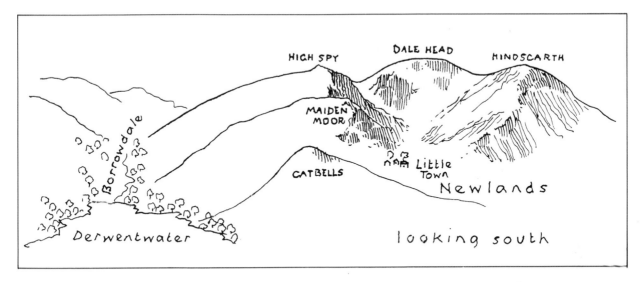

More than fifty years have gone by since I first set eyes on Newlands and in all that time the valley seems not to have changed in any way. Today it is the same sweet Arcadia I knew so long ago, lovely and secluded, an idyllic place of flowers and trees, of emerald pastures and sequestered farmsteads, all cosily sheltered by rough mountains, and having as its greatest blessing an undisturbed peace, a freedom from tourists in the mass and related commercial enterprises, and enjoying a way of life that in essence has never altered.

The Newlands valley runs closely parallel to Borrowdale yet is a world apart. Borrowdale at all seasons of the year and especially in summer is heavily populated by visitors attracted by Derwentwater and the exquisite scenery of the lake's environs, but the charms of Newlands are subtle and appeal more to a discerning minority. A lofty range of hills between the two is an effective barrier, segregating one from the other and allowing each to live its life without dependence on its neighbour.

The range of hills springs from the western shore of Derwentwater, rising first to the shapely cone of Catbells and continuing at an increasing elevation over Maiden Moor and the summit of High Spy, with Borrowdale now far below the eastern flank and Newlands a deep and narrowing trench at the foot of the precipitous western slopes. The high ground then swings round to its focal point, the massive bulk of Dale Head which, as its name implies, terminates the valley, and next turns north along the Hindscarth ridge, thus confining the upper reaches between steep acclivities. It is this 'horseshoe' that provides the walk to be described: a circuit of the skyline around the wild recesses of Newlands beyond the limits of cultivation.

(Opposite) The upper reaches of Newlands

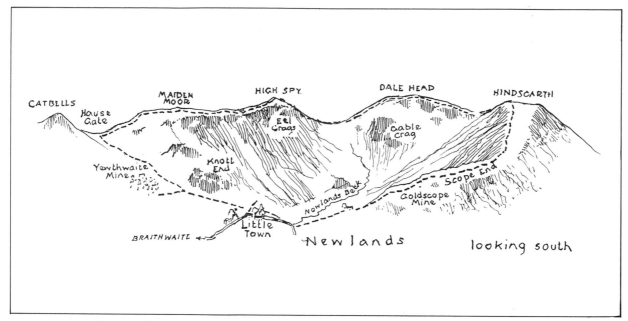

CATBELLS · House Gate · MAIDEN MOOR · HIGH SPY · Eel Crags · DALE HEAD · Cable Crag · HINDSCARTH · Yewthwaite Mine · Knott End · Newlands Beck · Scope End · Goldscope Mine · Little Town · BRAITHWAITE · Newlands · looking south

Knott End from Newlands Church

I prefer to begin and end the walk at the hamlet of Little Town, where a path joins a rising cart-track on the open fell below the crags of Knott End; at a wall-corner, the cart-track turns left and a path going straight ahead is followed, passing an area despoiled by the disused Yewthwaite Mine where there are dangerous open shafts, a tragic death occurring in one of them in 1962. Directly ahead is the depression of Hause Gate and upon reaching it a glorious view of Derwentwater and Borrowdale is suddenly revealed. Cameras should not be clicked here, however, as an even better viewpoint will soon be reached.

From Hause Gate a track to the right mounts steadily to Maiden Moor, aiming for a prominent cairn that appears to be the summit, but isn't. This cairn is a viewpoint par excellence: it commands an out-of-this-world prospect of Derwentwater backed by Blencathra, a scene that nobody carrying a camera can possibly resist.

Derwentwater from Maiden Moor

Dale Head from High Spy

The top of Maiden Moor is an easy promenade over level ground with little of immediate interest, and although the Ordnance Survey state the height as 1887 ft there is doubt as to the precise spot that yielded this information. All is grass here: there is no stone to sit on nor an outcrop to recline against, and the best features of the retrospective view are now hidden by widening convex slopes, so that there is no cause to linger. Walkers who feel they have earned a halt are recommended to stroll across to the Newlands edge of the summit plateau and find a couch near the rim of the formidable Bull Crag and enjoy a bird's view of the valley; it will be noted that Bull Crag is a part only of a continuous escarpment along this side of the fell. It is, in fact, more exciting to continue the walk along the edge of the escarpment than it is to keep to the popular path. Further on, the moor narrows to a crest and then an engineered path climbs to the summit cairn on High Spy, 2143 ft, a fine vantage point immediately above the mile-long precipice of Eel Crags, down which, from safe stances, there are spectacular views of the head of Newlands. But the most imposing object in sight, its full stature now revealed, is Dale Head, its steep northern face, wrinkled by tiers of crags, effectively bringing the valley to an abrupt end.

Next follows the first descent of the day, a long downhill walk to the moorland east of Dale Head, a confusing terrain of hillocks and hollows; here the valley path comes up out of Newlands and can be used for a quick return to Little Town in case of an onset of bad weather or to save time or tired legs. Other paths go down to Borrowdale, left, and forward to Honister Pass. The place to aim for is Dalehead Tarn, indicated from afar by its shimmering waters, and here, looking back, the profile of Eel Crags can be seen taking shape below the summit of High Spy.

Dalehead Tarn and High Spy

From the far end of Dalehead Tarn the ascent to the summit of Dale Head starts, there being a track for most of the way. This climb is steep and, like all climbs, longer than expected. I well remember, in the days when I was a raw apprentice on the hills, ill-prepared and ill-equipped, toiling up this slope in a state of near exhaustion: there was no track then and the ascent seemed interminable; for the last few hundred yards I was reduced to crawling upwards on hands and knees. As always on the hills, a five-minute halt was enough to restore sufficient energy to enable me to go on my way. In those far-off days, too, my routine was to descend steep grass by shuffling down on my bottom, a practice I still adopt on occasion because a tough and rubbery bottom is a valuable agent of friction, a sheet anchor with superb resistance to the pull of gravity. Once this method of downward progression ended in calamity when a concealed rock neatly removed the seat of my pants, a matter of indifference while I was alone on the hills but in the streets of Keswick later, and on the bus going home, I had to hide my embarrassed flesh in a buttoned-up plastic raincoat although the day was sunny and warm and everybody else was in shirt sleeves. Since then, my advice to others is to keep the body erect when walking steeply up or down.

The toil of the ascent is immediately forgotten on arrival at the summit of Dale Head. In every direction the panorama is magnificent, especially excelling in the full-length view of Newlands, the wild upper valley merging into the sylvan scenery beyond and distant Skiddaw closing the picture perfectly. This I consider to be the finest aerial view of a valley from a Lakeland summit. The well-constructed cairn of neat courses of slate stands on the brink of a sharp drop and makes a striking foreground. I have had reports that this cairn has suffered wanton damage of late but hope they are not true. I have an affection for summit cairns. To me, they represent ambitions and achievements. I feel bereaved by their loss.

Dale Head is a mountain mutilated by prospectors. The Honister flank is pitted with quarries and the Newlands face bears traces of a disused copper mine where the bright green veins of copper malachite can still be seen in the rocks and stones. It is a mountain of interest to geologists, for beneath the carpet of grass there is a fusion of the Skiddaw slates and the volcanic rocks of central Lakeland, some evidences of this joint being seen on the actual summit.

Summit cairn, Dale Head

(Below) Eel Crags and High Spy from Dale Head; (opposite) The Newlands valley from Dale Head

Dale Head is the turning point of the walk. A narrowing ridge, scarped on both sides and having lovely views of the Buttermere valley and fells, is traversed northwest to a depression where the ridge is left and a plateau crossed due north for half a mile to the summit of Hindscarth, 2385 ft, a fell with a broad top but extremely steep flanks on both sides. The summit cairn is an untidy pile of stones amongst embedded rocks; of greater interest is a larger and well-built cairn of some antiquity 200 paces away with the interior hollowed to act as a wind-shelter. There is now a long descent north, with cliffs falling away on the right, to the narrow ridge of Scope End directly ahead, where a delightful track through heather winds down towards the valley.

The upper part of the Newlands valley is rich in minerals and there are many places where man has scratched the ground for buried treasure, mainly lead and copper, and on Scope End, gold. Here was the famous Goldscope Mine, about which I wrote in an earlier publication as follows:

Goldscope Mine

Goldscope Mine was abandoned a hundred years ago after intermittent operation over a period of six centuries. One of the oldest mines in the district, it was also the most important in output, having rich veins of lead and copper. Silver and gold, too, have been extracted. Its early development, on a large scale, was undertaken by Germans; and its long history has been marked by many adventures and much litigation.

Upper Pan Holes

External evidence of the mine is indicated mainly by spoil-heaps on the Newlands Beck side of Scope End: immediately above is the main adit of Lower Pan Holes (from which a stream issues) with a second opening a few yards higher, under a tree. Further up the fellside is a curious slanting gash in a rockface — the Upper Pan Holes. On the other (Scope Beck) flank of the ridge are several levels.

Scope End is therefore pierced from both sides and the main level runs into the fell for such a considerable distance (over 300 yards) before becoming impassable, due to roof-falls, that it is reasonable to suppose that in the later years of operation it would be possible to walk right through the heart of it. In the darkness of these inner workings is a great shaft, which was sunk to such a depth ultimately that the pumping of water from it became too costly — this, not exhaustion of the minerals, was the reason for closure.

Lower Pan Holes

Hindscarth and Scope End

Having survived an exploration of the Goldscope Mine, the descent of Scope End is continued to the farm of Low Snab at its foot, where the farm access road goes through fields to Newlands Church, a small and humble edifice plain or pretty according to the eyes of the beholder and thence to the main valley road, reached at a bridge over Newlands Beck. Little Town is up a short hill to the right where, looking back, there is a splendid view of Hindscarth and Scope End, fitting subjects for the last photograph of the day.

12 THE COLEDALE ROUND
FROM BRAITHWAITE (9 MILES)

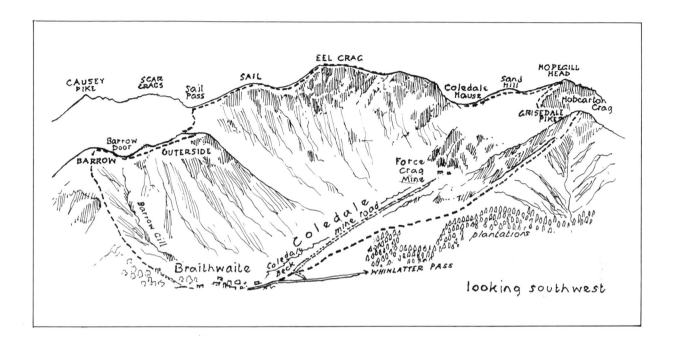

Nobody ever goes into raptures about Coledale. It lacks the characteristics of other Lakeland valleys, being without a farmstead, trees and green pastures and having no sylvan corners, no sinuous curves and no lovely paths. There is nothing to explore: all is seen at a glance and is not inviting. It is a long straight trench along which runs a rough road to the Force Crag barytes mine at its distant head, where the valley terminates in a spectacular tumble of cliffs and waterfalls: the end is dramatic, the approach dull and tedious. Coledale is not a place for a picnic.

The valley has one great advantage for the walker. Although a long and uninspiring trudge, the mine road offers a fast passage to the heart of a group of fells of considerable merit. And it is tightly enclosed by a ring of rugged heights that can be linked at a high level on a continuous walk all round the valley, a walk that ranks amongst the best in sustained interest and in the excellence of the views from each of the six summits attained.

The valley of Coledale is without charm but will be remembered with affection by those who walk around the mountain skyline of its perimeter and by so doing enjoy one of their most rewarding days on the tops.

(Opposite) The head of Coledale

On the principle of getting the hardest part of the climbing done first to give tired limbs an easy return to base, a policy I strongly advocate, I suggest that the walk starts from Braithwaite with an ascent of the mountain that dominates the village, Grisedale Pike. The climbing commences at once. Every step beyond the last cottage is upwards until the summit is reached, a long and relentless fight against gravity for which a girding of the loins is an essential preliminary.

Grisedale Pike from Braithwaite

Where the road turns right for Whinlatter, eager walkers have blazed a steep track straight up the fellside, but it is easier to go up the road a short way and use the mine road which turns left at a gravel pit to reach the walkers' path at a higher level. Now the climbing starts in earnest with a steep pull up to the 1200 ft contour. Here there is relief from intense effort as the gradient eases to the final pyramid of the Pike, the last section entailing more collar-work for half an hour until the summit is reached at 2593 ft, the cairn standing on a plinth of slate amidst a litter of fragments that tinkle musically when walked upon. A halt here is deserved and may be spent enjoying a wide prospect of the coastal plain and the Solway Firth, but most attention will be focussed on the next stages of the walk, well displayed between south and west.

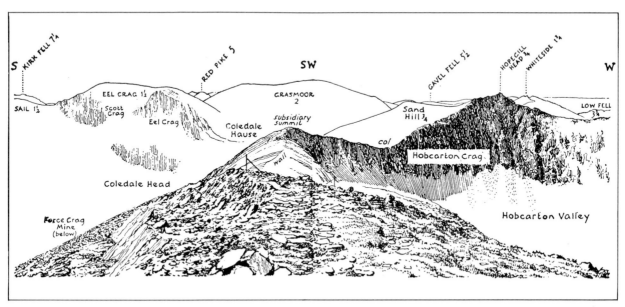

S KIRK FELL 7¼   RED PIKE 5   SW   GAVEL FELL 5½   HOPEGILL HEAD ¾   WHITESIDE 1¼   W
EEL CRAG 1½   GRASMOOR 2
SAIL 1½   Scott Crag   Sand Hill ¾   LOW FELL 3¾
Eel Crag   subsidiary summit   Hobcarton Crag
Coledale Hause   col
wall
Coledale Head   Hobcarton Valley
Force Crag Mine (below)

Keswick and Derwentwater from the summit of Grisedale Pike

Hobcarton Crag appears ahead as an increasingly formidable object as the walk is resumed down an easy ridge to a slight depression, beyond which a gradual climb along the edge of the cliffs reaches the peaked summit of Hopegill Head, 2525 ft, a wonderful vantage point immediately above a wild downfall of crags interspersed with lush terraces of bilberry. This is a hallowed place for botanists, being the only known habitat in England of the red alpine catchfly (*Viscaria alpina*), but searches for this rare plant are most certainly not recommended: the near-vertical rocks are of Skiddaw slate, fractured and splintered and totally unsafe for exploration. It is significant that no rock-climbing takes place here.

Viscaria alpina

Hobcarton Crag

Eel Crag above Coledale Hause

On one occasion I had a remarkable experience on the top of Hopegill Head. I approached the summit by way of the rocky northern ridge and, while yet some distance away, became aware of a great commotion at the cairn. I could hear a symphony of twittering and the swish of wings, growing in volume as I drew nearer, and as I topped the last rocks and brought the cairn in sight the cause was revealed: some thirty or forty swifts were darting and diving around the cairn, obviously in a state of great excitement because they completely ignored my presence only a few yards away; they had other things to engage their attention. They swooped around my head with alarming insistence, coming within inches before wheeling away; the experience was rather frightening, like something from a nightmare or a horror film. This was the only time I came within five yards of a summit cairn yet was unable to reach it: that short distance was made untenable by the diving swifts, but I was near enough to see that the pile of stones was covered by flying ants and that I was disturbing a feast. On other occasions I have found colonies of winged ants on summit cairns but unattended by predators, and once on the top of Caw in the Duddon Valley I found the cairn completely plastered with ladybirds, the stones appearing to be stained a bright red. These migrating flights of insects seem to have a liking for coming to rest at summit cairns, bless their little hearts, just as I have.

The rocky top of Hopegill Head is the finest situation visited on the walk and is left with reluctance to pass over the subsidiary height of Sand Hill and descend a grass slope to the wide depression of Coledale Hause, which carries a path coming up out of Coledale across a watershed and down to Lanthwaite by way of Gasgale Gill. The only feature of interest here is an old water cut made to divert supplies from Gasgale Gill for use at the Force Crag Mine in Coledale. Across the hause are the stony slopes of Eel Crag, the next objective.

Eel Crag has two summits, a lower one at 2649 ft reached by an unpleasant scramble over loose stones from Coledale Hause (which can be avoided by going up alongside Gasgale Gill until strips of grass appear on the left) and the main one at 2749 ft, the latter having a triangulation column. The name by which the fell is commonly known, Eel Crag, is unfortunate and inaccurate, the name properly being that of a rock buttress overlooking Coledale. The Ordnance Survey give the name of the fell as Crag Hill, but I never heard anyone use this. It is the hub of a mountain group, with four ridges radiating from it. The Coledale face drops away sharply and is much broken by crags; even steeper is the southern flank falling to Sail Beck, a pathless wilderness of eroded cliffs and scree and heather where no man ventures.

(Above) Sail Beck and Knott Rigg from Sail   *(Opposite) Coledale Head from Sail Pass*

Beyond the main cairn of Eel Crag, a ridge leaves the summit and goes sharply down eastwards, becoming narrow and rocky but without difficulty and is followed by a short rise to the summit of Sail, 2530 ft and then a long descent to Sail Pass which is crossed by a little-used path linking Stoneycroft in Newlands and Buttermere.

Beyond Sail Pass, the ridge continues over Scar Crags and ends abruptly at Causey Pike, but these heights are outside the ambit of Coledale, and at Sail Pass the path descending left below Long Comb is taken, soon arriving at the site of Lakeland's only cobalt mine, long abandoned. Continuing, now on the old mine road, there is a crossing of easy ground in the wide expanse of High Moss. This old road becomes of cart width and leads directly down to Stoneycroft in Newlands, two tarmac miles from Braithwaite, and offers a quick return to base. But walkers with a reserve of energy should climb the slope of Outerside, rising to the left of High Moss, and so reach its summit at 1863 ft. Here there is an aerial view of Coledale and a comprehensive prospect of the whole walk so far done and still to be done. Otherwise the top is undistinguished.

Grisedale Pike from Outerside

Outerside is rarely visited but a thin track through the heather heading north-east and having the Coledale edge on the left goes pleasantly down to the depression of Low Moss and then bypasses the minor height of Stile End, curving round it to the pronounced gap of Barrow Door. A path going down to Braithwaite passes through this gap, and if followed to the left gives a quick return to the village alongside the surprising ravine of Barrow Gill. But there is another summit to be visited to complete the itinerary: at 1494 ft this is the lowest top of the day but, thanks to a carpet of heather, a delightful belvedere. This is Barrow, easily reached by a rising track from Barrow Door and much too good to be missed.

(Above) Barrow Door

View from the summit of Barrow

From the summit of Barrow a bewitching path descends its northern ridge, at first winding through heather and lower down on grass amidst bracken, the sort of path that tempts one to linger even though ravaged by hunger and knowing a good meal awaits ahead. There is an exquisite vista of Newlands down to the right, marred at one point where the debris of the old Barrow Mine falls from the ridge and scars the fellside.

The end of this delectable path is reached at the farm of Braithwaite Lodge, where an access road goes down to the village. Now for that meal!

13 SCAFELL PIKE
FROM BORROWDALE   (10 MILES)

Ridges, in general, provide the best fellwalking in Lakeland as elsewhere: they are the high-level traverses that link mountain summits without too much descent and re-ascent between them. Ridges are usually the easiest lines of progression in rough terrain; they are the natural passages along the tops, and invariably reward the walker with ever-changing distant panoramas and aerial views of ethereal beauty as lakes and bright fields edged with trees and copses come into sight far below; and, in sharp contrast, tarns nestling in dark mountain hollows are revealed as sparkling jewels in sunlight and black pools under cloud. Often there are sensational glimpses of craggy slopes plunging down into shadowy depths where streams appear as winding silver threads. The narrower the ridge, the greater the enjoyment. Ridgewalking is fellwalking at its best.

There are a few exceptions. For example, the ascent of Scafell by the West Wall Traverse and the fellside crossing to Pillar Rock, each of which leads into situations of unsurpassed grandeur amongst towering crags and give a thrilling sense of adventure without attendant hazards, are not ridge walks but intimate explorations of rock scenery that yield even greater satisfaction to those who seek a measure of excitement in their days on the fells.

Another notable exception is the ascent of Scafell Pike from Borrowdale. This is a classic expedition, and I consider it to be the finest fellwalk in the Lake District. Not because Scafell Pike is the highest ground in the country, not because its summit is especially distinguished, nor even because of the far-reaching panorama it commands, but for the infinite variety of the natural features and landmarks met along the way and the impressive surroundings throughout. It is an ascent of great merit, entailing much rough walking, as befits a climb to this loftiest of all Lakeland fells, and progress is slow, yet every step, if not always a joy to tread, is a step towards the fulfilment of an admirable ambition: to stand on the highest inches in England.

Moreover, there are two routes to the top from Borrowdale, both of rare distinction and abounding in interesting situations, so that the return may be made by using the alternative. By doing so, two splendid fellwalks can be enjoyed in one outing and with a visit to Lakeland's highest cairn as a special incentive, the whole makes a challenging itinerary, a test of endurance for senior citizens and of stamina for youngsters, but well within the capacity of fellwalkers in the average to good bracket; and an achievement that will make the day a day to remember with satisfaction. But there are two buts, the first is to await a spell of settled weather and clear visibility, the other is to start early.

(Opposite) Scafell Pike from Great Gable

Seathwaite, a small farming community

Seathwaite, where the walk starts and ends, is a small farming community, the last outpost in Borrowdale, and the wettest inhabited place in the country in terms of rainfall, averaging about 130 inches a year. Encompassed by steep fells, its river, the Derwent, becomes a raging torrent when in spate and the devastation caused by flood waters is clearly seen in the choke of boulders along its course and in the scattering of debris on the adjoining fields.

Seathwaite is a gateway to the grandest mountains in Lakeland and is a very popular starting point for walks on the fells. The few buildings stand at the terminus of the tarmac road up the valley, and it is not uncommon for dozens of cars to be close-parked on the verge here, while walkers pass through the farmyard from early morning until dusk. Seathwaite is a most friendly place and the farm animals, even the dogs, show no aggression but give the impression that, while everybody is welcome, they are rather bored by the constant procession of visitors. Rainfall statistics notwithstanding, every fellwalker has happy memories of Seathwaite in the morning of a day of adventure and at its close.

From Seathwaite, a path goes forward to Stock-ley Bridge, a much-trodden pedestrian highway, dusty and scoured of vegetation and seldom with-out foot traffic. Many visitors to the bridge are ill-shod and not intent on fellwalking expeditions: they settle on the rocks by the stream and after a picnic return to their cars at Seathwaite.

Over the bridge on the facing slope a network of blazed tracks indicate the popular route to Sty Head. This is another example of a well-made path suffering damage by boots descending at speed. The original path, grooved and paved and nicely graded, has been destroyed, only a few small sec-tions remaining in pristine condition.

Stockley Bridge

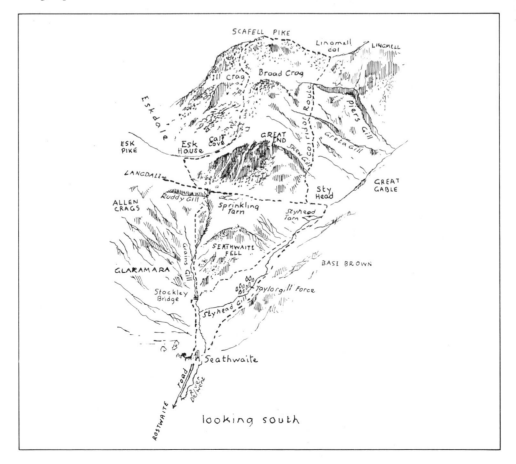

looking south

The path to be taken after crossing Stockley Bridge is not the scarred route facing but one turning upstream and entering the narrow confines of Grains Gill, leaving behind the picnic parties and the crowds aiming for Sty Head. Grains Gill is flanked on the left by Glaramara and on the right by Seathwaite Fell; it is quiet and pleasant, with a few trees and water splashes, but near the top, where the stream issues from a ravine, the ground steepens sharply, this being the most arduous part of the walk. Emerging on gentler terrain at the head of the gill, the well-known path linking Great Langdale and Wasdale is reached and, at this point, coming down on the left, is Ruddy Gill, so named because of its red subsoil indicating haematite; this is a continuation of the vein seen exposed at Ore Gap on Bowfell.

Ruddy Gill

(Above) Grains Gill

Great End from Sprinkling Tarn

After struggling up and out of Grains Gill, a breather has been earned and this may best be enjoyed by a short stroll to the right along the Wasdale path to Sprinkling Tarn, a most attractive sheet of water with an indented rocky shore, its scenic quality enhanced by the massive cliffs of Great End nearby and soaring above; Great Gable is also in the picture. This is a delightful place, well provided with heathery couches amongst grey boulders on the water's edge. The tarn is an enchantress; the temptation to linger is strong but must be resisted. Too many walkers bound for Scafell Pike have given up the ghost here, daunted by the sight of Great End and bewitched by the beauty and solitude of the tarn.

'Onwards!' must be the cry. Much remains to be done.

(Above) Esk Pike; (opposite) Borrowdale from Great End, with Sprinkling Tarn

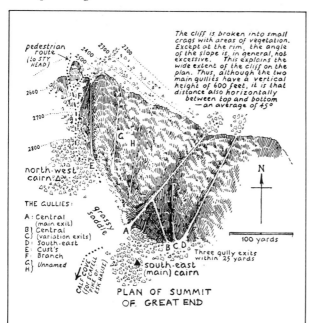

pedestrian
route
(to STY
HEAD)

2400
2500
2300
2600
2700
2800

north-west
cairn

The cliff is broken into small
crags with areas of vegetation.
Except at the rim, the angle
of the slope is, in general, not
excessive. This explains the
wide extent of the cliff on the
plan. Thus, although the two
main gullies have a vertical
height of 600 feet, it is that
distance also horizontally
between top and bottom
—an average of 45°

C   H

E

grassy
saddle

N

100 yards

THE GULLIES:

A: Central
(main exit)
B: Central
C: (variation exits)
D: South-east
E: Cust's
F: Branch
G: Unnamed
H:

CALF COVE
(for SCAFELL
PIKE or ESK HAUSE)

A

B C D
Three gully exits
within 25 yards

south-east
(main) cairn

PLAN OF SUMMIT
OF GREAT END

Great End blocks the way to Scafell Pike, but is obviously unassailable by direct assault, and after a reluctant farewell to Sprinkling Tarn the walk is resumed by returning to the head of Grains Gill and following the Langdale path until a cairned track branches off to the right: this is a fairly new short cut to Esk Hause and is a useful time-saver. It rises across a stony slope in the direction of Esk Pike, rounding the cliffs of Great End, and arrives at the grassy saddle of Esk Hause.

At Esk Hause the ground falls away sharply into the wild upper reaches of Eskdale and the great bulk of the Scafells comes in sight, the prominent peak of Ill Crag, a satellite of Scafell Pike and often mistaken for it from this viewpoint, being seen springing from the depths in a succession of crags. Now the path turns to the right and ascends a grassy hollow, Calf Cove, to the skyline above.

Before going on along the path from Calf Cove, an assessment should be made of the strength remaining in the legs and of the hours of daylight still available, because there is an opportunity at this point to make a worthwhile digression to the top of Great End, 2984 ft, at the cost of an extra mile of rough walking up and down the stony slope to the right. On reaching the summit cairn, the justification for this deviation will be fully appreciated: a superb retrospective view of Borrowdale unfolds, extending from Sprinkling Tarn, now seen as an inky blot a thousand feet below, to the fields of the mid-valley and Derwentwater backed by the Skiddaw group. A perambulation along the edge of the cliffs, looking down its impressive gullies, is certainly equally thrilling.

The summit of Great End is rarely visited. It is, in my opinion, a summit much to be preferred to that of Scafell Pike, not only for the Borrowdale view, which is superior to any seen from the Pike but for its quietness and solitude and the excitement and interest of the cliff-top exploration.

At the top of Calf Cove the path to Scafell Pike turns left and is unmistakable, bearing the imprints and footprints and decaying litter of legions of pilgrims and an over-abundance of cairns. At first the going is easy, on grass, but then the ground takes the form of a wide stony ridge with only minor undulations. Next follows 150 yards of close-packed boulders, unavoidable and difficult to negotiate, calling for care. Beyond is an easier section, on gravel and small stones, as the path bypasses the top of Ill Crag, seen on the left and now appearing insignificant, and descends to a col beyond which the path rises as a rough stairway of boulders to skirt the summit of Broad Crag. Stones and outcropping rocks are everywhere in this arid wilderness, cairns marking an uncomfortable passage through them, and patches of mountain greenery are rare indeed. Another small col is reached and ahead now is the final pyramid of Scafell Pike. The path picks a stony way up this last rough slope, steeply initially before easing into a tilted desert of awkward and angular boulders, a dead landscape of sterile rock. Human voices, seeming quite out of place in this lifeless no-man's-land, indicate that the summit is near, and their owners are duly found littering the massive cairn in varying stages of exhaustion and exultation.

The approach to Scafell Pike

The summit of Scafell Pike

Ever since the Ordnance Survey pronounced the height of Scafell Pike as 3210 ft and thereby officially established its superiority in terms of altitude over all other land in the country, its summit has been a magnet for all active visitors to the Lake District, a Mecca that simply must be attained, the objective above all others, the ultimate achievement. Over the years, it has been the venue of ceremonies and celebrations, of bonfires and birthday parties, and the rejoicings continue today with every successful ascent.

Nature's design for the roof of England is a desolation of stones of all shapes and sizes, a barren waste where only mosses and lichens can find sustenance, an inhospitable desert without grace, without charm and without colour other than the drab grey of volcanic rocks.

Man's contribution to the scene is a huge circular stone platform, a plaque commemorating the gift of the summit to the nation; an Ordnance column, and litter. There is no beauty here.

Extract from "The Southern Fells".

Soliloquy.........

In summertime the cairn often becomes over-run with tourists, and a seeker after solitary contemplation may then be recommended to go across to the south peak, where, after enjoying the splendid view of Eskdale, he can observe the visitors to the summit from this distance. He may find himself wondering what impulse had driven these good folk to leave the comforts of the valley and make the weary ascent to this inhospitable place.

Why *does* a man climb mountains? Why has he forced his tired and sweating body up here when he might instead have been sitting at his ease in a deckchair at the seaside, looking at girls in bikinis, or fast asleep, or sucking ice-cream, according to his fancy. On the face of it the thing doesn't make sense.

Yet more and more people are turning to the hills; they find something in these wild places that can be found nowhere else. It may be solace for some, satisfaction for others : the joy of exercising muscles that modern ways of living have cramped, perhaps; or a balm for jangled nerves in the solitude and silence of the peaks ; or escape from the clamour and tumult of everyday existence. It may have something to do with a man's subconscious search for beauty, growing keener as so much in the world grows uglier. It may be a need to readjust his sights, to get out of his own narrow groove and climb above it to see wider horizons and truer perspectives. In a few cases, it may even be a curiosity inspired by ~~Wainwright's~~ Pictorial Guides. Or it may be, and for most walkers it will be, quite simply, a deep love of the hills, a love that has grown over the years, whatever motive first took them there : a feeling that these hills are friends, tried and trusted friends, always there when needed.

It is a question every man must answer for himself.

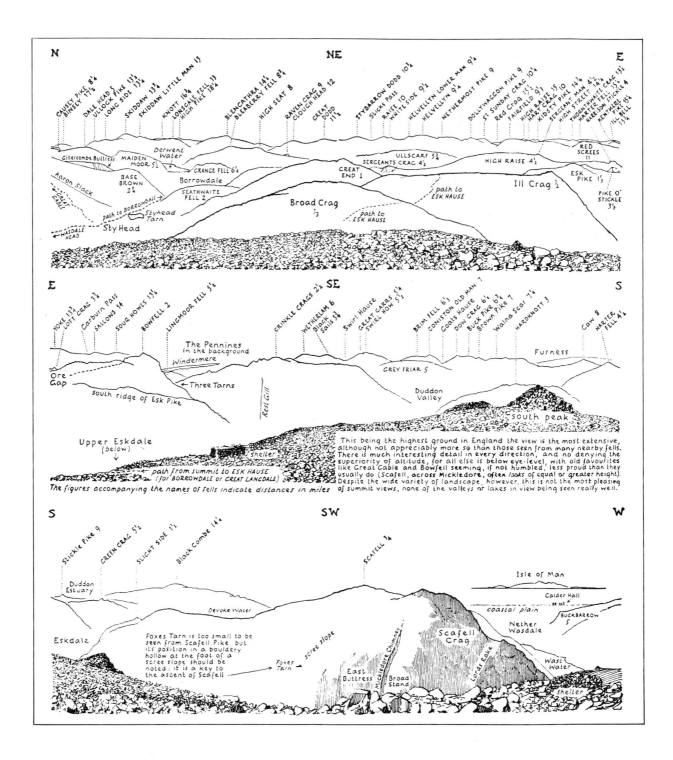

This being the highest ground in England the view is the most extensive, although not appreciably more so than those seen from many nearby fells. There is much interesting detail in every direction, and no denying the superiority of altitude, for all else is below eye-level, with old favourites like Great Gable and Bowfell seeming, if not humbled, less proud than they usually do (Scafell, across Mickledore, often looks of equal or greater height). Despite the wide variety of landscape, however, this is not the most pleasing of summit views, none of the valleys or lakes in view being seen really well.

The figures accompanying the names of fells indicate distances in miles

Foxes Tarn is too small to be seen from Scafell Pike, but its position in a bouldery hollow at the foot of a scree slope should be noted: it is a key to the ascent of Scafell

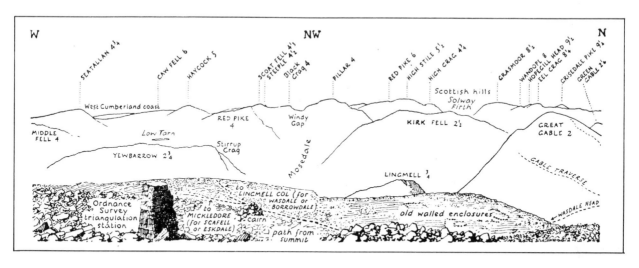

W — NW — N

SEATALLAN 4¾ CAW FELL 6 HAYCOCK 5 SCOAT FELL 4½ STEEPLE 4½ Black Crag 4 PILLAR 4 RED PIKE 6 HIGH STILE 5½ HIGH CRAG 4¾ GRASMOOR 8½ WANDOPE 8 HOPEGILL HEAD 9½ EEL CRAG 8¾ CRISEDALE PIKE 9½ GREEN GABLE 2½

West Cumberland coast

Scottish hills
Solway Firth

RED PIKE 4

MIDDLE FELL 4

Low Tarn

Windy Gap

KIRK FELL 2½

GREAT GABLE 2

YEWBARROW 2¾

Stirrup Crag

Mosedale

CABLE TRAVERSE

LINGMELL ¾

Ordnance Survey triangulation station

to LINGMELL COL (for WASDALE or BORROWDALE)

to MICKLEDORE (for SCAFELL or ESKDALE)

cairn

old walled enclosures

WASDALE HEAD

path from summit

Scafell from Scafell Pike

Piers Gill

Skew Gill

Rejoicings over, limbs rested, and encouraged by the prospect of easier walking, all mercifully downhill, the return to Seathwaite is started along a distinct but stony path heading west but soon bifurcating, the left branch aiming for Mickledore and Scafell, the right branch, the one to be taken, trending north towards Lingmell and descending to the grassy depression of Lingmell Col. Here a turn to the right, guided by many cairns, soon reaches the head of Piers Gill, an awesome fissure enclosed by vertical cliffs and a notorious trap for inexperienced walkers who enter its lower confines and find themselves stranded in its gloomy depths and unable to proceed, the way being barred by huge chockstones and waterfalls between overhanging crags: an unfortunate adventurer who slipped and fell into the ravine in 1921 was found only after eighteen days of searching by rescue parties, he having survived his injuries and kept himself alive by a trickle of water.

The path skirts the top of the gill and resumes along a grassy shelf with fearful declivities on the left and bouldery slopes on the right. This is the Corridor Route, formerly known as the Guides' Route and originally used by climbers bound for Scafell Crag. It gives a remarkably easy passage through very rough terrain and opens up splendid views of Wasdale Head down on the left and of the tremendous pyramid of Great Gable ahead. The top of another ravine is passed – this is Greta Gill, which drops away sharply on the left and has a magnificent waterfall lower down, unseen from the path – and then follows a steeper descent to the foot of Skew Gill, a huge cleft that splits asunder the stony breast of Great End.

Hopes that there would be no more uphill walking are dashed when the scree debouching from Skew Gill is crossed because the grassy slope beyond must obviously be climbed. This is positively the last ascent of the day, however, and no great obstacle; at the top of the incline the path coming down from Sprinkling Tarn is met as the cliffs of Great End recede, and a turn to the left along this path leads to much-trampled ground very familiar to all who walk on the fells. This is Sty Head Pass, a busy pedestrian thoroughfare and crossroads and a popular springboard for mountain excursions, and the easiest link between Borrowdale and Wasdale. Once it was the subject of fierce controversy when insensitive authorities planned to build a road across it but were howled down by others who had more care and feeling for the environment and were forced to abandon their ridiculous ideas.

Sty Head is for walkers and must remain their exclusive preserve.

Great Gable from the Corridor Route

(Above) Lingmell from Sty Head; (below) Great End from Styhead Tarn

From Sty Head, paths radiate in many directions. To the left as approached (south, turning west), there is a long descent to Wasdale Head, straight ahead begins the climb to the top of Great Gable, and north-east lies Styhead Tarn and the path to Borrowdale, all distinct and profusely cairned. The latter is the one to take. It skirts the western shore of Styhead Tarn, which lacks the scenic attraction of Sprinkling Tarn but is nevertheless a favourite halting place: few walkers go past without stopping for a paddle in its clear waters or for a last look back at the impressive mountain background. This is a wonderful spot, a place of silence and solitude. Fancy wanting to build a motor road through this lonely sanctuary! Motorists must learn to walk if they wish to see the glories of Sty Head.

Taylorgill Force

After leaving Styhead Tarn, Borrowdale-bound, the path runs alongside the issuing stream, Styhead Gill, which becomes the River Derwent down in the valley, and crosses a wooden footbridge to continue the descent to Stockley Bridge. It is infinitely preferable, however, to go forward on the west bank of the stream on a thin track instead of crossing the footbridge. This alternative enters a wooded ravine graced by the slender waterfall of Taylorgill Force, the last highlight of the day. The track precariously hugs the base of a wall of crags, and in a few places needs care, before emerging into marshy fields and slanting down to a bridge by which the Derwent is crossed and Seathwaite entered under an arch in the farm buildings.

Thus ends the best fellwalk of all.

The mountain landscape of Lakeland is a chaotic upheaval of soaring peaks and lofty ridges springing steeply from deep glacial valleys, a compact mass of high ground rising sharply in wild desolation from a pastoral surround and clearly defined by its geological structure. Much of the upland area is volcanic and the evidences are manifest in a widespread scattering of boulders and stones amongst outcrops where the underlying rock breaks the surface, yet the summits follow no set pattern and are strongly individualistic. There are no smooth grassy hills in the heart of the district: the terrain is rough everywhere, with steep and craggy slopes scoured by scree-filled gullies and choked ravines. Featuring on almost every mountain are precipitous crags, great buttresses of naked rock that both attract and repel, awesome pinnacles fissured by frost and rain. These fearful cliffs are the exclusive preserve of the rock-climber and have no place in the itineraries of the ordinary fellwalker.

The most formidable of these natural bastions is Scafell Crag which towers in supreme majesty above a stony hollow in the fellside: a vertical wall of clean rock some 500 ft high, divided by gullies into five buttresses, the whole appearing to be totally unassailable. 'Nobbut a fleeing thing could get up theer,' said the innkeeper at Wasdale Head when his visitors of a hundred years ago contemplated the possibility of climbing it, yet, despite his assertion, those early pioneers, brave men all, succeeded in devising several routes of extreme severity up those forbidding cliffs, and today there is a network of lines of ascent available only to expert cragsmen.

The aspect of the Crag from below is intimidating, even frightening, and it is so palpably impossible for common or garden mortals to scale that none dares venture up the rocks from the safe ground at the foot, readily acknowledging that those who do so are a superior breed. But Nature has provided a breach in the defences of the Crag by which active walkers may gain access to its innermost secrets, make intimate acquaintance with magnificent and spectacular rock scenery, and emerge unscathed at the top: an achievement earned only by arduous effort and much expenditure of energy. This is the only route on Scafell Crag where walkers can tread safely without encountering serious climbing and without danger to life and limb. Lord's Rake and the West Wall Traverse are special privileges of the fellwalker and make him feel that perhaps he is not too inferior after all.

(Opposite) Scafell from the path to Mickledore from Scafell Pike

(Above) Wasdale Head

(Right) Pikes Crag and Scafell

I think Wasdale Head must take pride of place amongst the valleys of Lakeland, not for scenic beauty but because of the sheer grandeur of its mountain setting. It is deeply inurned below steep and shaggy slopes, a patchwork of bright fields intersected by walls of massive width built of stones cleared from the pastures, an emerald strath circumscribed by rough fellsides overtopped by giants: the Scafells, Great Gable and Pillar. There is an inn and a few farmhouses and cottages catering for visitors. Wasdale Head is the best base of all for earnest fellwalkers and climbers.

I remember the inn when it was little changed from the days when that redoubtable dalesman, Will Ritson, was mine host a hundred years ago. On my first visit, it was still a haunt of climbers: boots and ropes cluttered the passages, drying jackets and breeches were draped over doors and chairs, all guests were seated for meals at a large wooden table and given no choice of food, in a room where the furniture showed signs of distress after being subject to demonstrations of climbing techniques; the talk was of climbing and little else, just as in Ritson's time. Ritson was a great character. Rough in speech, spirited in action, a practical joker of ingenuity, he was in no way subservient to the many distinguished men who regularly stayed at the inn and formed the fraternity of rock-climbers, nor was he abashed by their erudite knowledge. It used to be said at that time that Wasdale had the highest mountain, the deepest lake, the smallest church and the biggest liar in England. The biggest liar has gone but his ghost still lives there.

Today, alas, the inn has been brought into line with modern demands. Motorists have discovered Wasdale Head, and sandals are as likely to be seen there as heavy boots. But, seen from the heights around, the valley is as it always was: a place apart, a place unique.

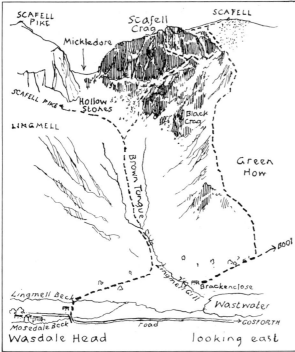

The walk starts at the road corner south of the inn where a signposted path leads to a footbridge crossing Lingmell Beck and then rises along a colourful fellside, the view back to Wasdale Head, with Pillar in the background, being very pleasing as one mounts higher. The path turns left above Lingmell Gill, a stream that bears the scars of devastating cloudbursts, its channel choked by boulders swept down from the heights above by the fury of past floods. But at this point, the attention is rivetted on the exciting skyline that comes into view ahead, formed by the serrated pinnacles of Pikes Crag and, across the Mickledore gap, the shadowed cliffs of the massive upthrust of Scafell Crag.

The gill is crossed at the foot of Brown Tongue, a widening strip of grassland between watercourses, up which climbs a track that would be tedious were it not for the rugged grandeur of the scene ahead, increasing in impressiveness with every step and a spur to progress.

The slope eases at the top of Brown Tongue and the main path inclines left, bound for Scafell Pike. By going forward, a profound hollow is entered amongst a litter of boulders and scree fallen from the enclosing crags. The surroundings are awesome. Pikes Crag soars into the sky on the left, ahead is the gap of Mickledore, topping long fans of scree and rocky debris, and towering on the right the tilted cliffs of Scafell Crag dominate the scene and seem to threaten collapse. This grim fastness is Hollow Stones, and its deep confinement between high and near-vertical walls of rock will make sufferers from claustrophobia and others of timid disposition decidedly uncomfortable. Everybody with a camera will want a picture of Scafell Crag but, seen from below, the aspect is considerably foreshortened, and to view its huge proportions in perspective, a detour along the path rising to Scafell Pike will reveal the full extent of its immense height.

Scafell Crag

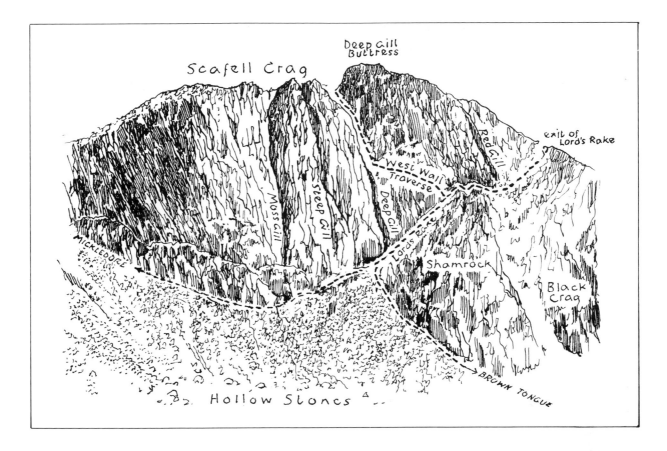

Hollow Stones is the place to gird up the loins before starting the great adventure of ascending to the top of Scafell Crag by the only route available to non-climbing pedestrians, a route of many highlights but accomplished only by sustained and arduous effort. The way goes up the long slope of scree on the right, a toilsome ascent where walkers choose any line they fancy up a ladder of loose and shifting stones, the best footing being found by scrambling upwards along the base of the crags of the Shamrock, so named because from below it appears to be part of the solid mass of Scafell Crag but in fact is severed from it by the deep channel of Lord's Rake, not yet visible. Although the scene around appears to be sterile and dead and unchanged since the landscape took shape in ages past, rockfalls do occur from time to time, caused by frost or heavy rain, and in 1958 a series of violent electrical storms of unusual severity brought down a tremendous tumble of stones and boulders that spread a new covering over the existing scree, and for years after this recent fall could be clearly distinguished by its lighter colour from the drab grey of the older stones.

At the top of the slope any further upward progress seems to be barred by the vertical wall of Scafell Pinnacle directly in front, but at this point a wide channel of stones opens on the right, rising very steeply as straight as a die to a small col on the skyline, and enclosed between a sheer wall of rock on the left and the topmost crags of the Shamrock, the latter forming a high parapet. This is Lord's Rake.

Lord's Rake is unmistakable. It is the only possible way of progressing further upwards from the top of the slope above Hollow Stones, but if confirmation is sought it will be found a few paces to the left, a cross carved in the rock of the Pinnacle marking the spot where four climbers fell to their deaths in 1903, this being still the worst climbing accident in the history of rock-climbing in the district. It should be noted that Lord's Rake does not lead into the heart of the mountain but rises obliquely across the face. Almost at once after entering the confines of the Rake, a huge cleft opens on the left: this is Deep Gill, the most direct route to the summit but seen at a glance to be impossible of ascent by walkers, who are committed to a fierce struggle up the Rake in a chaotic jumble of slippery stones and jammed boulders. Many and varied are the profanities that have been uttered on this desperate treadmill, even by persons of refinement, and all can be forgiven. Despair is lightened occasionally by sightings of starry saxifrage nodding to passers-by from moist crannies in the rocks, but the Rake has no other pleasures. After a strenuous battle against gravity for eighty yards, and just below the col, escape from the Rake is made up a short steep track on the left, where the rock wall relents to permit access to easier ground above. This is the start of the West Wall Traverse.

Lord's Rake

Deep Gill

Deep Gill Buttress and Scafell Pinnacle

After the tortures of Lord's Rake, the West Wall Traverse is sheer delight. Here is grass, at last, on a sloping and rising shelf that doubles back above the lower reaches of the Rake, now out of sight below its confining crags. The rock scenery is spectacular, fascinating, awe-inspiring. The ramparts of Deep Gill Buttress soar into the sky on the right, and directly ahead at close range is the upper part of Scafell Pinnacle, a graceful column of rock tapering to a spire high above. It is a wonderful privilege to be so intimately in the company of such magnificent cliffs. The track on the shelf is rough and boulder-strewn but easy to follow. At the end of the Traverse, it rounds a vertical buttress and enters the upper section of Deep Gill above its difficulties and the top exit is in sight.

The upper section of Deep Gill, a rough channel between impending crags, is tremendously impressive but the climb to the top, although steep, has no problems. It emerges on a level sward on the open fell, a heavenly resting place after all that has been endured. On my first visit, the exit from the gill was defended by an overhanging cornice of vegetation but this final obstacle has been pulled away and the last few yards of ascent, although very steep, are now negotiated by a new track.

The top of the gill, apart from the comfort of its grassy couches, is a wonderfully satisfying place. The view down the gill and across a profound gulf to Great Gable and the fells beyond is of absorbing interest, but the highlight of the scene is Scafell Pinnacle, its topmost rocks now seen in detail nearby on the right, the apex of a sublime pillar of rock that has its roots many hundreds of feet below at the entrance to Lord's Rake.

Scafell Pinnacle from the top of Deep Gill

The summit of Scafell

Wastwater

The cairn on the summit of Scafell, 3162 ft, is in view from the top of Deep Gill and is reached in five minutes by a simple stroll across a slight grassy saddle. The top is not particularly distinguished but commands a far-reaching view, being especially good to the south and west where there is a wide prospect of the coast and the sea beyond.

The descent from Scafell, compared with the complexities of the ascent, is simple and straightforward. To avoid the screes falling from the summit, a return is made to the saddle and a stony path going down on the left is followed. To add a spice of interest, a thinner track soon branching to the right and skirting the edge of the crags should be taken in a search for the upper exit of Lord's Rake which is not easy to locate but should be pinpointed and memorised for future expeditions on Scafell: it is a vital link with Hollow Stones and the only pedestrian way off the mountain on its north side, other than the West Wall Traverse, that bypasses Scafell Crag completely and reaches the easier ground below it. The track passes the gaping cleft of Red Gill, down which on my first visit I slithered and tumbled under the wrong impression that it was Lord's Rake, an experience survived without mishap but with pride dented by the mistake. The entrance to the Rake is in fact lower down the slope, around a corner, where its course can be clearly traced, descending to the screes debouching from Red Gill and then rising below cliffs to the col seen earlier in the walk when climbing up the Rake from the other end.

Here end the day's excitements and the walk continues very easily on grass down the long featureless slope of Green How to join the old corpse road linking Wasdale Head and Boot. This is followed down to the right, passing Brackenclose, owned by the Fell and Rock Climbing Club, and going around the head of Wastwater to the valley road, with Wasdale Head a mile distant.

15 GREAT GABLE
FROM HONISTER PASS   (6 MILES)

Great Gable is regarded with affection by all fellwalkers in Lakeland and indeed is probably the peak most favoured for a mountain excursion. The name itself is a challenge and is appropriate, suggesting strength, shapeliness, impressiveness and a commanding presence, and it has all these attributes in full measure. Whenever seen in a view, the distinctive summit is a magnet that draws the feet towards it, appearing from some directions as a slender spire, from others as a dome overtopping the neighbouring fells, and from Wasdale Head, where it was obviously named, it rises sharply from the valley as a massive, steep-sided pyramid that compels the attention of all visitors. The top is an irresistible objective and those who reach it enjoy a sense of achievement. Great Gable has status and confers status on the walkers who attain it.

The mountain is the centre of an area of 3000 acres of high fells acquired by the Fell and Rock Climbing Club as a memorial to the members who lost their lives in the 1914-1918 war, and was given to the National Trust in 1923. In June 1924 a dedicatory tablet, affixed to the summit rocks, was unveiled at a moving ceremony in the presence of a gathering of five hundred fellow-members and friends. Since then, a Remembrance Service has been held here in November each year. The selection of Great Gable as the venue of this annual pilgrimage is testimony to the esteem in which it is held by those who love the hills.

The ascent may be made from several points, the most popular being by the Breast Route from Sty Head, a good way up but too often made noisy by throngs of visitors who do not appreciate that the charm of the mountains lies in their silence and solitude. The direct climb from Wasdale Head is unremittingly steep and threads a stony passage through the fringe of crags high on this flank: it is a weary treadmill and not recommended. The best route, combining a long and interesting walk with the ascent and giving a convenient opportunity to visit other subsidiary summits without digressing, starts from and returns to the top of Honister Pass. I select this route, not because of the advantage gained by taking a car up to the pass which, at 1190 ft, considerably reduces the amount of climbing to be done on foot, but for the scenic excellence of the journey, the easy travelling and the superlative vistas of the Butter- mere valley and fells seen on the way.

(Opposite) Great Gable from Wasdale Head

(Left) Honister Crag;   *(Opposite) The Buttermere Fells*

Honister Pass is industrial. Here are the cutting sheds of the immense slate quarries that are slowly carving away and tunnelling into the tall cliffs of Honister Crag, the operation, on a near-vertical plane, being served by an amazing network of steeply inclined roads by which the slate is brought down in great blocks from the quarries high above.

In earlier days, the slate was conveyed down to the sheds by a steep tramway controlled by winding gear in a building near the top known as the Drum House, of which only the foundations remain. It is the track of this old tramway that now provides the way upwards for travellers on foot, and it is a rough and steep start to the walk. Nobody enjoys struggling up and slithering down this straight cut in the fellside but it is a necessary prelude to the expedition and the effort entailed is forgotten when the top is reached and an exciting skyline of fells comes into view. At this point, the more adventurous of walkers may digress to the right to the rim of the quarries and get a startling aerial view of the upper workings from safe stances above. Others, less active, or with no head for exposed heights, should not be tempted from the path which, at the site of the Drum House, turns left across an open moorland.

From the Drum House onwards, the walking is very easy as the path rises gradually along the western flank of Grey Knotts and soon opens up a glorious prospect of Haystacks and the High Stile range, with Pillar beyond and the lake and valley of Buttermere to the right, a picture of great beauty revealing new features as the walk progresses. Although the immediate surroundings are not of great interest, the mile from the Drum House to the Brandreth fence commands charming views to the west, making this easy section of the walk a delightful promenade.

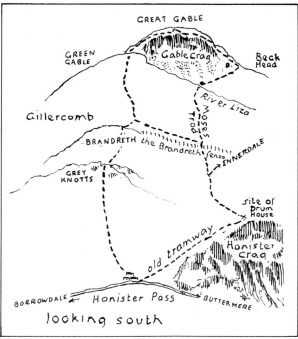

The path from the Drum House had a commercial origin. Before the construction of the gravitation tramways at the Honister quarries, the slate was moved by man-handled sledges down to the Pass, where the road at that time was in a primitive state and not easily negotiable by wheeled traffic, then exclusively horse-drawn. It was more convenient for supplies destined for South Cumberland and the port of Ravenglass to be transported by packhorses across the high fells to Wasdale, the route being planned to avoid steep gradients and rough places. This practice ceased about 1850 when the Honister road was improved, but the path has been kept in being by walkers and is commonly known as Moses' Trod.

Moses is a well-established figure in local tradition, which described him as a Honister quarryman who, after his day's work, illegally made whisky from the bog-water on Fleetwith at his quarry hut, smuggling this potent product to Wasdale with his pony-loads of slate. There is no evidence of his family name, or even that he ever lived, but no reason either for doubting the existence of a man of whom so many legends still survive in the district. He has given his name to many features along the path or in its vicinity. Up amongst the rocks of Gable Crag was a stone hut, now derelict, known as the Smuggler's Retreat, and below it is a rock-climb called Smuggler's Chimney, not climbed by Moses but so named after the first ascent in 1909 out of deference to his memory. On the side of Great Gable overlooking Wasdale, on the route of his descent to that valley, is an upright boulder still known as Moses' Finger.

The path today is most often used as a route of ascent to Great Gable and, after a branch goes away on the right bound for Ennerdale, reaches the Brandreth fence of which only the iron posts remain.

Moses' Finger (8 feet high)

The Brandreth fence

About here, the line of Moses' Trod is obscure, the more distinct path turning left to climb to the ridge between Brandreth and Green Gable en route for Great Gable, but by going forward at the turn on the same contour the Trod becomes clear and can be resumed. I recommend that this should be done: the Trod offers an alternative approach to Great Gable and calls for less effort than the ridge route. Still maintaining a steady contour, the Trod goes to-wards the great arc of Gable Crag, now starkly in view directly ahead.

Great Gable from Moses' Trod

The Trod crosses a stream, Tongue Beck, hereabouts providing a splendid view of Pillar and the afforested valley of Ennerdale, and then reaches the headwaters of the River Liza in a gloomy and austere setting. The infant river comes down from Stone Cove, a well-named wilderness of boulders between Green Gable, now up on the left, and Gable Crag, which extends in a massive arc high above and directly ahead and forms an impregnable barrier to the summit of Great Gable behind. The terrain is hostile, fans of scree covering the steep slope below the crag. After crossing the stream, Moses' Trod aims diagonally to the right and crosses the depression of Beck Head thence descending to Wasdale, but this is an unnecessary digression when the target is the top of Great Gable, and a slanting route upwards, heading for the skyline to the right of Gable Crag, leads to the stony ridge coming up from Beck Head, and here a steep and stony track goes up to the left and emerges on the tilted plateau of the summit, the highest point being clearly in view and reached along a track indicated by many cairns.

The summit of Great Gable; (right) The war memorial tablet

The summit of Great Gable is an upthrust of bare rock surmounted by a large cairn, a hallowed place since its adoption as a war memorial; the dedicatory tablet, which has a relief map of the area carved on it, is affixed to a rock on the north side. I have a personal interest in this summit: it was here that a Southport fellwalker spent a day in 1966 collecting signatures on a petition recommending me for a national honour following the completion of my series of Lakeland guidebooks, this being duly awarded. I was not to know the identity of this friendly and appreciative walker until fourteen years later when it was disclosed to me by a correspondent who knows him.

As may be expected from the superior altitude of the summit, 2949 ft, the view from it is excellent in all directions.

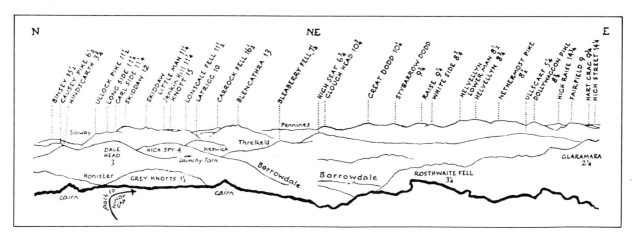

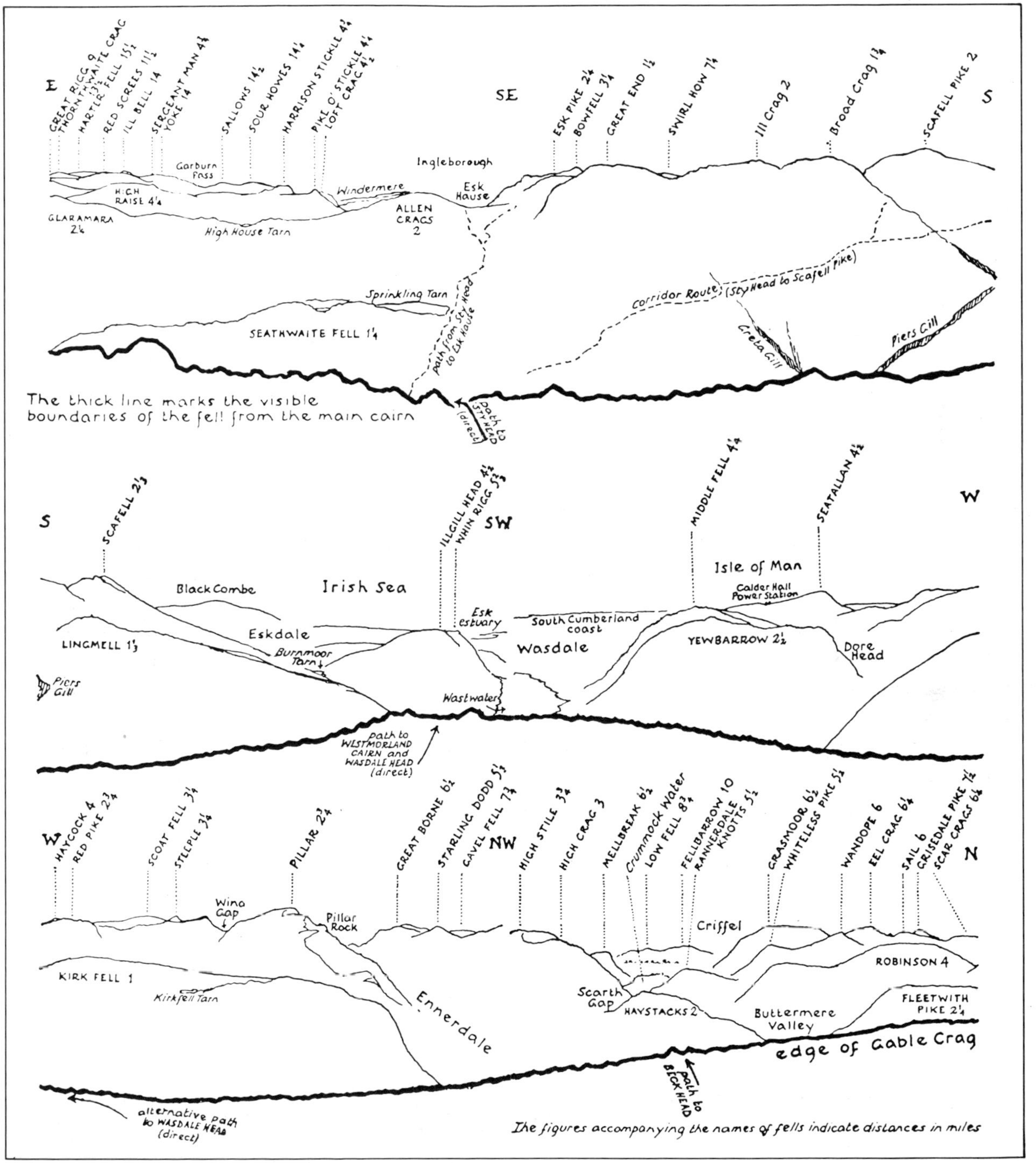
E
SE
S
GREAT RIGG 9
THORNTHWAITE CRAG
HARTER FELL 15½
RED SCREES 11½
ILL BELL 14
SERGEANT MAN 4¾
YOKE 14
SALLOWS 14½
SOUR HOWES 14¼
HARRISON STICKLE 4¾
PIKE O' STICKLE 4¼
LOFT CRAG 4½
ESK PIKE 2¼
BOWFELL 3¼
GREAT END 1½
SWIRL HOW 7¼
Ill Crag 2
Broad Crag 1¾
SCAFELL PIKE 2
Garburn Pass
Ingleborough
HIGH RAISE 4¼
Windermere
Esk Hause
ALLEN CRAGS 2
GLARAMARA 2¼
High House Tarn
Sprinkling Tarn
SEATHWAITE FELL 1¼
path from Sty Head to Esk Hause
Corridor Route (Sty Head to Scafell Pike)
Greta Gill
Piers Gill
The thick line marks the visible boundaries of the fell from the main cairn
path to STY HEAD (direct)
S
SW
W
SCAFELL 2⅓
ILLGILL HEAD 4¼
WHIN RIGG 5½
MIDDLE FELL 4¼
SEATALLAN 4½
Isle of Man
Black Combe
Irish Sea
Calder Hall Power Station
Esk estuary
South Cumberland coast
Eskdale
LINGMELL 1⅓
Burnmoor Tarn
Wasdale
YEWBARROW 2½
Dore Head
Piers Gill
Wastwater
path to WESTMORLAND CAIRN and WASDALE HEAD (direct)
W
NW
N
HAYCOCK 4
RED PIKE 2¾
SCOAT FELL 3¼
STEEPLE 3¾
PILLAR 2¾
GREAT BORNE 6½
STARLING DODD 5½
CAVEL FELL 7¾
HIGH STILE 3¾
HIGH CRAG 3
MELLBREAK 6½
Crummock Water
LOW FELL 8¾
FELLBARROW 10
RANNERDALE KNOTTS 5½
GRASMOOR 6½
WHITELESS PIKE 5½
WANDOPE 6
EEL CRAG 6¼
SAIL 6
GRISEDALE PIKE 7¼
SCAR CRAGS 6¼
Wind Gap
Pillar Rock
Criffel
KIRK FELL 1
Kirkfell Tarn
Ennerdale
Scarth Gap
HAYSTACKS 2
Buttermere Valley
ROBINSON 4
FLEETWITH PIKE 2¼
edge of Gable Crag
path to BECK HEAD
alternative path to WASDALE HEAD (direct)
The figures accompanying the names of fells indicate distances in miles

(Opposite) Wasdale from Great Gable with Wastwater in the distance; (right) View past Windy Gap; (below) Gable Crag from Green Gable

The summit plateau should not be left without first taking a short stroll of 120 yards south-west in the direction of Wasdale to a prominent cairn (the Westmorland Cairn)· standing on the edge of a downfall of crags and having an arresting view of Wasdale Head, a patchwork of small fields half a mile below, and of Wastwater in the distance beyond. There is also to be seen from this point the massive build-up of the Scafells from valley level to the sky-line ridge, with the great gash of Piers Gill prominent. Nearby, below the cairn, the upper rocks of the Napes appear as a serrated fringe in front of a profound void.

All paths on the top of Great Gable are abundantly cairned. The way off for the return journey to Honister heads north at first but is deflected east by the brink of Gable Crag, dropping steeply amid rocks to join a path slanting to the neat col of Windy Gap. Stone Cove is now down on the left and descending on the right is the ravine of Aaron Slack, carrying a track to Sty Head. Across the gap, there is a short climb to the top of Green Gable, 2603 ft. The summit is pleasant, with unseen cliffs falling from the west edge. The dominant feature in the scene from this viewpoint is Gable Crag, its full height and impressiveness clearly revealed at close range.

From the top of Green Gable, the way onwards is clear, continuing along the spine of a ridge that forms a watershed between the gathering grounds of the rivers Liza and Cocker to the west and those of the Derwent to the east. There is now, for the first time on the walk, an outlook over the deep trench of Borrowdale beyond the hanging valley of Gillercomb, steeply buttressed and carrying Sourmilk Gill down to Seathwaite around the abrupt height of Base Brown. A path branches off in this direction, but the way goes forward, still aiming north, and descends to a depression beyond which rises the slope of Brandreth. At this depression, the path inclines left and descends to join Moses' Trod at the Brandreth fence, from where the route of the outward journey can be reversed to the Drum House and Honister Pass, but a better alternative that avoids any retracing of steps is to go up to the summit of Brandreth, 2344 ft.

The top of Brandreth is stony and featureless, having nothing of nearby interest, and only the extensive panorama is likely to delay progress. The summit cairn is sited at a meeting of three broken fences, the one heading north-east pointing to the next objective, Grey Knotts, reached by a simple walk along a wide ridge.

The summit of Brandreth, looking to Great Gable

(Above) Tarn on the summit of Grey Knotts;
(right) Honister Pass from Grey Knotts

The summit of Grey Knotts, 2287 ft, is, in contrast to that of Brandreth, quite attractive, having a series of tors of grey rock and a few small tarns, the habitat of bog bean. This is a lovely place for the last rest of the day and a final appraisal of the beautiful views in all directions; this too is the place to wave farewell to Great Gable. In mist, the summit can be confusing and it is important not to drift eastwards where there are crags. In clear conditions there is no difficulty, the north edge revealing a view of Honister Pass and the cutting sheds and the parked cars a thousand feet below. There is no distinct path down but no hazards arise from making a beeline over rough and bumpy ground to the luxury of the tarmac road.

16 THE MOSEDALE HORSESHOE
FROM WASDALE HEAD　　(8 MILES)

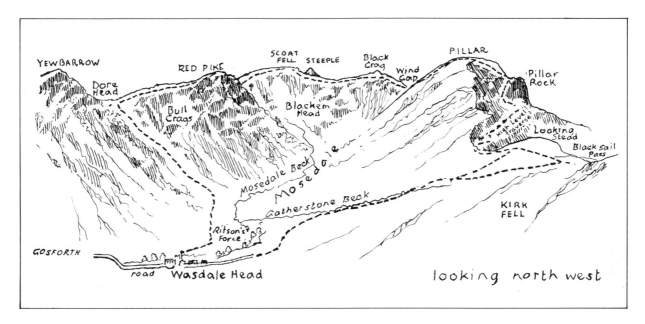

looking north west

There are five Mosedales in the Lake District, the name signifying a dreary and desolate valley, often marshy, and the choice is appropriate for most of them. But not for the best known, the Mosedale that lies in a deep recess opening from the head of Wasdale but out of the sight of visitors to that valley. Desolate and wild it certainly is, but no lover of mountain scenery would ever consider it dreary. The dale is encompassed by lofty fells of extreme roughness and grandeur, the highest being Pillar, one of Lakeland's giants, but it is not Pillar that catches the eye when Mosedale is surveyed from its entrance but the shadowed front of Red Pike, a cataract of beetling crags of intimidating appearance, and to a lesser degree the steep slopes of Scoat Fell beyond. Except for a stony track coming down from a col at the head, the valley has no paths other than those made by sheep, nor is likely to have, the terrain being too uninviting to attract sightseers although an exciting place for adventurers and explorers.

Mosedale is terminated abruptly at Blackem (or Black Comb) Head, an untrodden wilderness, a tangle of crags and rocky gorges and hidden waterfalls where the starry saxifrage lives happily without disturbance. But above, along the skyline, is a path that makes a high-level circuit of the tops around the valley, an exhilarating expedition with no obstacles to easy progress. This splendid walk can be, and should be, augmented by two worthwhile detours from the ridge path, one to the wonderful and famous Pillar Rock, cathedral-like and majestic, and the other to the lovely summit of Steeple. The walk to be described will include these detours.

(Opposite) Pillar from High Stile

Mosedale from the path to Gatherstone Beck

It is preferable to do the round of Mosedale anti-clockwise for two reasons: first, to avoid the steep initial climb to Dore Head which is too overfacing after a hearty breakfast and, secondly, to approach Pillar Rock from the best direction for seeing it to full advantage.

The walk starts along the lane beyond the inn at Wasdale Head and reaches open ground at the foot of Kirk Fell, where a good path turns to the left above the tree-lined course of Mosedale Beck. This contours the slope before gradually inclining upwards to Gatherstone Beck.

On one occasion I was coming down this path when I came across four elderly walkers, two men and their wives, who were halted in some distress; in fact, one of the women was lying on the ground. She had broken an ankle, they told me: what could they do? I offered to report the accident at Wasdale Head, which I did, and was asked to accompany two local volunteers and help to carry a stretcher. I agreed with some reluctance, having already had a tiring walk that day, and off we went. The stretcher had an iron frame and was heavy. It was heavier still when the casualty was loaded on it but we managed to bring her down to the inn where, to my amazement, she limped across the yard to the party's car and they drove away without a word of thanks. Obviously she had not broken an ankle but merely suffered a sprain and could very well have been supported down by her companions. I am sure that incidents of this sort happen often, the rescue teams being called out unnecessarily. Too many people these days seem to regard voluntary help, not only on the hills, as a social service to which they are entitled as members of the Welfare State; they have lost the inclination to fend for themselves. While the rescue teams prefer to do their Good Samaritan work without pay, I feel strongly that those who need their help, or think they do, should make a generous donation to the funds of these brave and unselfish men.

The path rises steadily and crosses Gatherstone Beck, a very attractive watercourse enlivened by sparkling cascades along a bouldery channel, and continues to climb on the opposite slope, swinging right above zigzags to reach Black Sail Pass where a turn to the left alongside an old fence leads up to the grassy plateau of Looking Stead. Or, above the zigzags, advantage can be taken of a short cut branching left and climbing more directly to the skyline at Looking Stead. Now the east ridge of Pillar is clearly seen and there is a view down into Ennerdale, a dark shroud of coniferous forest. I remember the time when this valley was bare of trees and was colourful and pleasant. Its former beauty has gone.

(Left) Gatherstone Beck; (below) Ennerdale from Looking Stead

The ridge is now followed and if persisted in will duly reach the summit of Pillar, but a watch should be kept for a track going down the fellside on the right at the foot of a steep rise in the ridge. This track avoids a small crag directly ahead by rounding it below and rising again beyond. Originally, before this track was devised, it was usual to cross the face of the crag, rather precariously, by shuffling along a horizontal crack.

This is the start of the High Level Traverse to Pillar Rock and the start of one of the best miles in Lakeland, a route of engrossing interest. With little variation in contour, it proceeds along an easy shelf below an array of formidable crags high on the left, the fellside on the right dropping steeply into Ennerdale. The track is delightful and steps are accelerated by the exciting prospect of an early sighting of Pillar Rock, as yet sensed rather than seen. The crowning moment arrives at the top of a small rise where stands Robinson's Cairn, the soaring cliffs of Pillar Rock here being fully revealed ahead: a wonderful sight, spectacular and awe-inspiring.

The cairn is a memorial to John Wilson Robinson, a pioneer fellwalker and rock-climber, a man sincerely devoted to the fells, an enthusiast of great energy who regularly walked from his home at Lorton to join his friends at Wasdale Head for a day's climbing and then walked back home in the evening: a prodigious performance involving some twenty miles of rough up and down tramping apart from the day's activities at Wasdale Head. A memorial tablet, beautifully worded, is affixed to a nearby rock.

The High Level Traverse

Pillar Rock from Robinson's Cairn

Wordsworth wrote of Pillar:

> You see yon precipice; it almost looks
> Like some vast building made of many crags;
> And in the midst is one particular rock
> That rises like a column from the vale,
> Whence by our shepherds it is called the Pillar.

The foot of Pillar Rock can be reached from Robinson's Cairn by a simple crossing on grass amongst outcrops but would lead into a trap from which no escape was possible. This is definitely not the way to go. Instead the track, which now turns left and ascends into a cove, should be adhered to closely and followed along an easy terrace rising to the right above a tremendous downfall of rock. This is the Shamrock Traverse, so named because the crag immediately below, which is severed from Pillar Rock by the deep cleft of Walker's Gully, appears from the east to be part of the main mass.

Excitement becomes intense as the Shamrock Traverse rises to confront the upper part of Pillar Rock, the High Man, and reveals its intimate detail at close range. The scene is overpowering. Thoughts are of nothing else but the immense tower of rock immediately ahead. Worldly worries are totally excluded from the mind, and even toothache can be forgotten in such sensational surroundings. The scene is sublime, yet brutal, without a shred of beauty, and indeed to timid observers will seem a place of horror, awful and ugly.

The Shamrock Traverse

High Man, Pillar Rock

There is no cause for concern if the sketchy track is kept underfoot as it mounts through a tangle of boulders to crag-free but stony ground above the Rock which, on looking back, now appears as a huge dome partly screened by an intervening height. The track continues steeply upwards.

I was once toiling up this slope and nearing the top when I was hailed by a party of men far below on the fellside, and it was obvious from their gesticulations that this was no ordinary greeting, but the distance was too great for their shouts to be intelligible. I went on, rather mystified, and was to learn later that the men were searching for a walker who had set out for Pillar the previous day and not returned. They must have thought that I may have been the missing person, but they continued their search and found the man lying dead at the foot of Walker's Gully.

Gradually the gradient eases and the track emerges on the grassy plateau of Pillar's summit, the Rock being lost to sight and, after the intricacies of the ascent, the open landscape is a welcome change.

The top of Pillar is the only smooth place on this rugged mountain and, except for a summit cairn at 2927 ft and a triangulation column, has little of interest. The view, however, is excellent, the full length of the Scafell range and Great Gable being particularly well seen.

One of my evergreen memories is of a February day fifty years ago when I first visited Pillar. I climbed straight up from Ennerdale, which at that time had not been planted with conifers and was bare and desolate. I had not gone far when I was enveloped in a clammy mist, visibility being reduced to a few yards only. I had hoped to see Pillar Rock, having been thrilled by graphic reports of rock-climbing adventures on this wonderful monolith, but the blanket of mist blotted out everything except a few yards of ground around me. This flank of Pillar is one of the roughest in the district, a succession of craggy outcrops, and upward progress was laborious. Robbed of sight I struggled ever upwards, mercifully without meeting any insuperable obstacle. The mist did not relent, even for a moment, and the silence was profound: this was not a day for larks to be flying and singing. I did not bump into Pillar Rock and saw no sign of it. I began to sense that I was well off-course, this being confirmed when at long last I entered a scree gully that led me to the skyline of the west ridge some distance from the summit. I had spent four hours struggling up the rugged fellside like a blind man, seeing nothing beyond my grasp. I do not recall a mist as dense and immovable as this . . .

The incident would not be worth the telling but for a remarkable transformation that occurred as I walked up to the summit. All at once, with a suddenness that transfixed me, I stepped out of the wet mist into brilliant and dazzling sunlight and above was a cloudless blue sky. I went up to the summit, now starkly clear. It was a walk in space. Just below me was the mist, stretching into the far distance but now having a ceiling and being no longer grey but a pure white. Clearly defined on this vaporous curtain was the shadow of a man. It was my shadow, walking when I walked, stopping when I stopped: the first time I had witnessed such a phenomenon. I spent a few minutes waving to the man in the mist, always getting a simultaneous response and then, as I went on down the east ridge, there was a gradual movement in the mist, then a swirling and boiling of the vapours followed by a swift dispersal and disappearance. In a matter of minutes, the mist vanished to disclose the valley below and the fells beyond. The rest of the day, as I went down to Wasdale Head and over to Eskdale, was gloriously sunny and warm.

Windgap Cove

The remainder of the route around the Mosedale skyline can be prospected from the top of Pillar and promises straightforward walking. First comes a rough descent south-west to the narrow col of Wind Gap, neatly dividing Mosedale and Ennerdale and carrying a path between the two valleys, the Ennerdale side being a scene of wild desolation with a ring of crags surrounding the lonely hollow of Windgap Cove.

Across the col, there is a sharp rise to the top of Black Crag, the path then levelling to give easy progress on grass above the crag, which falls precipitously into Windgap Cove. From the edge of the cliffs, a striking view is obtained of the slender pinnacle of Steeple, here seen springing high out of gloomy depths, its lofty and delicate proportions justifying its name. The gulf between, bounded by the crags of Scoat Fell, is the grim recess of Mirk Cove, an area of devastation uninviting and repelling.

The High Stile range, forming a mountainous barrier between the parallel valleys of Ennerdale and Buttermere, is one of the most beautiful of ridge walks. It is, moreover, free from complexities, rising on a straight north-west – south-east axis without deviations. Three summits overtop the general level of the ridge, High Stile being the central and highest, and High Crag and Red Pike, little lower in altitude, being sturdy supporters on each side. Both flanks are steeply scarped, High Stile and High Crag having precipitous crags on the Buttermere side, and there are conifer plantings along their bases although not extending high enough above Buttermere to mar the impressive grandeur of the scene. Red Pike is gentler and has a scattering of deciduous trees on its lower slopes. The range makes a tremendous background to the Buttermere valley and lake, this being the finest aspect, a picture of surpassing beauty even by Lakeland standards. Approaches from Ennerdale are much less attractive, the afforested area being much more extensive and developed without regard to the environment, and the slopes above too steep and rough to be considered; a path climbs to Red Pike from a break in the plantations but lacks interest and scenic quality. It is the ascent from Buttermere that reveals the grandest features of the range and excels in loveliness and charm: every step is a delight.

Duplication of place names occurs in many instances in Lakeland, often causing confusion. This Red Pike is commonly referred to as the Buttermere Red Pike to distinguish it from the one overlooking Mosedale.

It is usual to reach the ridge by using a well-worn path climbing above the village of Buttermere to the summit of Red Pike, thereafter following the ridge over High Stile and High Crag and descending the screes of Gamlin End to Scarth Gap. The path up to Red Pike is very popular, having a midway attraction in Bleaberry Tarn, but tends to be over-populated by visitors on summer days. There appears to be no other line of ascent to the ridge, but there is, just one, and this I recommend to active walkers who prefer solitude and do not mind a rough scramble. This is certainly the way for me.

I found this route when once scouting in Burtness Comb for a way to the top of High Crag as an alternative to the customary line of ascent from Scarth Gap up the unpleasant and slippery screes of Gamlin End. I noticed what appeared to be a continuous shelf rising steeply across the face of High Crag's tremendous north buttress, a thousand feet high, and on exploring further had no difficulty in following it upwards to broken ground just below the north top, the summit then being a short distance forward. I was pleased with this discovery for several reasons: it seemed to be a virgin route, having no traces of earlier visitors; it gave a feeling of adventure and real mountaineering; it led directly to the top of the mountain; it was profoundly quiet, there being nobody within sight or sound, and never again did I need to toil up or down Gamlin End. This is the route I shall describe.

(Opposite) High Stile from Gatesgarth

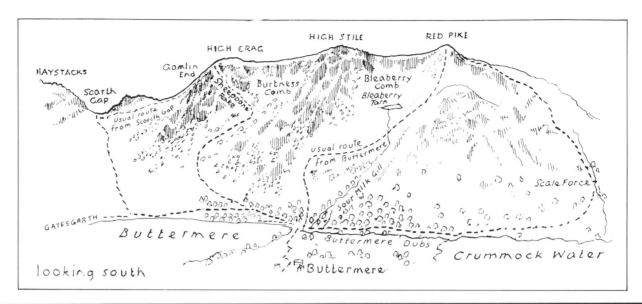

HAYSTACKS

Scarth Gap

Gamlin End

HIGH CRAG

HIGH STILE

RED PIKE

Steeppone Rake

Burtness Comb

Bleaberry Comb

Bleaberry Tarn

Usual route from Scarth Gap

Usual route from Buttermere

Scale Force

Sour Milk Gill

GATESGARTH

Buttermere

Buttermere Dubs

Buttermere

Crummock Water

looking south

From Buttermere village, a lane leads to a bridge crossing the stream issuing from the lake and beyond is a choice of paths, the one to be taken turning left through the lakeside wood. This is departed from 120 yards beyond a cross-wall where a forest ride branches to the right, soon reaching a stile in another wall, over which a track travels in company with it, rising to the wide opening of Burtness Comb, also known as Birkness Comb. This track has been fashioned by rock-climbers bound for the crags around the Comb, a favourite area for their sport. When the wall turns away left, a line of cairns indicates the way forward to the inner recesses of the Comb and discloses the ring of cliffs ahead. On the left is the tremendous precipice of High Crag, and rising across it will be noticed a shelf or gangway that offers a tenuous line of escape to the skyline high above. This is the way to go: it deserves a name and I call it Sheepbone Rake, which is appropriate because the only officially named feature hereabouts is Sheepbone Buttress, a crag alongside. A rough slope is climbed to the foot of the Rake and the route continues steeply up it as a scramble on grass with no impediments other than fallen boulders and no insuperable obstacles. The situation, poised between crags above and crags below, is sensational but safe. At the top, broken ground is encountered and a climb to the right reaches the north cairn of High Crag and the summit a short walk beyond.

(Opposite) Buttermere   *(Below) High Crag from Burtness Comb*

The summit cairn of High Crag, decorated with discarded iron fence posts, stands at 2443 ft on the extreme eastern edge of the ridge and commands uninterrupted views in that direction, the finest aspect being of the head of Ennerdale backed by Great Gable and Kirk Fell, the latter overtopped by the Scafell group. Nearer and below eye level are Scarth Gap and Haystacks, with Fleetwith Pike a bold object to their left, the extensive panorama culminating in the distant skyline of the Helvellyn range.

The head of Ennerdale

Burtness Comb

With the hard work of the day over, the exhilarating ridge walk to follow can be contemplated with anticipatory pleasure. It is a joy to tread, not only for its intrinsic delights but also for the beautiful views it provides as the walk proceeds. There is a short descent from High Crag and the path then skirts the edge of the crags falling into Burtness Comb, the most arresting feature being the vertical face of Eagle Crag, one of the many so-named in the district, confirming that these magnificent birds were once permanent residents. There are spectacular glimpses down into the depths of the Comb along this edge. Lakeland really needs a uniform name for its mountain hollows: the Welsh have 'cwm', the Scots 'corrie', but here they are variously named as 'comb', 'combe', 'cove' and even 'hole'. Burtness Comb is one of the most typical of these hollows forming a hanging valley, wild and lonely, above the cultivated pastures of the lowland farms.

When the Comb is passed, a simple but stony path rises gradually to the highest point on the ridge, the summit of High Stile, 2644 ft, presenting a view that evokes raptures of delight from its cairn perched on the brink of an abrupt drop and justifying an hour's rest to absorb the beauty of the scene.

(Opposite) Crummock Water; (above) Fleetwith Pike from High Stile; (below) Red Pike from High Stile

The cairn on High Stile is left, always with reluctance, and the walk resumed, a short descent leading to the obvious continuation of the ridge towards Red Pike. There are impressive peeps down the gullies of Chapel Crags as the path rounds another comb, a twin to Burtness but less rocky. This is Bleaberry Comb, identified by the dark pool of Bleaberry Tarn on the floor of another hanging valley, and across it can be seen the usual route to Red Pike coming up from Buttermere. The ridge path prefers the open fell top, but more interest will be found by skirting the edge of the escarpment and smug satisfaction derived from the sight of walkers toiling up the scree of the tourist route below. Then, after a slight ascent, the summit of Red Pike, 2479 ft, is reached.

It will have been noticed on the walk from High Crag that all the excitement and beauty of the ridge is concentrated on the Buttermere side, the Ennerdale flank contributing nothing, but hereabouts Pillar is an imposing object across the latter valley.

A direct return may be made to Buttermere from the summit of Red Pike by using the tourist path, but the ridge is not yet ended although declining steadily from here onwards. By continuing in the same direction, another comb is brought into view, also having a rim of crags descending into a hanging valley and generally following the pattern of the others. This is Ling Comb, a place of heather, but unfrequented, a Cinderella that nobody comes to see. The rim of the escarpment is known as Lingcomb Edge. It is followed down to its extremity, where a heathery slope is descended to the watercourse of Scale Beck, seen forming a defined channel on the left. A path materialises alongside the stream, becoming steep in its lower stages and eroded by visitors to the lovely waterfall now just below.

High Stile from Red Pike

Scale Force

On a walk of many highlights, here is another. The waterfall is Scale Force, the highest in the district and one of the finest. It plunges in a single leap of over 100 feet down a dark ravine hemmed in by perpendicular walls bedecked by ferns and trees: a wonderful sight.

A beaten path descends from the outlet of the ravine towards Crummock Water, which, in Victorian times, had a boat-landing to which ladies and gentlemen were rowed across the lake from Buttermere as part of a popular excursion to the waterfall. This facility has long been defunct and so have the ladies and gentlemen, at least in sartorial appearance. Most of today's visitors are rough shod and not at all elegant, and for them there is no alternative to the lakeside path that continues pleasantly amongst trees to the bridge at Buttermere but is notoriously wet underfoot. Still, wet feet don't matter at the end of a perfect day.

18 HAYSTACKS
FROM BUTTERMERE   (7 MILES)

Dear Haystacks! Here is a rugged height, little in stature and small in extent, encircled by much loftier fells, some of international renown, yet standing quite unabashed by their greater presence in the landscape and not acknowledging inferiority to any of them. Like a shaggy and undisciplined terrier in the midst of a company of sleek foxhounds, Haystacks looks irascible, defiantly aggressive, and a bad-tempered little monster, not caring a damn for anybody or anything, and if blessed with lungs would probably demand attention by yapping and barking all day long. It is unusual in structure, not conforming to any pattern and stoutly asserting its right to be called a mountain despite a lack of height, a superior mountain because it is certainly not prepared to concede that any of its neighbours, not even Great Gable and Pillar, which look down at it, are more imposing or important. It probably feels infuriated by appearing last in this book, knowing jolly well that its rightful place is first.

So why does Haystacks win the affection of all walkers? You have to climb to the top and wander about to understand. Above the wall of defending crags is a fascinating landscape, a confusing labyrinth of miniature peaks and tors, of serpentine tracks in rampant heather, of lovely tarns and tarnlets, of crags and screes, of marshes and streams, of rocks for climbing and rocks not for climbing, of surprises around every corner, with magnificent views all around. Adrenalin runs fast in this natural wonderland. For a man trying to forget a persistent worry, the top of Haystacks is a complete cure.

Haystacks is absolutely right in demanding special attention, although perhaps exaggerating in claiming a degree of superiority over all other fells in the district. To say that there are few to match it would be a fairer assessment of relative merits.

The approach should always be made from Buttermere village to introduce into the walk the sylvan beauty of trees and water as an appetising starter and to emphasise the contrasting wildness soon to follow. A shorter version is possible from a car parked near Gatesgarth at the head of the lake, but Haystacks deserves better than to be cut short and needs the gradual appreciation that the longer route gives. Buttermere's lake is too regular in outline to rank with the best, but its rocky shoreline, fringed by trees, is quite delightful and served by an enchanting path that has Haystacks in view all the way.

(Opposite) Haystacks from the north shore of Buttermere

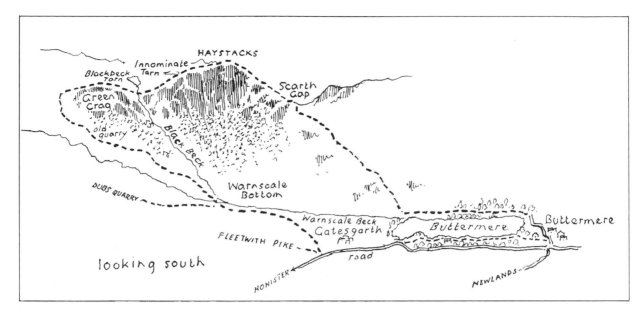

The lakeside path leaves the village at once and keeps closely to the north shore, at one point passing through a tunnel cut in the rocks, and is everywhere charming. Near the head of the lake, the path joins the Honister motor road and this is then followed past the large farm of Gatesgarth, the last outpost in the valley and, like Seathwaite in Borrowdale, well known to all walkers, to the point where an intake wall goes off to the right at the foot of Fleetwith Pike. The white cross now prominently in view on the lower slopes of the Pike was erected as a memorial to Fanny Mercer, killed in a fall on the nearby rocks in 1887. Here the road is left and a path taken alongside the wall to enter the gloomy amphitheatre of Warnscale Bottom, the cliffs of Haystacks being directly ahead and high above.

Haystacks and High Crag

A direct assault on Haystacks from Warnscale Bottom is seen at a glance to be totally out of the question, and a rising detour must be made to avoid and get above its daunting crags. Had it not been for an old Ordnance map, I would probably never have been aware of a disused track that climbs across the fellside to an abandoned quarry below Green Crag. One day I set out to try to trace it, and found it to be still distinct in places with ancient cairns still surviving to mark its many zigs and zags: a fascinating stairway. To get a footing on this track, it is necessary to cross Warnscale Beck, which is easier said than done, near its confluence with Black Beck. Upon reaching the quarry and the end of the track, the slope beyond is climbed to the ridge where a turn to the right, again on a good path, skirts the summit of Green Crag and brings into view an exciting prospect ahead. Blackbeck Tarn is seen occupying a lonely hollow on the left, its issuing stream falling away sharply into a ravine, and the path winding sinuously forward, crossing the outflow and rising along the base of crags to the top of Haystacks, now seen cut away abruptly by precipitous cliffs.

Haystacks from Green Crag

(Above) Blackbeck Tarn; (below) Innominate Tarn looking towards Great Gable

After fording Black Beck and looking fearfully down its steep channel, the path hugs the base of a wall of rock and, when clear of this, a choice of routes is available. By wandering to the left over a rough carpet of heather and mosses the Brandreth fence will be met and the walk can be extended by inclining to the right and climbing through a maze of outcrops to the summit. Or, by scrambling up the broken slope to the right, the rim of the crags plunging down to Warnscale Bottom comes suddenly underfoot with dramatic effect, the edge then being followed upwards above a sensational downfall of steep gullies and steeper buttresses, having throughout in stark contrast the gentle beauty of Buttermere as a backcloth, until the summit is reached. Or the main path may be continued, aiming more directly for the highest point of the fell and passing the lovely Innominate Tarn, a delectable spot.

typical summit tors

perched boulder on a rock platform

the summit

The summit cairn stands on a rocky tor amid a confusion of boulders, its modest elevation of 1900 ft seeming to be incongruously low, for surely this is the top of an Alpine giant? The views are magnificent, Great Gable and Pillar and High Crag all being prominent in a glorious panorama. No wonder that Haystacks has such a good opinion of itself.

Buttermere from Haystacks

Scarth Gap

The temptation to linger on the top of Haystacks until the sun goes down must be resisted for the descent to Scarth Gap, passing a charming rocky tarnlet, is rough and getting rougher as more walkers become addicted to Haystacks, sliding screes having to be negotiated before easy ground is reached at the gap. But, having survived this ordeal, the way back to Buttermere is simple, a good path descending grassy slopes to the head of the lake, whence a much-trodden track goes alongside the shore, entering a plantation and continuing distinctly through trees to the bridge over the stream issuing from the lake, where a lane leads to the village. What a day it has been!

(Opposite) High Crag from Haystacks   *(Below) Buttermere*

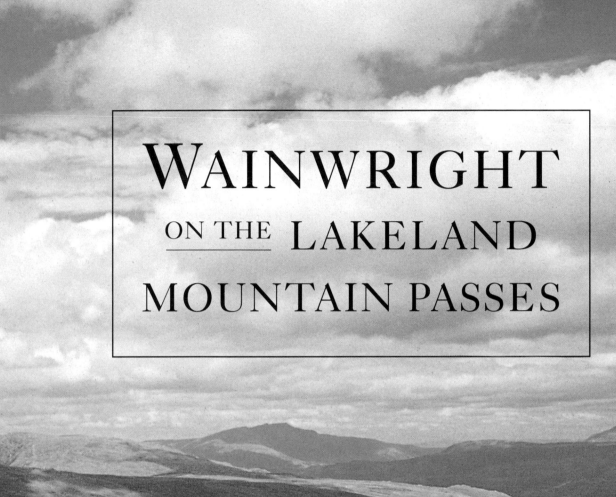

WAINWRIGHT

ON THE LAKELAND

MOUNTAIN PASSES

MAPS BY BORIS WELTMAN

CONTENTS

INTRODUCTION

THE LAKE DISTRICT is a compact mass of high and rugged ground soaring abruptly from surrounding valleys and the coastal plain of Cumbria, almost as distinctive and well defined as a volcanic island rising from the sea. Within its natural boundaries, mountains and fells crowd together, there being over 200 separate and named summits. As in all mountainous terrain, the peaks are linked by ridges intersected by skyline gaps or depressions that permit ease of crossing from one valley to another; a few carry roads but most are accessible only on foot. These relatively simple ways of crossing high ranges are known as passes. Long before men explored the lofty summits for pleasure, the passes were used by nomadic tribes and later by the early settlers and, where negotiable by packhorses, by enterprising traders as commercial routes.

Left *Helvellyn from High Tove*   Above *The road over Honister Pass*

Lakeland is not fashioned for motorists: cars can penetrate the interior only in a few places. It is largely a preserve of walkers. The most exhilarating and rewarding form of pedestrian travel is fellwalking, a pastime that has grown greatly in popularity in recent decades, but it is available only to the physically fit. Most visitors to the district, however, are content to stroll along the lovely valleys and beside the lakes, preferring not to risk the hazards of the higher ground above; some even have a primeval fear of mountains as places of danger. But there is an intermediate class of walkers who admire mountain scenery and favour the loneliness of the wild recesses, yet because of disability or lack of energy in their later years cannot aspire to the ultimate summits and dare not venture too far upwards. Such are catered for by the passes, away from the sight and sound of traffic, where the peaks can be viewed in intimate detail and in the silence of solitude.

Deepdale

For those who can walk in moderation and choose to do so sedately and without fear of going astray, the passes offer ideal expeditions. People get lost on the mountains but very rarely on the passes. Here distinct paths have formed through centuries of use although they are often still narrow and rough; cairns provide comfort in places of doubt; the natural configuration of the ground, rising on both sides, confines walkers to the trodden ways, and the streams descending from the passes are infallible guides to direction. All these reassuring factors make the passes practicable in any weather conditions except deep snow, and on days when heavy cloud rules the tops out of bounds the passes can be walked in safety.

The passes may of course be walked in either direction. In this book, I have described them in the direction most usually followed or which provides the greater interest or excellence in forward views. In a few cases where passes have no official name, I have given them appropriate ones.

Every skyline gap or depression on a mountain ridge, sometimes referred to as cols, may be regarded as a pass of sorts if approachable on both sides, and there are hundreds of such places in Lakeland. Most of those remote from tourist paths will have been crossed by shepherds or foxhunters or Ordnance surveyors at one time or another, but many are virgin and have never been trodden by man. These latter are outside the scope of this book which is concerned only with those that carry distinct paths and are in common use.

Some of the passes are short and can be reversed to the starting point in the course of a day's walk. But most are of several miles and a single crossing is enough for one day. Walkers who are travelling from one bed-and-breakfast to another in a different valley have no problems, but those encumbered by cars must plan to return to them. The best arrangement in such cases is to team up with friends who also have their own transport, the two parties leaving their cars at either extremity of the pass at agreed parking places and doing the walk in opposite directions, swapping car keys as they meet midway, thus ensuring a comfortable return to base.

No day in the Lake District needs be wasted because of inclement weather. The mountains are inhospitable in bad conditions and better avoided, and touring the gift shops in the valleys and sheltering in doorways and cafés quickly palls. The friendly passes offer the perfect answer. You'll still get wet, of course, and despair at the shroud of mist that masks the beauty all around, but the exercise will do you good and after a rousing supper in dry clothes you will vote the day a very satisfactory one after all. Walking the passes is the next best thing to walking on the mountains and often no less rewarding.

Each pass is the subject of a separate chapter, the description of the route being accompanied by a simple location map with a mile-scale, north being at the top. Heights are given in English feet and distances in English miles despite the current regrettable practice of quoting them in foreign metres and kilometres to which the author, a jingoistic Englishman, refuses to comply. This book is about the English Lake District. Let's go on thinking of it as English!

1 BLACK SAIL PASS, 1800'
Wasdale Head – Ennerdale

WASDALE HEAD, the most impressive inhabited place in Lakeland, is so deeply inurned amongst high mountains that there appears to be no easy escape from it other than by reversing the usual line of approach on the road alongside Wastwater. Only the glen of Lingmell Beck coming down on the right below the shapely pyramid of Great Gable seems to offer a possible way out of the valley: this is the walkers' way to Sty Head. Less obvious is a route entering the side valley of Mosedale on the left: this climbs to a skyline depression or saddle between Kirk Fell and Pillar and descends from there into Ennerdale.

This is the Black Sail Pass.

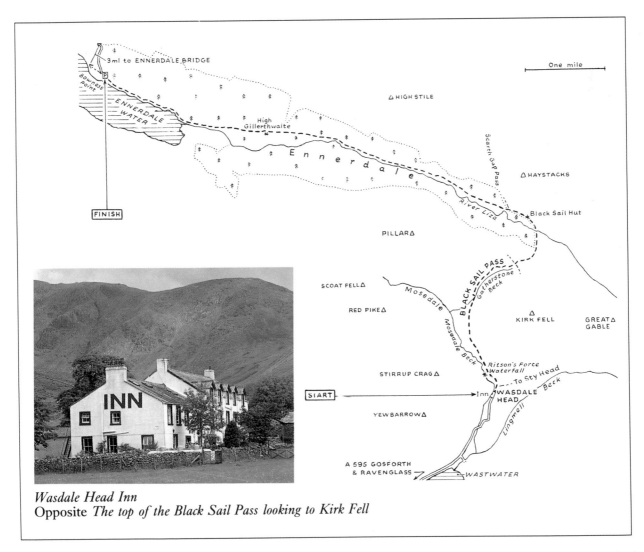

Wasdale Head Inn
Opposite *The top of the Black Sail Pass looking to Kirk Fell*

Wasdale Head

THE ROUTE STARTS from Wasdale Head Inn which has reverted to its former name after being known as Wastwater Hotel for many years, inappropriately because the lake is a mile distant. Modernisation has destroyed the old atmosphere of this venerable inn, a Mecca for the pioneers of rockclimbing of a hundred years ago.

When I first went there, the passages were littered with climbing ropes, hobnailed boots and drying clothes. Meals were served at a long table, with no choice of food, in a room hung with enlarged photographs by Ashley Abraham, whose camera work incidentally has never been bettered, of the classic rock climbs around Wasdale and the brave men who made the first ascents. The talk then was exclusively of adventures on the crags. Mine host in those early years of the sport was Will Ritson, a great character and practical joker: it was said of Wasdale Head in those days that it had the highest mountain, the deepest lake and the biggest liar in the country, the latter distinction being earned by Ritson himself.

Those times are over. Today all is changed. The inn has been tidied, the horses and traps have been replaced by cars, and sandals are as likely to be seen as heavy boots. I liked it better as it was.

A short lane leaves the inn heading towards Kirk Fell which most closely overlooks the dale, and a good path turns left above the intake walls and enters Mosedale. Just below, lined by trees, is Mosedale Beck, momentarily excited by a waterfall known as Ritson's Force; across the stream rise the towering slopes of Yewbarrow, surmounted by the cliffs of Stirrup Crag. Ahead, the desolate hollow of Mosedale comes into view, dominated by the ramparts of Red Pike and terminated by Scoat Fell.

The path trends to the right as the slopes of Kirk Fell decline. It climbs steadily to come alongside the tumbling waters of Gatherstone Beck, its name apparently derived from the boulders that litter its bed. This is forded, the path rising on the far bank in zigzags before straightening into a steady climb

towards the depression ahead. A newer track branching to the left is used by walkers ascending Pillar. Views here on Gatherstone Head are restricted to Yewbarrow behind and Kirk Fell across the beck, but gradually the gradient eases and a ruined wire fence marking the top of Black Sail Pass is reached.

Mosedale   Above *Ritson's Force*

At the top of the pass a splendid view unfolds ahead. Ennerdale is below in a dark shroud of conifer plantations contrasting sharply with the bare slopes of the upper reaches of the valley. Haystacks is directly in front and the lofty High Stile ridge rises in fine array to the left. At this point, however, the most arresting sight is Kirk Fell nearby, its shattered and craggy slopes soaring into the sky with dramatic effect: it looks rough, and it is.

The fence crosses the top of the pass, keeping to the watershed; westwards it serves as a perfect guide to Pillar, eastwards it climbs sharply into the fastnesses of Kirk Fell, bravely accompanied by a thin track.

The path goes forward and descends into Ennerdale, coming alongside the edge of the plantations and crossing the River Liza by a footbridge. Now in sight are the two giants of Ennerdale, Great Gable and Pillar: the former descends in smooth slopes from the rim of crags fringing its perfect dome while Pillar is very rough from top to toe and has an unbecoming skirt of spruce fir.

Black Sail Hut is a few minutes further on.

Opposite *Black Sail Hut*   Above left *View in Ennerdale and* (right) *the River Liza*

The Black Sail Hut, once a shepherd's bothy but now converted and extended into a Youth Hostel, is a lonely outpost indeed, far from other habitations, but a first-class centre for fellwalking expeditions. A cart track, now used as a forest road, leads down the valley through the plantations, some relief from a monotonous trudge being afforded by the lively Liza alongside. Another Youth Hostel at High Gillerthwaite is passed after an hour's walk in the close company of trees, the forest road continuing to run alongside the north shore of Ennerdale Water, where there is a fine retrospective view of Pillar, to a public car park at Bowness Point. If no car is waiting, the walk can be continued by a lakeside path to the little community of Ennerdale Bridge to sample the fleshpots on offer there, these consisting of an inn, a shop and an infrequent bus to Whitehaven.

2 BOARDALE HAUSE, 1200'
Patterdale – Boardale or Martindale

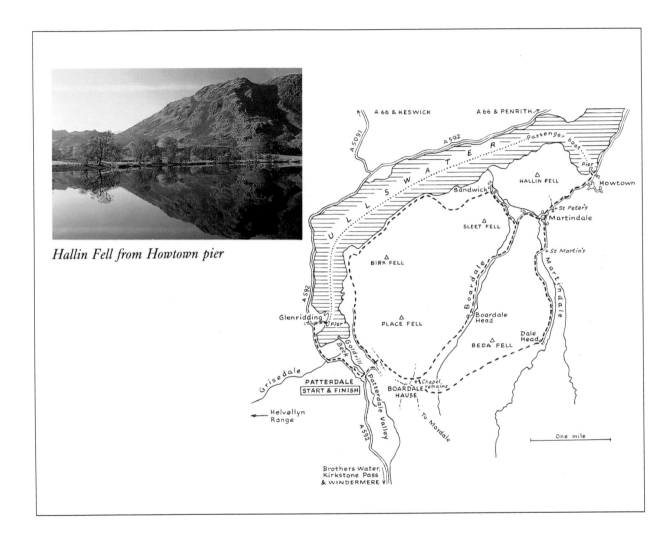

Hallin Fell from Howtown pier

T HE EASTERN SIDE of the upper reaches of Ullswater rises abruptly in the steep and rough slopes of Place Fell, effectively barring a direct approach to the valleys that lie in the folds of the hills beyond. These valleys are hidden from the sight of the crowds of tourists who visit the lake, are unsuspected and remain unspoilt. By road, they can be reached by a long and circuitous journey around the north end of the lake and, having no through routes, are of little appeal to motorists, but walkers are blessed with a choice of two lovely paths. One runs along the lakeside, rounding the north end of Place Fell, and is in my opinion the most beautiful walk in Lakeland; the other climbs to and crosses a low ridge at the south end.

This latter pass is Boardale Hause.

Opposite *Patterdale from Boardale Hause*

Deepdale from Boardale Hause

FROM PATTERDALE VILLAGE, a side road crosses Goldrill Beck and gives access to the open fellside. The well-trodden path to the right is followed, taking the higher branch when it forks and climbing steadily to the easier ground of Boardale Hause.

The views on this ascent are of superlative beauty. Ahead is Brothers Water and Kirkstone Pass, deep-set amongst encroaching heights; behind is a glorious prospect of the Patterdale valley with the massive bulk of the Helvellyn range towering beyond the deep trench of Grisedale. Ullswater completes a delightful picture.

Boardale Hause is a walkers' crossroads, five paths leaving here for different destinations and needing care in selection. On the hause is a ruined enclosure resembling a derelict sheepfold, but in fact it is the site of a medieval chapel, as a few carved stones lying around testify. On large-scale maps, this is named Chapel in the Hause. Its isolated situation on the ridge, midway between Patterdale and Boardale, was presumably intended to give equal facility of access to the good folk of both valleys. Some years ago, the confusion of paths was further compounded by the construction of an aqueduct across the hause when the pipe-laying operations and tractors carved new routes over the top, but nature is doing its best to remove the scars.

Boardale Hause is the popular springboard for the ascent of Place Fell and a track climbs to the left with the summit as objective; another goes right for the long upland crossing to Mardale, but the main path, for Boardale and Martindale, leads forward over the crest, forking at once for Boardale, to the left, and Martindale, to the right.

The path into Boardale (spelt Boredale by early writers and map-makers) descends to the head of this valley which takes the form of a narrow defile between the slopes of Place Fell and Beda Fell. A good track goes down to the first habitation, Boardale Head, where it matures into a narrow road which, after a further mile or so, branches left to Sandwick; here the lakeside path may be taken to return to Patterdale, thus completing the circuit of Place Fell. The right fork links with Martindale and goes on to Howtown.

The path to Martindale is in no hurry to descend and circles around the head of Boardale to the south ridge of Beda Fell, beyond which it declines steadily into the much larger valley of Martindale, where there is a long-established deer sanctuary. It reaches the first habitation at Dale Head, a farmhouse notable for its massively buttressed walls. Here starts a pleasant road that proceeds along this quiet and lovely valley in the shadow of Beda Fell and joins the road from Boardale. Before the junction, a detour to the old church of St Martin is recommended: this was built in 1653 on the site of an ancient chapel, but was closed in 1881 because of decay. A new church, St Peter's, was built in 1882, but a few summer services are still held in the old church which has been restored.

Boardale

Dale Head

Below *The old church of St Martin*

From the road opposite St Peter's church a wide grass path – a joy to tread even in bare feet – leads to the top of Hallin Fell, and if time permits a half-hour's diversion, this simple stroll should not be missed. This is the easiest of all fellwalks and the visual rewards more than recompense the slight effort needed. Martindale is seen full length and in all its glory, and a bird's-eye view of Ullswater presents itself when the highest point is reached at 1271'. The summit is crowned by a fine obelisk of cut stone twelve feet tall. The man who built it not only indicated the top of the fell but erected for himself a permanent memorial.

There is a rise in the road beyond St Peter's church and at the top Ullswater is revealed ahead. The lakeside hamlet of Howtown is also in view amongst trees at the foot of a long descent made easier for cars by a series of wide loops.

Martindale from Hallin Fell

Howtown has a pier and is a calling place for the passenger boats that ply on Ullswater in summer. With pre-knowledge of the timetable, arrival can be timed to meet the boat for Glenridding, a mile from Patterdale, which gives a very pleasant return to the starting point of the walk. There is no more beautiful scene in the district than the head of Ullswater and no better way to enjoy its delights than to approach leisurely over the water.

Opposite *The road curling down to Ullswater*   Below *The pier at Howtown*

3 THE BURNMOOR CORPSE ROAD, 900'
Wasdale Head – Eskdale

BEFORE THE EARLY settlers at Wasdale Head were granted the present small patch of consecrated ground their fatal casualties had to be conveyed for burial elsewhere, at first to the mother church at St Bees and later to the churchyard just outside the village of Boot in Eskdale. The route adopted for these sad journeys to Boot lay over the low moor around Burnmoor Tarn, this being preferred to the longer and circuitous way on the primitive roads of that time. The coffins were strapped to the backs of horses, wheels being unable to negotiate the rough ground. The route was known as the Corpse Road and, now classed as a bridleway, is in popular use by today's walkers.

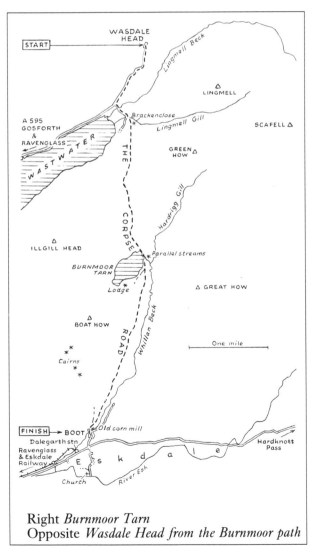

Right *Burnmoor Tarn*
Opposite *Wasdale Head from the Burnmoor path*

TURN OFF the road from Wasdale Head near the head of Wastwater where a lane to the left crosses an area that still bears traces of a devastating cloudburst in Lingmell Gill many years ago when an avalanche of boulders and rubble thundered down on the fields below, the debris being later partially cleared by prisoners of war. Beyond is the handsome building of Brackenclose, headquarters of the Fell and Rock Climbing Club since 1937. From here the route heads south on a gradual incline between the rising slopes of Green How and Illgill Head, to reach the bare summit of the pass, where Burnmoor Tarn and the fells around Eskdale come into view. The path goes on to the tarn.

Burnmoor Tarn is a large and unattractive sheet of water in a desolate landscape; a former gamekeeper's lodge is the only habitation in sight. The path skirts the eastern shore and here an odd natural curiosity will be seen: the main feeder of the tarn, Hardrigg Gill coming off Scafell, and the issuing stream, Whillan Beck, occur side by side and only a few paces apart without any apparent watershed between them.

After a marshy tract the path commences a long straight descent to Boot in the close company of Whillan Beck with the scene ahead becoming more pleasant with every step.

Walkers with archaeological interests and time to spare should deviate by climbing the low moor on the right to its summit, Boat How, thence descending south through an area of Bronze Age occupation with at least five stone circles and many ancient cairns as evidence. At the foot of the slope a bridleway will be reached, this going down to join the main path as it enters Boot.

Illgill Head   *Ruins near Boat How*

On the outskirts of Boot, before going down to the main street, the fellside immediately south is of nostalgic interest, being scarred with the remains of disused iron mines that were served by a narrow-gauge industrial railway along the base of the fell. The track is plain to see, although robbed of its lines, as is the site of the former Boot Station, passengers also being carried on the railway. This section was closed when the mines were abandoned, but half a mile down the valley the railway is open for passenger traffic; miniature trains offer a sylvan ride from Ravenglass to a new terminus at Dalegarth, where there is a shop and café. This popular railway is the Ravenglass and Eskdale Railway, affectionately known as Ratty, and links with the main railway at Ravenglass.

The old railway track at Boot

The village of Boot is entered by crossing a bridge over Whillan Beck and here is a building of character: the old corn mill, long disused but restored to working order by Cumbria County Council in 1975.

The scenery upstream is charming and a short walk on a woodland path from the bridge brings into view a delightful section of the beck, its waters tumbling in cataracts amongst rocks.

Boot is the 'capital' of mid-Eskdale although having only a few cottages and a tiny population. It is a friendly place and apart from its visual delights, has an hotel, shops and cafés that cater mainly for the summer invasions of visitors brought by the miniature railway to the terminus nearby. And there is a church and graveyard worth visiting, and of course the lovely River Esk. Boot is favoured.

The corn mill at Boot

Whillan Beck

4 CARLSIDE COL, 2250'
Millbeck – Barkbeth

ANYONE TRAVELLING between the Vale of Keswick and the countryside west of Skiddaw will almost certainly make the journey by road and only the odd eccentric with time to kill will consider the alternative walking route described in this chapter, this involving a steep and stony scramble in terrain unfamiliar to tourists. The route provides an introduction to the twin valleys of Southerndale and Barkbethdale coming down from Skiddaw, rarely visited and known intimately only by the local farmers. Other walkers are not likely to be met. Solitude reigns.

THE WALK STARTS at the pleasant hamlet of Millbeck nestling amongst trees at the base of Skiddaw where a path leads north and soon comes alongside the stream issuing from the obvious defile ahead. Directly in front is the dark pyramid of Carsleddam, a heathery offshoot of the greater fell of Carl Side beyond. The stream, Slades Beck, comes round the obstacle on the east side, down a stony ravine with Skiddaw Little Man towering high above and the parent fell ahead. The walk by the stream is so totally enclosed that it becomes claustrophobic: there is little of beauty in this arid scene. When confronted by the great mass of Skiddaw the route trends left and climbs steeply and stonily to an obvious col on the skyline where a deserved halt may be taken and the way onward prospected. Carl Side rises on the left, terminating a ridge formed by Long Side and Ullock Pike. A track bound for Skiddaw crosses the col and ascends a stony slope littered with slate fragments, some loose, some in embedded upright flakes. Nearby is the insignificant Carlside Tarn.

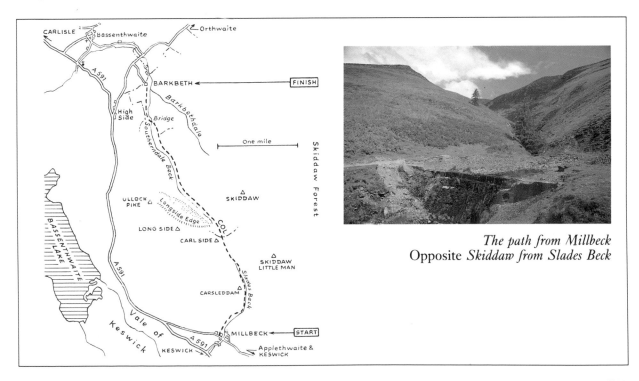

The path from Millbeck
Opposite *Skiddaw from Slades Beck*

Above *Long Side and Ullock Pike from Carlside Col*
Left *Southerndale*

Over the crest of the col the way is downhill on
steep pathless slopes into the head of Southerndale,
a shy valley completely dominated by the ramparts
of Longside Edge high above, from which fans of
scree scar the fellsides. When Southerndale Beck
takes shape, a thin track above its eastern bank will,
if it can be found, ease the walk down the valley to a
bridge, and here there is an impressive retrospect of
the valley with Skiddaw now in view.

From the bridge, a rough lane, with thorn bushes
and trees which soften the landscape, leads to the
farmstead of Barkbeth at the foot of a parallel valley,
Barkbethdale, along which is an imposing view of
Skiddaw.

A farm access lane goes down to a tarmac road
leading left to High Side, which has a bus stop on
the Keswick–Carlisle service. Or alternatively, a
side road goes to the nearby village of Bassenthwaite
(locally called Bass) which is likely to have refreshments on offer.

Above *The path to Barkbeth*   Below *Barkbeth Farm*

5 COLEDALE HAUSE, 2000′
Braithwaite – Lanthwaite

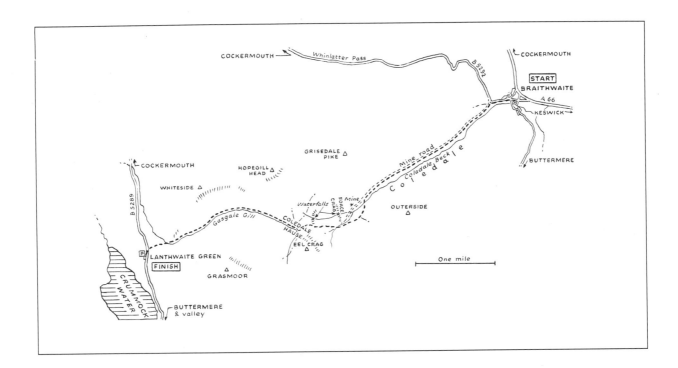

THE NORTH-WESTERN fells form a compact mass, the individual summits being closely linked, and although the boundaries of the group are clearly defined by surrounding valleys, there are no easy ways through the high ground.

The only recognised pass in common use is Coledale Hause, the usual route to it being along the straight channel of Coledale, leading into the heart of wild uplands, an approach also popular as a fast way to the summits of the enclosing heights, especially when starting from the village of Braithwaite. The through route is interesting rather than impressive, views being restricted, but the journey is a splendid half-day's expedition.

Opposite *Coledale*
Right *Braithwaite*

STARTING FROM Braithwaite, advantage can be taken of a long and easy mine road leading straight as an arrow in the direction of the hause. The village is left by the Whinlatter Pass road and around the first corner the mine road leaves on the left. There is a short cut to it blazed by the boots of the thousands of walkers bound for Grisedale Pike which dominates the scene, but the original start is much easier. The mine road enters the long valley of Coledale and heads purposefully for a barytes mine at its terminus: this section is tedious but gives a fast approach on a good surface along the base of Grisedale Pike; opposite is the shapely peak of Outerside rising sharply from Coledale Beck alongside the road. When the mine is within easy reach, the beck is crossed and a rising path ascends grassy slopes to outflank the imposing barrier of Force Crag directly behind the mine and forming a precipitous background. The dark cliffs are relieved by the silver thread of Low Force cascading over the rim.

As height is gained along the path, another wall of crags comes into view above the other, these upper cliffs also having a slender waterfall, High Force.

Force Crag

Coledale and Force Crag mine from High Force

Now having the impending mass of Eel Crag on the left, the path continues to climb easily to the flat expanse of Coledale Hause, passing many industrial relics on the adjacent ground. On the hause itself is a disused water cut that formerly diverted the stream of Gasgale Gill, coming down on the left, from its natural course over the watershed to provide supplies for the mines.

Most walkers arriving at the hause leave the path here to ascend Eel Crag or Grasmoor on the left, or Hopegill Head or Grisedale Pike on the right; all these fine summits are often visited in a circular expedition from Braithwaite using the hause only as a crossing place.

The through route to Lanthwaite and Crummock Water goes forward over the watershed and descends steeply into the ravine of Gasgale Gill on a path now much rougher underfoot but compensated by the lovely vistas appearing through the portals of the gill as the walk proceeds.

All around is wild desolation, ahead is enchantment.

As height is lost, the confining fells rise starkly into the sky. On the left is Grasmoor, the highest of the group, its steep slopes not inviting ascent; and on the right, even more repelling, are the crags and scree runs of Whiteside in an awesome downfall.

Between the two heights, the stream and the path run close together and emerge in a rocky passage at the exit to the gill; immediately a beautiful prospect is revealed as an easy slope goes down to the road at Lanthwaite Green. The formidable slopes of Grasmoor fall away abruptly to permit a view of the Buttermere valley with the High Stile ridge supreme. Over the pastures of Lanthwaite, rise the twin summits of Mellbreak, a stretch of Crummock Water also being seen.

The whole scene is exquisite and becomes more so on close acquaintance; only the procession of cars along the road disturb the tranquillity of this loveliest part of Lakeland. The road remains narrow despite the influx of summer motorists who must continue to suffer inconvenience: it would be sacrilege to widen and improve this road to modern standards, so destroying the charm of a delightful journey in scenery of superlative beauty.

Mellbreak and Lanthwaite   Above *Gasgale Gill*

Above *High Stile and Crummock Water*   Below *Crummock Water and Loweswater*

6 DALEHEAD TARN, 1900'
Newlands – Honister Pass

THE HEAD OF Newlands is so tightly encircled by mountains that there seems at first sight to be no way of crossing this barrier except by serious climbing. And these mountains are formidable. Blocking the direct route south is Dale Head, defended by cliffs always in shadow and effectively terminating the valley. Nor are its near neighbours of kinder appearance: high on the left is the mile-long escarpment of Eel Crags, a place for rockclimbers only, and to the right rise interminable slopes, capped by cliffs and scree, to the top of Hindscarth, neither having anything to offer the average walker.

Newlands Beck points the way of escape. It is seen coming down easier ground to the left of Dale Head and a path follows its course upwards without difficulty and leads on to an easy descent to the road at the top of Honister Pass.

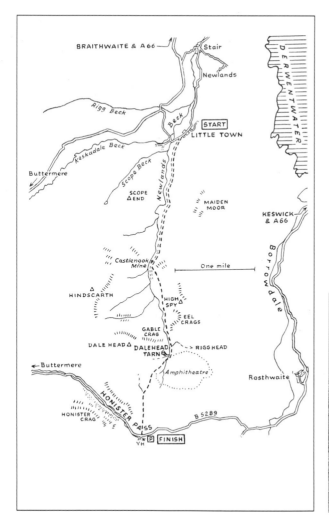

A CART-TRACK leaves the road at Little Town in Newlands and heads south following Newlands Beck upstream for two miles along the floor of the valley with little gain in height. The track is distinct, having been used for centuries by traffic from the many mines hereabouts, all now disused, and in modern times by the boots of walkers. On the left is Maiden Moor, with relics of lead mines and quarries, and on the right Scope End rises abruptly in a dark covering of heather that conceals the spoil of the once-famous Goldscope Mine; although the levels driven into the fellside can still be found, they should not be entered.

Opposite *The upper Newlands valley*
Below *Dale Head*

Hindscarth and Scope End from Little Town

This mine was abandoned over a hundred years ago after intermittent operation for six centuries: one of the oldest mines in the district, it was also the most important in output, having rich veins of lead and copper, and silver and gold have also been extracted. Its early development on a large scale was undertaken by German miners, and its long history has been marked by many incidents and much litigation.

Higher in the valley the old mine of Castlenook occupies a prominent headland alongside the track and beyond is revealed the final reaches in the form of a grassy ampitheatre deep-set amongst rising fellsides. Directly in front, leaving nobody in doubt that Newlands has come to an end, towers the immense facade of Dale Head with Gable Crag conspicuous. On the left skyline is the intimidating array of Eel Crags, and Hindscarth on the right is capped by a barrier of broken cliffs and has no welcome to offer. The ampitheatre, however, is a rewarding place for those with an interest in things past: there are mine shafts and ruined huts, and it is still possible to trace a well-graded path going up to the old copper mine on Dale Head, now in sad decay but worthy of inspection.

Newlands Beck is seen coming down from a depression to the left of Dale Head and a path follows it up to a plateau of easy but undulating and confusing ground. A track branches left to Rigg Head and descends to Rosthwaite past the extensive disused quarries.

For Honister, the path goes forward, still alongside the stream, passing Dalehead Tarn which cannot be seen but is indicated by a tributary issuing from it. A thin track leaves the side of the tarn bound for the summit of Dale Head which towers behind.

It will now be appreciated by walkers that the name of Dalehead Tarn heading this chapter is not really appropriate. The true pass or watershed is seen half a mile further on above a slight slope, the stream still descending from it. The path continues easily, crossing an old wire fence to join the main path from Honister Pass to the top of Dale Head. At the watershed, a glorious panorama of well-loved mountains is suddenly displayed ahead with stunning effect across the trench of Honister, and makes a magnificent background as the path descends gradually to the road at the top of Honister Pass.

Right *Dalehead Tarn*
Below *The view south from the watershed*

7 DEEPDALE HAUSE, 2150′
Dunmail Raise – Deepdale

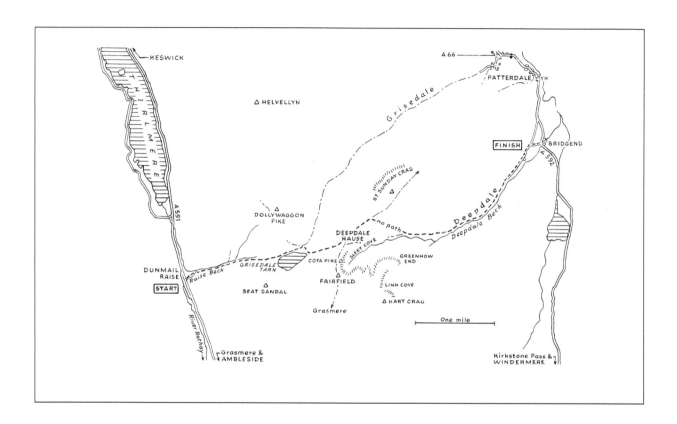

WHEN I FIRST explored the eastern fells, there was no semblance of a path from Grisedale Tarn to the obvious depression of Deepdale Hause on the high skyline between St Sunday Crag and Fairfield. Since those early days, a thin track has formed, not, however, intended to assist the crossing of the hause into the valley of Deepdale beyond but to reach the excellent path going up from the hause to St Sunday Crag after following the ridge down from Fairfield. Rarely indeed is the hause used as a pass into Deepdale since most walkers arriving at the tarn from Grasmere prefer the easier route provided by continuing along the bridleway down Grisedale and so to the Patterdale valley, of which Deepdale is a part. But if Grisedale is busy with pedestrian traffic, as it often is, Deepdale Hause is the key to a lonely alternative with mountain scenery of a high order, and for the person who likes undisturbed solitude it has special appeal for there is very little possibility of meeting other walkers. Here a buzzard may circle overhead and sheep will be grazing but no other sign of life need be expected. On its wild upper reaches, Deepdale becomes your very own.

Opposite *Deepdale Hause from Grisedale Tarn*

GRISEDALE TARN is invariably reached by way of the popular Grasmere–Patterdale path but there is a shorter and quieter route to the tarn from the west. This starts from the A591 on the top of Dunmail Raise.

Clear of the tarmac and the things that speed along it, the moor is crossed to come alongside Raise Beck issuing from a rough watercourse forming the north boundary of Seat Sandal. The beck, a happy tumble of cataracts, is no longer destined exclusively for the Rothay, as nature intended, but has been diverted to feed Thirlmere. A stony track climbs along the bank emerging, as Seat Sandal declines, into open grassland with Grisedale Tarn in full view ahead, backed by the St Sunday Crag and Fairfield range with Deepdale Hause clearly identifiable. Nearby is the massive bulk of Dollywaggon Pike carrying a dusty path to Helvellyn.

From the outlet of the tarn, a beeline can be made for the hause, keeping a lookout for the new track to ease the ascent of the rough fellside. When attained, there is a comprehensive view of the Helvellyn range seen over the great gulf of Grisedale, but the most imposing feature within close proximity is the sharp pinnacle of Cofa Pike, concealing its parent fell, Fairfield.

The Helvellyn range from Deepdale Hause   Above *Raise Beck*

Used as a pass, a descent must now be made into the head of Deepdale without the help of a path, and the scenery is immediately awesome: the crags of Cofa Pike plunge precipitously into Sleet Cove and beyond is seen the massive wall of Fairfield in a succession of cliffs and scree gullies which terminate in the towering buttress of Greenhow End. There is no difficulty in finding a way down the valley: after initial steepness, the descent is on easy grass and Deepdale Beck soon forms to give infallible guidance – indeed, one has a feeling of watching a tremendous convulsion of nature from a comfortable seat in the front row of the stalls.

When the wild upper recesses are left behind, a path materialises and leads around the base of St Sunday Crag in surroundings of lessening drama to the cultivated fields, trees and scattered homesteads as the A592 road and creature comforts are reached in Patterdale.

Above *Cofa Pike*

Below *The northern precipices of Fairfield*

8 DUNMAIL RAISE, 782'
Grasmere – Thirlmere

THE MAIN ARTERY of communication in the Lake District is the A591 road which takes advantage of the only easy breach in the high fells. Recent road improvements have made this a fast highway for cars but, because of the weight of traffic, heavy lorries are precluded from using it.

The name of the pass derives from Dunmail, the last King of Cumberland, who was defeated in battle in 945 by King Edmund of England, and whose remains, according to legend, are buried beneath the huge pile of stones on the summit of the pass. This cairn or mound was preserved during a realignment of the road some years ago and now occupies an island formed by a dual carriageway.

Freed from the delays caused by heavy vehicles, cars use the road as a racetrack. Pedestrians are advised to keep off the tarmac as much as they can and may do so as described below.

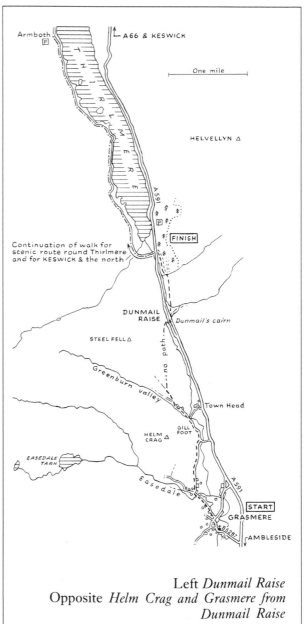

Left *Dunmail Raise*
Opposite *Helm Crag and Grasmere from Dunmail Raise*

INSTEAD OF following the A591 north from Grasmere, travellers on foot would do far better by taking the side road to Easedale, leaving it at the first junction on the right where a quiet and pleasant byway runs below Helm Crag to the secluded dell of Gill Foot and continues along a track that leads into the side valley of Greenburn. This is left near the last two cottages in favour of a path climbing the south ridge of Steel Fell. When clear of the intakes, which still feature a pillbox where the folk of Grasmere intended to repel German invaders who never came, a beeline can be made to Dunmail Raise, now clearly in sight, by contouring the pathless fellside and crossing an area of drumlins left by a glacier. Walkers arrive exactly at the top of the pass, indicated by Dunmail's cairn.

The alternative to continuing on the road is provided by a stile in the wall on the east side, which admits to a field where the old road can be joined to cross an ancient bridge at the foot of a series of waterfalls before entering a conifer plantation and debouching on the main road opposite the junction of the scenic route around Thirlmere. If instead the A591 is followed down to Thirlmere, a tear-jerking plaque set in the wall on the right, and not noticed by speeding motorists, deserves a brief halt: this pays a glowing tribute to a horse that gave his master a lifetime of faithful service and 'whose only fault was dying'.

Walkers bound for places north of Thirlmere, or Keswick, should escape from the A591 and take to the scenic route, a much quieter and more attractive alternative starting at the junction where a signpost still points to Armboth although nothing is left of Armboth now but its name which is used for the car park and the fell (*see* page 100).

9 ESK HAUSE, 2490'
Eskdale – Borrowdale

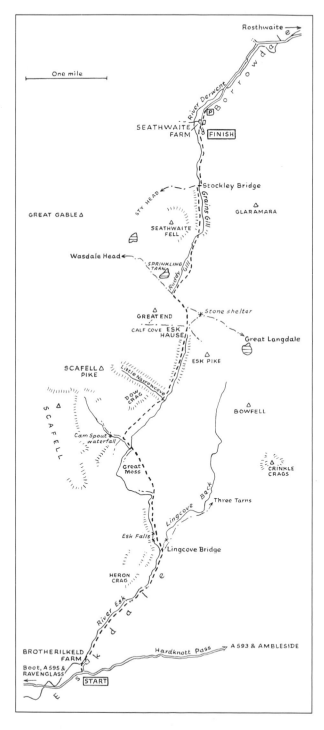

ESK HAUSE – the true Esk Hause, not the misnamed one – forms a watershed between the two lovely valleys of Eskdale and Borrowdale, and is the highest pass in Lakeland. This distinction is not recognised by popularity, for although it crosses magnificent terrain it is rarely used as a pass. In fact, I have never seen anybody engaged on the through route and, truth to tell, I have never done it myself. One reason for its neglect may be that the course of the route runs alongside the Scafell range and most red-blooded walkers, in fine weather, cannot resist the greater appeal of the high-level traverse of the ridge.

The head of Eskdale is confusing topographically, a tangle of rough ground in a bowl formed by the Scafells, Esk Pike, Bowfell and Crinkle Crags, and one of the wildest areas in the district. But the route to Esk Hause is clearly defined by the River Esk, this being followed closely to its source just below the hause and pointing the way exactly. Over the hause, territory much frequented by walkers is reached and the loneliness of the approach is dispelled.

But make no mistake. An afternoon start is too late. Esk Hause deserves a full day.

ESKDALE'S ROAD is left at the foot of Hardknott Pass near Brotherilkeld Farm, the only habitation seen on the journey until Seathwaite Farm is reached at the end of the day. A distinct path goes up the valley in typical Lakeland scenery and comes alongside the delightful River Esk, a watercourse of pools and splashes and happy gurgles, but today its charms must be resisted: it must not detain. The long precipice of Heron Crag, high on the left, is passed and a confluence of waters is reached, the picturesque stone arch of Lingcove Bridge being just beyond and spanning Lingcove Beck coming down from Bowfell.

Opposite *Esk Hause*

Above *Brotherilkeld looking towards Bowfell*

Below *Lingcove Bridge*

Hereabouts, the Esk changes direction, the river issuing from a spectacular gorge through which plunge the Esk Falls. The gorge is manifestly inaccessible and is avoided by crossing Lingcove Bridge to a path rising along the fellside high above. Almost at once the great wall of the Scafells comes into view ahead, a thrilling moment calculated to stop in his tracks anyone carrying a camera. The path goes forward towards the imposing scene and reaches a vast marshland, the Great Moss, once a deer preserve owned by Furness Abbey. Now the Scafells are seen in full stature and majesty, rising sharply from the flat strath of the Moss. A popular route of ascent is indicated by the waterfall of Cam Spout directly ahead, but the route to Esk Hause follows the river up the valley opening on the right and after gingerly picking a way through the marshy ground, join a firm path.

Above *Esk Falls*

The Scafells from Great Moss

The path continues upriver, the valley narrowing as the fells crowd in on both sides. The formidable cliff of Dow Crag, sometimes referred to as Esk Buttress, is prominent on the left and succeeded by the great chasm of Little Narrowcove, a rough and menacing ravine beset by crags and bringing a tributary down to join the Esk, which is now in its infancy. As it traverses stony ground the path becomes intermittent as it still keeps close to the stream. The eastern flanks of the valley throughout this section of the walk from Great Moss belong to Esk Pike.

The hause is now seen ahead above a rough steep slope; the stream and the path give up the ghost, having fulfilled their roles as guides, and a final stiff pull lands the walker on Esk Hause, with a new landscape in front of him.

Above *Esk Pike*

Below *Looking north from Esk Hause*

Grains Gill

On the grassy expanse of Esk Hause life becomes exciting again. The ground in front falls away gradually towards Borrowdale between the massive dome of Great End, half left, and Esk Pike high to the right. Well-worn paths are met here. A track blazed by thousands of boots each year winds up into Calf Cove on a popular route to Scafell Pike; another goes off to climb Esk Pike. Another, also part of the Scafell Pike route, comes up over easy grass from a wind shelter of stones on the path crossing below between Great Langdale and Wasdale Head; this shelter is commonly regarded as Esk Hause, quite wrongly.

To proceed, it was formerly necessary to go down to the shelter and turn along the Wasdale path, but a fairly new track has been trodden from the hause and descends directly to the Wasdale path at the top of Grains Gill after passing alongside Great End and revealing a view of Great Gable. Grains Gill is the key to the last few miles of the walk. At its head, alongside the Wasdale path, it has the name of Ruddy Gill, the red subsoil having an iron content. Five minutes further towards Wasdale, the path comes alongside the shores of a delightful sheet of water, Sprinkling Tarn, a great time-waster and not on today's crowded itinerary: it should be saved for a leisurely visit and a long halt. Having resisted this detour, the stream issuing from Ruddy Gill is crossed and a steep descent follows, skirting a deep ravine from which the stream emerges as Grains Gill. This too is forded to a path that goes down with the stream to Stockley Bridge; the stream becomes the River Derwent below the bridge. The crowds met here should not be assumed to be a welcoming party; nothing is further from their minds. Some are picnickers; some casual strollers. We are back in tourist country. A wide, dusty and often busy path leaves the bridge for the short journey to Seathwaite Farm, always a welcome sight. There is a car park here which is the terminus of the Borrowdale valley road.

Above *The top of Floutern Pass looking to Buttermere*   Below *Ennerdale from Floutern Pass*

10 FLOUTERN PASS, 1300′
Ennerdale – Buttermere

IF WALKERS WERE called upon to vote for the Lakeland pass they considered least attractive, there is little doubt that Floutern Pass would top the poll with a thumping majority. This pass is the easiest and shortest way of crossing the fells between the Buttermere valley and Ennerdale Water. It starts well and finishes well but the intermediate stages are without charm or beauty and contain an extensive quagmire from which few walkers escape dryshod. Nor have the surrounding fells any visual appeal: they are barren, lack character, are without features of interest, undistinguished in outline and share in the general hopelessness of the landscape. It is the sort of place that once visited will ever afterwards be approached with trepidation. Some reward for misery will be gained by walking the pass in the direction here indicated, suffering being forgotten in the sylvan beauty of Buttermere with Scale Force as a special bonus to revive drooping spirits. Floutern, frankly, is a mess.

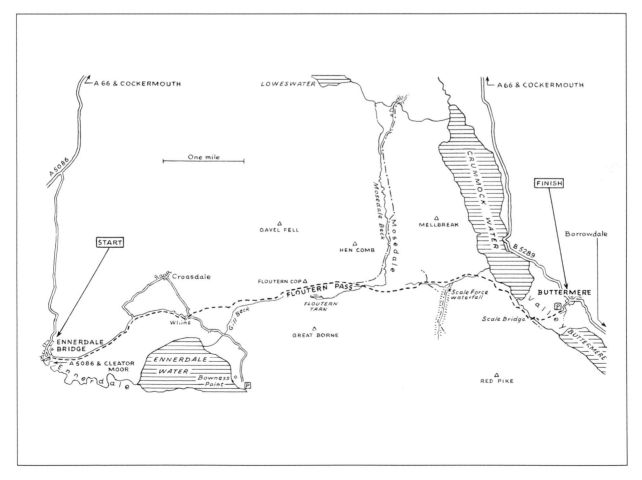

THE VILLAGE of Ennerdale Bridge is left by the Croasdale road, from which a lane cuts a corner to reach a no-through road, much used in summer, going down to a large car park at Bowness Point on the side of Ennerdale Water. The path to Floutern Pass leaves this road at Whins and climbs steadily alongside Gill Beck to a wire fence crossing the watershed and marking the highest point of the walk. The views fore and aft are in total contrast. Behind are the green pastures and thriving husbandry of Ennerdale with a glimpse of its lovely lake, a pleasing scene, but ahead is seen a dreary wasteland without invitation or welcome – Bunyan's Slough of Despond in person, but with a hint of better things in the far distance. Only the diminutive peak of Floutern Cop nearby tries to give distinction to the scene. On the right, the ground rises to Great Borne, also known as Herdhouse or Herdus, and Floutern Tarn comes into sight as the walk proceeds, being revealed as an elongated sheet of water with attractions only for anglers and not worth a visit.

The path descends into a vast hollow, dark with peaty marshland and threaded by the stream issuing from the tarn. The stream has the good sense to escape into a side valley, one of Lakeland's five Mosedales, and a path goes with it along the base of Mellbreak to the sweet countryside of Loweswater. But walkers bound for Buttermere must contemplate the morass ahead and find a way across it, gingerly treading the wet ground and making abortive searches for firm footing in a series of trials and errors before soaked feet make a nonsense of patient investigation and a beeline is ploughed to the greenery ahead. Finally clear of the glutinous mud, a slight slope is climbed and at the top a view is revealed that makes it all seem worthwhile.

The marshes of Floutern Pass

Crummock Water and the Buttermere Fells
Right *Scale Force*

After the damp rigours of the Floutern crossing, the prospect from the top of the rise beyond is a soothing balm. Crummock Water appears in a frame of colourful fells to make a lovely picture. On the descent, a popular path turns off to the rocky chasm of Scale Force, its 125-ft plunge making it the highest of Lakeland's waterfalls and the highlight of the Buttermere area. Victorian ladies and gentlemen visiting the force were brought by boat to a landing on the shore of Crummock Water, but today's Elizabethans must use a wet path through the lakeside trees. This is the path that ends the walk from Ennerdale, crossing Scale Bridge to enter Buttermere village in surroundings of such exquisite beauty that Floutern seems like a bad dream. But if the path is crowded and noisy, as is all too often the case, even lonely Floutern will be seen to have some merit after all.

11 GARBURN PASS, 1450′
Troutbeck – Kentmere

THERE IS little doubt that in late medieval times before the present lines of communication were established, a primitive road cut across the fells in the south-east corner of the Lake District between Windermere and Shap. The initial section of this ancient highway took advantage of a dip in the high skyline of the Ill Bell range to cross from Troutbeck to Kentmere, the depression being known as Garburn Pass, originally spelt Garbourn. Ordnance Survey maps still name the long lane leading to it as Garburn Road. Today, reduced in status to a bridleway, it is a route only for walkers, pony trekkers and motorbike scramblers.

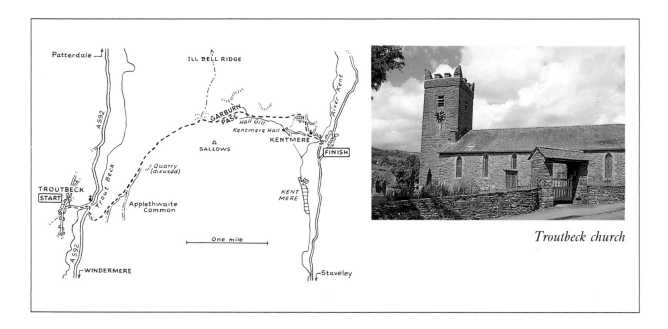

Troutbeck church

A SHADY LANE leaves the A592 near Troutbeck church and climbs steadily among trees to reach open country where it is joined by a rough road coming from the south. The fellside here is Applethwaite Common, the venue of annual sheepdog trials.

The lane continues to ascend between stone walls and soon reaches the disused Applethwaite Quarry. Most old quarries are gloomy and repelling, with an air of desolation, but this one, masked by trees, is worthy of inspection since it still retains its weighbridge and other relics of abandoned industry. This apart, there is little to relieve the tedium of the steady climb except for an excellent aerial view of the Troutbeck valley, improving with every step.

When the summit is gained, there is a comprehensive panorama to the west, the high fells of Lakeland forming the distant horizon. A rough track turns off here over marshy ground to the Ill Bell ridge, but the cart-track goes forward through a gate between sturdy stone walls.

Opposite *Looking to The Tongue and Threshthwaite Mouth*

Above *Applethwaite Quarry*

Below *Garburn Pass looking down to Windermere*

With the Kentmere valley now in sight, the descent there commences on a deteriorating but distinct path following Hall Gill down below an escarpment of crags high on the left. In pleasant surroundings, the pele tower of Kentmere Hall comes into sight below and the new Kent Mere beyond. As the first buildings appear ahead, a huge isolated rock may be noticed in a field over the wall on the right: this is Badger Rock, also known as Brock Stone. It resembles a small cliff, large enough to provide rock climbs, but is in fact a boulder fallen from the heights above.

Pass through a picturesque complex of cottages and farm buildings to a tarmac road which leads to Kentmere church and the village beyond.

Pele tower at Kentmere Hall

Above *Badger Rock*

12 GATESCARTH PASS, 1950'
Longsleddale – Mardale

MOTORISTS TRAVELLING north from Kendal along the A6 are rewarded for preferring this old turnpike to the modern M6 by a brief glimpse of a lovely valley opening between bare fells on the left after five miles of the journey. This valley is seen emerging, straight as a furrow, from a distant mountain surround, and patterned by pasture and woodland and an occasional white farmhouse. With the River Sprint running alongside, it is a delightful place.

This is Longsleddale, the most easterly of the major valleys of Lakeland and lacking nothing of the beauty of the others; indeed, preserving the romantic charm that some have lost. Because of its seclusion and the absence of a through passage for vehicles, and having neither an inn nor a shop in its eight-mile length, it has happily suffered little from the intrusion of tourists: its one road remains narrow between fragrant hedges and stone walls. It is an oasis of pastoral tranquillity amidst inhospitable fells, looking very much as it did three centuries ago. Man has nurtured it, not spoilt it. The only disturbance to its rural security occurred some fifty years ago when Manchester Corporation cut a five-mile trench along the eastern slopes to contain their aqueduct from Haweswater, but they restored the ground commendably and nature has since clothed the scars. More recently a second aqueduct was planned but the project was abandoned after angry protests from the inhabitants. The people of Longsleddale may be few in number but they love their valley and are right to be proud of it. Longsleddale is delightful.

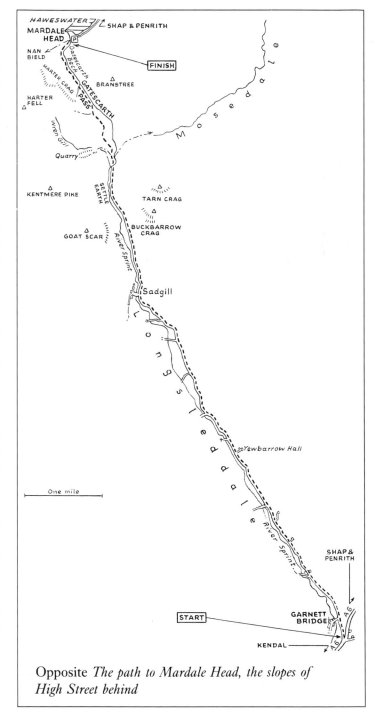

Opposite *The path to Mardale Head, the slopes of High Street behind*

Longsleddale
Right *Garnett Bridge*

THE VALLEY ROAD branches from the A6 and descends sharply to the only hamlet, Garnett Bridge, where a cluster of cottages around a former bobbin mill makes a picturesque study for the camera. Then the road goes on, mile after mile, passing the oldest building in the dale, the medieval pele tower of Yewbarrow Hall, and the little church before finally reaching the farmsteads of Sadgill. Here the road ends. Cars can go no further and are often parked on the verges by the bridge, sometimes awkwardly to the annoyance of the few residents of this lonely outpost. Car parks never improve the scenery and usually detract from it, but at Sadgill Bridge a small one is now needed.

At Sadgill, the view ahead is of wild grandeur. The mountains crowd in, revealing the desolate upper reaches of the valley through the rugged portals of Goat Scar and Buckbarrow. The crossing of Gatescarth Pass starts here, for travellers on foot only. The tarmac road gives place to a rough cart-track between stone walls. The green pastures continue for a further half-mile. In 1845, a reservoir was planned here with the authority of an Act of Parliament to regulate the flow of the river to the water-powered mills lower down the valley, but it was never proceeded with because of the huge cost. Cultivation ends abruptly where a gravel dam, built to retain the stones brought down by the river, crosses the valley floor.

Now the track starts to climb into a scene of grim desolation. On the left rises the precipitous face of Goat Scar, this being succeeded by the gloomy mountain hollow of Settle Earth, a haven for foxes; the summit above is Kentmere Pike. On the right towers Buckbarrow Crag, its discharge of stones littering the ground; amongst them but not discernible from the track is a massive boulder rivalling in size the famous Bowder Stone in Borrowdale. The height above is Tarn Crag which has on its summit the crumbling remains of a stone survey post, one of three erected above the line of the aqueduct from Haweswater, here in a tunnel over a thousand feet below the surface.

The steeper sections of the track are roughly paved with stones set in horizontal courses to serve as brakes for the horses bringing down heavy loads of slate from Wrengill Quarry, long disused. Alongside tumbles the infant Sprint in a series of cataracts and waterfalls.

The head of Longsleddale

The cart-track escapes from its confining walls when the gradient eases and a gate is reached, the wall on the right turning up the fellside and that on the left continuing on the line of march. The landscape here is dreary, the walk proceeding with open grassland on the right, rising gradually to a depression on the skyline. A path branches in this direction over rough and marshy ground: this is the way to Mosedale.

A stile in the accompanying wall admits to the vast disused Wrengill Quarry, and for walkers with an interest in industrial archaeology a detour over the wall will be most rewarding.

Wrengill Quarry has vertical man-made cliffs, tunnels, a derelict tramway, water channels, a terrace of cottages and ancillary buildings, all in sad decay.

On my first visit, the cottages were substantially intact. I once spent a night here amongst the skeletal ghosts of an abandoned industry, an eerie experience in the graveyard of dead workings. The only pleasure I can remember on this occasion was provided by the extensive carpet of wild thyme on the cliff tops: I uprooted a few plants for my garden at home but they obviously preferred the loneliness of Wrengill Quarry and soon withered in an alien habitat in suburbia.

At the far extremity of the quarry, Wren Gill enters in a fine waterfall, disappearing into two potholes and continuing underground before emerging as the River Sprint.

The quarry was last worked by prisoners during the First World War. It is a sad place today.

Waterfall in River Sprint

Summit of Gatesgarth Pass
Right *Harter Crag*

Resuming the walk to Mardale, the track rises steadily over grass slopes, now unenclosed, and ascends in a series of zigzags, engineered centuries ago to ease the passage of laden packhorses. Higher, the gradient lessens and the summit of Gatescarth Pass is reached at a gate in a wire fence crossing the watershed. A new landscape opens up ahead framed by the crags of Harter Fell and the steep declivities of Branstree. The prospect is pleasing as the track descends into Mardale, at first gently and, when the ground steepens, in a succession of sharp zigzags so delightful to follow that there is no inducement to short cuts; consequently there is little erosion and the path remains in pristine condition. Gatescarth Beck is a lively companion alongside.

To the left, split by a great gully, tower the cliffs of Harter Crag. It was here that a pair of golden eagles, the first seen in Lakeland for 150 years, built an abortive eyrie two decades ago. Later they adopted a nesting site on another crag a mile away where, under the watchful eyes of wardens of the Royal Society for the Protection of Birds, they settled successfully and reared families.

High Street and Haweswater come into view during the descent and the path from Nan Bield joins in for the final hundred yards to the public car park at Mardale Head situated at the terminus of the road alongside Haweswater.

13 GOATS HAUSE, 2100'
Coniston – Duddon Valley

GOATS HAUSE, as the name implies, is undoubtedly a pass, and it is true that by crossing it a walker may travel between Coniston and the Duddon Valley, but few ever will because the Walna Scar 'road' is so obviously the most direct way from one to the other. Only for anyone wishing to extend the walk and having a couple of hours to spare can Goats Hause be recommended. The route, however, has one great merit: it passes through one of the grandest scenes in the district where the awesome precipices of Dow Crag soar high above Goats Water. Also introduced is Seathwaite Tarn, a large sheet of water shyly hidden in a fold of the hills and not often seen by Lakeland's visitors.

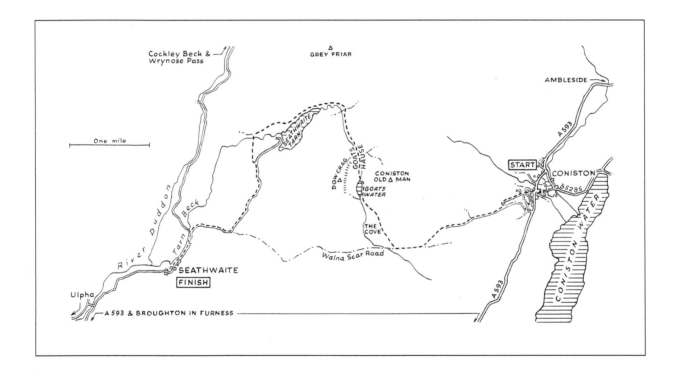

APPROACHING FROM Coniston, leave the Walna Scar cart-track just beyond the rock gateway where a track branches to the right and rises into a hollow, The Cove, with Dow Crag coming into sight ahead. When Goats Water is suddenly reached after a rise in the path, a dramatic picture unfolds with stunning effect. Dow Crag is now revealed in full stature as an array of massive buttresses split by deep gullies and overtopping steep slopes of scree and boulders falling to the water's edge. Goat's Water is uninviting, its outlet choked by boulders and its shores fringed with debris from above.

Opposite *Dow Crag*

When I first visited this impressive scene, there was an upright memorial stone, roughly inscribed CHARMER 1911, on a grassy bank amongst the boulders at the outlet of Goat's Water. Charmer was a foxhound killed in a fall on Dow Crag, and it is nice to reflect that a faithful dog was revered in this way. Then came the vandals. On a later visit, I found the memorial uprooted and cast among the stones in the bed of the issuing stream. Later still I could find no trace of it and hope it has been carried down by floodwaters to a safer haven. Charmer deserved better than this.

The rockclimbers' way to Dow Crag fords the outlet and slants upwards across the scree to a cave formed by a huge boulder at the foot of the cliff, this being the usual base of operations. Lesser mortals take a rough track along the eastern shore of the tarn, reaching easy slopes that rise to the dip in the skyline ahead. This is Goats Hause, traversed by a path linking Dow Crag and Coniston Old Man, the latter having been on the right throughout the walk thus far. There is a fresh landscape in front but it is the sight of Dow Crag that still rivets the attention.

Goats Water and Dow Crag from Goats Hause

Seathwaite Tarn
Right *Gully on Dow Crag*

Continuing, a long simple slope descends into the valley in front where Seathwaite Tarn, almost a mile in length, occupies the centre of the stage, the backcloth being formed by the bulky fell of Grey Friar, an outlier of the Coniston range. Around the head of the tarn, which has been adapted as a reservoir, are relics of the Seathwaite Copper Mines, a dead industry; there are open mine levels here that are dangerous to enter. This area is featured in Richard Adams' *The Plague Dogs*.

A path on the northern shore of the tarn leads to the reservoir access road and this is followed down, in scenes of increasing loveliness and thriving husbandry, to join the Walna Scar road before it meets the main valley road a pleasant half-mile north of Seathwaite. Dancing alongside in the final stages of the walk is Tarn Beck on its way to meet the River Duddon.

14 GRASSGUARDS, 1180'
Duddon Valley – Eskdale

FOR A WALK of sustained delight, the crossing of the broad ridge dividing the Duddon Valley and Eskdale must rank high in the itinerary of visitors enjoying a stay in the southern part of Lakeland. The start and finish are amid scenery of idyllic loveliness, sadly marred by recent extensive conifer plantations on the Duddon flank of Harter Fell but the forest so created is skirted rather than entered and does not detract from the pleasures of a summer walk.

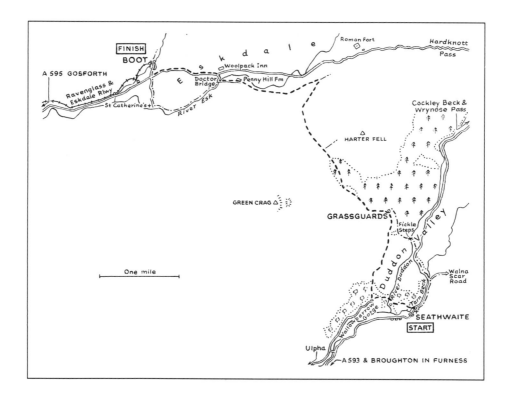

THE ISOLATED BUILDINGS of Grassguards may be reached by either of two routes from the Duddon Valley. From Seathwaite church a path leads through woodlands, crossing Tarn Beck, to a bridge that has replaced stepping stones on the River Duddon in a setting joyful to behold: here the river is seen issuing from the steep confining slopes of Wallowbarrow Gorge, a ravine bedecked with heather and trees, and always a place of bewitching beauty. Over the bridge, the path turns west to join a cart-track used by the scattered farms hereabouts and this climbs steadily to open countryside and Grassguards.

The alternative route leaves the road a mile north of Seathwaite and crosses a pasture to reach the river, where the huge stepping stones of Fickle Steps admit to the wooded slope on the far bank. This too is a charming spot although the crossing may cause some apprehension. Safely accomplished, a path rises through native trees to emerge at Grassguards.

Opposite *From the bridge in Wallowbarrow Gorge*

Upper Eskdale from Harter Fell; Hardknott Fort is visible in the centre

From Grassguards, the path heads north-west, with open undulating country on the left and, when the trees are left behind, the beckoning pyramid of Harter Fell rising in colourful slopes. An insignificant watershed is crossed, marked by a broken wall, and Eskdale starts to take shape ahead. When a track branches off, obviously bound for the summit of Harter Fell, the ascent of this fine mountain should be considered: the climb, amongst heather, is rewarded with fine views of Eskdale, the summit is exciting, the highest inches reached only by simple scrambling up naked rock. The northern panorama of the head of Eskdale, backed by the Scafells and Bowfell, with a nearer aerial view of Hardknott Roman Fort, is truly magnificent. If two parties have arranged to do the walk from opposite directions, it needs to be discussed beforehand whether Harter Fell is to be included; if so, the summit makes a grand meeting place.

Resuming the main path and with Eskdale gloriously displaying its lovely plumage in front, descend into the valley. It is well to keep strictly to the path and not attempt short cuts on the lower slopes, since the bracken of Eskdale is the highest in the district and impenetrably dense. At the foot of the descent, a lane is joined and followed down-river, to pass Penny Hill Farm – a place of happy memories where I was first introduced to the life of a Lakeland farmer – and arriving at Doctor Bridge over the River Esk. The lane joins the valley road near the Woolpack Inn, and the village of Boot is a short mile to the left.

But to enjoy some delectable river scenery, an enchanting path leaves Doctor Bridge and follows the Esk down-river as it rounds a wooded hill and leads to St Catherine's church, the parish church of Eskdale, a plain structure built in the seventeenth century and more remarkable for the contents of the graveyard than for those of the interior. Here is Tommy Dobson's grave, marked by a headstone inscribed with his own likeness, a fox, a hound and horn: a masterpiece in granite. Tommy's name has not lived on as has John Peel's, yet his local reputation as a Master of Foxhounds was even greater. Foxhunting was his whole life and his memorial reflects this passion.

A lane from the church leads to journey's end in the friendly village of Boot.

Tommy Dobson's grave
Below left and right *Penny Hill Farm*

Above *Far Easedale*

Below *Greenup Gill*

15 GREENUP EDGE, 1995'
Grasmere – Borrowdale

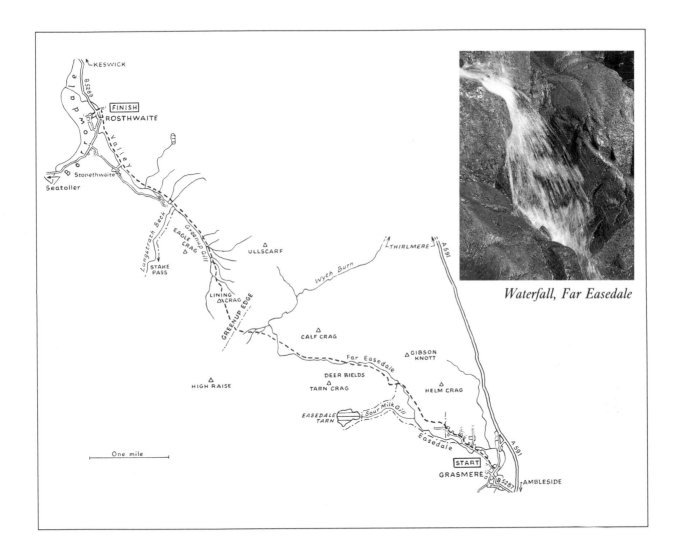

Waterfall, Far Easedale

TRAVELLERS ON FOOT between Grasmere and Borrowdale have little choice of route if they seek the shortest and most direct way. The central mass of fells must be crossed at a high level and the key to the easiest passage is Greenup Edge, a gap on the ridge joining High Raise and Ullscarf but, unfortunately for many walkers who have gone astray, not an obvious one when approached from Grasmere. The Edge is wild and lonely and provides a sharp contrast with the initial and final stages of the walk which are verdant and beautiful. Greenup Edge links two of the most popular parts of Lakeland and is in daily use.

LEAVE GRASMERE by the road to Easedale, from which a very popular path turns off to cross Easedale Beck and climb by the side of Sour Milk Gill, a delightful cataract, to Easedale Tarn. This is a prime objective of most sojourners at Grasmere – even in Victorian times when refreshments could be obtained at a stone hut near the outflow, but this has gone and today's visitors must take their own picnic lunches.

The route to Borrowdale, however, still with a tarmac surface, follows the main valley into Far Easedale, passing some desirable residences, and from it another well-trodden path leads upwards to another much visited objective, Helm Crag. This is better known as the Lion and the Lamb, to which the summit rocks bear a fancied resemblance.

These off-route attractions have no place in the itinerary of walkers bound for Borrowdale. The road is continued to its extremity where it becomes a rough lane alongside Far Easedale Beck which, when the last walls are passed, is crossed at Stythwaite Steps to a path heading upstream in open country. The path is unmistakable and cannot be lost even in mist, the sound of rushing water giving direction. Up on the left is the formidable Deer Bields Buttress, jutting from the lofty ridge that divides the two Easedales; on the right are the colourful slopes of Gibson Knott, continuing the skyline from Helm Crag. In places, the path crosses marshy ground where bog asphodel is rampant and then, after a rocky scramble, reaches the watershed marking the head of the valley of Far Easedale.

Looking towards Grasmere from the Easedale Tarn path

Easedale Tarn

Below *Summit of Greenup Edge*

The head of Far Easedale was formerly crossed by a wire fence of which a forlorn iron stepstile is the sole remaining relic. Beyond, the ground declines to a valley draining to the right, and walkers under the mistaken belief that the watershed is Greenup Edge may descend in that direction thinking it will lead down to Borrowdale. It won't: this is the valley of Wythburn going down to the head of Thirlmere, nowhere near Borrowdale, and containing extensive tracts of marshy ground indicated on Ordnance maps as The Bog. Greenup Edge is still half a mile distant and at a higher level; it can be discerned in front, slightly to the left of the ridge declining from the facing fell of Ullscarf. The path to it declines gently at first and then rises steadily, crossing several streams draining into Wythburn.

The path over Greenup Edge is a simple promenade on easy ground between the rough declivities of High Raise on the left and the smoother slopes of Ullscarf on the right, and either of these summits may be climbed from this point by walkers with energy to spare. But most will go forward for the distant glimpse of the Borrowdale heights and a bird's-eye view of the valley of Greenup Gill curving steeply down on the next stage of the journey.

With the flat top of the Edge left behind, the path starts the long descent, soon bypassing the rocky upthrust of Lining Crag and coming alongside Greenup Gill and fording the many tributaries joining in from Ullscarf. The descent continues below the cliffs of Eagle Crag (the best known of a dozen Eagle Crags in Lakeland, all named when golden eagles were resident in the district in past centuries) and out of its shadow reaches valley level at a lovely watersmeet where Langstrath Beck joins Greenup Gill from a wide opening on the left. Great slabs of rock are a feature of the confluence and they are a much favoured halting place. A drowning tragedy here is commemorated by a memorial bridge.

Right *Lining Crag*
Greenup Gill meets Langstrath Beck

Eagle Crag from Stonethwaite Beck

The finish of the walk is along the Stonethwaite Valley directly ahead, a mile of exquisite beauty where the distinctive charm of Victorian Lakeland is still preserved. Out of sight and sound of the Borrowdale traffic, the Stonethwaite Valley is an Arcadia of delight, its huddle of cottages and farm buildings an architectural gem, and living a life unchanged for centuries. The environs of wooded fellsides, sparkling streams and emerald pastures make Stonethwaite, in my opinion, the most charming of Lakeland's side valleys. Nothing is orderly as modern planners would have it; a carefree untidiness pervades the scene and hits exactly the right key in bewitching enchantment. The whole is an epitome of rural peace and serenity in a landscape of romance. Here is a surviving example of Lakeland's unique charm that has to such a large extent been destroyed by the very same people who come in search of it.

The path ends in the busy main street of Rosthwaite, a metropolis after Stonethwaite. Here, back in civilisation, advantage can be taken of the Borrowdale bus to go to Keswick for a connection to Grasmere if it is desired to return to the starting point of the walk. It must be grudgingly conceded that despite the damage done to the twentieth-century Lakeland scene by the internal combustion engine, buses can sometimes be a blessing.

16 GRISEDALE HAUSE, 1929'
Grasmere – Patterdale

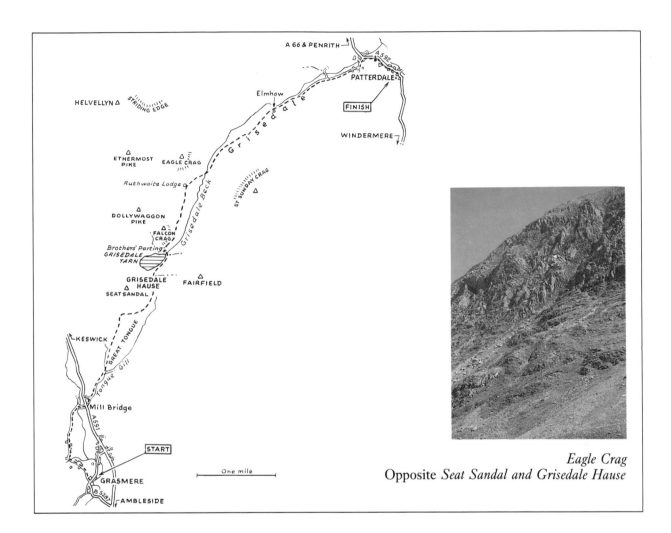

Eagle Crag
Opposite *Seat Sandal and Grisedale Hause*

T HE ROYAL ROAD for walkers journeying between Grasmere and Patterdale lies over Grisedale Hause, and indeed there is no other direct way that does not call for serious climbing. It is a route used for centuries by the dalesmen and later adopted in part for the ascent of Helvellyn when the fashionable method of reaching the summit was on the backs of ponies.

It is a splendid walk through the mountains in contrasting scenery, beautiful at the extremities and grimly austere in its higher sections, and is much used as a springboard for the ascent of the many popular heights that flank the route.

With the possible exceptions of the Sty Head and Rossett passes, Grisedale Hause may well be the most trodden of the high crossings amongst the fells that are and will always remain the exclusive preserve of travellers on foot.

Above *Grisedale Tarn*

Below *The Vale of Grasmere from Grisedale Hause*

A SIGNPOST on the A591 at Mill Bridge, just above the Travellers' Rest, points the way along a pleasant lane with Tongue Gill in close company. This ends when confronted by a steep conical slope that seems to bar further progress. This is Great Tongue, Tongue being a name common in Lakeland where a sharp upthrust of land divides a valley into two parallel descending sections. But here, as in most such cases, paths go round the obstacle on both sides. The left fork is usually taken, this being the way the ponies went, and the breast of Seat Sandal is ascended on a grass path before contouring to the stony rise below the hause. The right fork is easier initially but terminates in a steep rough scramble alongside waterfalls to join the other. The final rise to the hause is short but arduous on loose stones. At the crest, crossed by a sturdy wall, fine views fore and aft reward earlier effort.

The outlet of Grisedale Tarn

Ahead, Grisedale Tarn comes suddenly into view, backed by the featureless slopes of Dollywaggon Pike, up which winds a well-worn and dusty track; this was the former pony route to Helvellyn but nowadays is usually littered by countless humans, some struggling upwards, many fallen by the wayside. On the right beyond the tarn rise the even steeper slopes of St Sunday Crag, and between the two heights is the V-shaped gap that contains the valley of Grisedale. It is a barren landscape that greets the walker at Grisedale Hause, but look back to see, in total contrast, the verdant Vale of Keswick, Coniston Water and the undulating lesser fells of southern Lakeland.

From the hause, tracks go off to Seat Sandal, left, and Fairfield, right, but the main route goes forward, descending slightly to the outlet of the tarn, this being easily forded; here the path to Helvellyn turns left and the pass route to Patterdale follows the direction of the issuing stream, Grisedale Beck.

A short distance below the outlet, on a slope littered by fallen boulders is one of special significance; this is an inscribed boulder known as the Brothers' Parting, marking the spot where William Wordsworth said a last farewell to his brother John in 1805. They never met again, John being drowned in the ship he commanded shortly afterwards.

The path goes forward into Grisedale, descending slightly at first and revealing the shadowed cliffs of Falcon Crag high on the left before reaching a solitary stone hut, Ruthwaite Lodge, built originally as a shooting lodge but taken over by a mountaineering club. The stream cascading down the fellside nearby deserves a second glance: note the old mine level at the side.

From Ruthwaite Lodge the path descends more steeply to the floor of the valley, again crossing Grisedale Beck. Up on the left is the near-vertical precipice of Eagle Crag, a haunt not of eagles but of rockclimbers. Towering on the right are the un-remitting slopes of St Sunday Crag, nearly 2000 feet above and topped by a fringe of cliffs down which a woman fell to her death recently after going astray on the summit of the mountain.

From here on the walking is easy, the path becoming a cart-track and affording impressive retrospects of Dollywaggon Pike which now assumes the form of a slender pyramid, and neighbouring Nethermost Pike, starkly etched against the sky above a line of crags.

Above *Ruthwaite Lodge*

Below left *Eagle Crag* and right *Nethermostcove Beck*

Grisedale

Below *Patterdale church*

In scenery of increasing loveliness, the first buildings are reached at the farm of Elmhow. I once spent a night in a barn here without permission. The occasion was Coronation Day 1953, a public holiday, and I arrived at dusk after walking over the tops from Ambleside. I found a comfortable bed of straw but, being apprehensive of discovery, was unable to sleep and chain-smoked through the hours of darkness (I was on cigarettes in those days) without setting the barn on fire. I was off at dawn before the farmer started his morning rounds. I had to be in Kendal at nine o'clock to open the office, and walked over to Grasmere to catch the first morning bus. The day was memorable because it brought the news that Hillary and Tensing had reached the summit of Everest, an event that interested me more than the Coronation, for I had long cherished an impossible ambition to be the first man to reach the top of the highest mountain in the world. The news effectively burst a silly bubble.

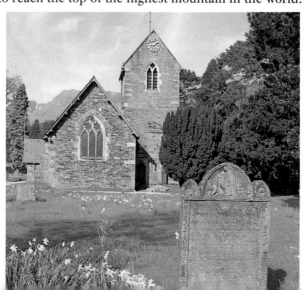

Further down the valley, the cart-track becomes a tarmac road used as an unofficial parking place for the cars of motorists who take to their legs for the ascent of Helvellyn by way of Striding Edge. The road leads down through an avenue of trees to join the A592 near Patterdale church, the village and refreshments for which the body has been clamouring being around the corner to the right.

The A592 has infrequent bus services and wise people wishing to avail themselves of these facilities will have studied the timetables in advance and kept an eye on their watches.

17 HARDKNOTT PASS, 1290'
Duddon Valley – Eskdale

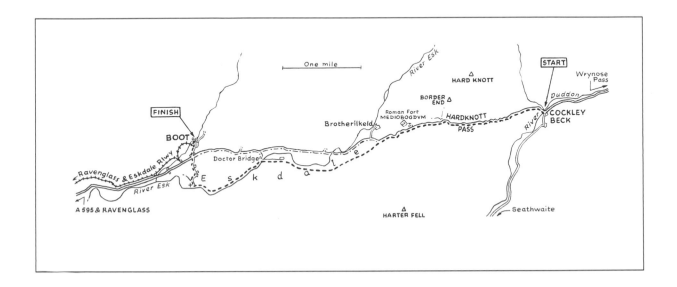

SEVEN OF THE mountain passes in Lakeland are crossed by motor roads, all of them having steep gradients on both sides, but quite the most notorious, challenging the skill and nerve of car drivers, is Hardknott Pass between the Duddon Valley and Eskdale.

Hardknott is almost a twin to Wrynose and usually both passes are crossed on the same journey, but motorists who have come over Wrynose from the east must expect a much stiffer climb over Hardknott and should approach it with the utmost concentration. It is no place for learner drivers. Height is not the problem, the altitude at the top being modest and lower than most of the others: it is the steepness of certain sections. Even the Romans baulked at the steepest part and sacrificed pride and principles by adopting a detour to circumvent the difficulties.

Opposite *The top of Hardknott Pass*
Right *The Scafell range from Border End*

THE ROAD STARTS to climb innocuously from the River Duddon at Cockley Beck Bridge but soon springs to life in a heart-stopping series of sharp and narrow hairpin bends with a gradient of 1 in 3, without respite until an easier incline to the top of the pass is reached. It is not unusual to find cars and their owners stranded on the unenclosed verges, or halted for breath on the more accommodating summit. Over the pass, with a glorious view of Eskdale ahead, there is a steep and awkward corner to negotiate before the road settles down in a long decline to the valley.

Towards the end of this descent, on an elevation to the right of the road, is the best preserved of the Roman forts in Lakeland: this is Mediobognvm, commonly referred to as Hardknott Castle, and should certainly be visited. Dating from the second century and identified beyond doubt by inscribed stones and

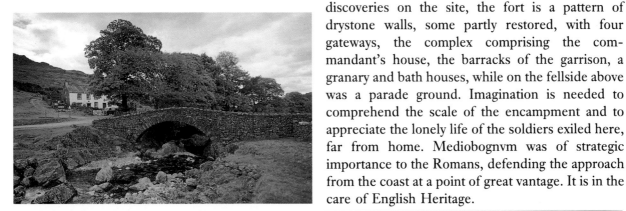

discoveries on the site, the fort is a pattern of drystone walls, some partly restored, with four gateways, the complex comprising the commandant's house, the barracks of the garrison, a granary and bath houses, while on the fellside above was a parade ground. Imagination is needed to comprehend the scale of the encampment and to appreciate the lonely life of the soldiers exiled here, far from home. Mediobognvm was of strategic importance to the Romans, defending the approach from the coast at a point of great vantage. It is in the care of English Heritage.

Above *Cockley Beck Bridge*

Hardknott Fort

Returning to the road, the descent continues to the floor of the valley, occupied by the River Esk and generously endowed with lush fields and lovely trees, and goes on to the village of Boot amidst scenery of unspoilt charm. At Boot, a miniature railway makes a delightful seven-mile journey to connect with the main line at Ravenglass.

Walkers over Hardknott Pass have little chance of escaping from the traffic on the Duddon side, the verges being too rough and boggy for easy progress, but upon reaching the top they should leave the road and scramble higher to the crest of Border End for a magnificent prospect of the Scafells and Bowfell and the other wild mountains circling upper Eskdale. After visiting the Roman fort, they should proceed down the valley by footpath from the bottom of the hill, enjoying the idyllic surroundings of the River Esk flowing nearby. At Doctor Bridge, the road may be joined for the last mile to Boot or, pleasanter, the river may be followed around a wooded hill on an enchanting path to the humble parish church of Eskdale, where the remarkable memorial to Tommy Dobson in the graveyard should be inspected (*see* page 73). A short lane then leads to the village.

Above *Remains of Hardknott Fort*

Eskdale

18 HART CRAG COL, 2520′
Rydal – Deepdale

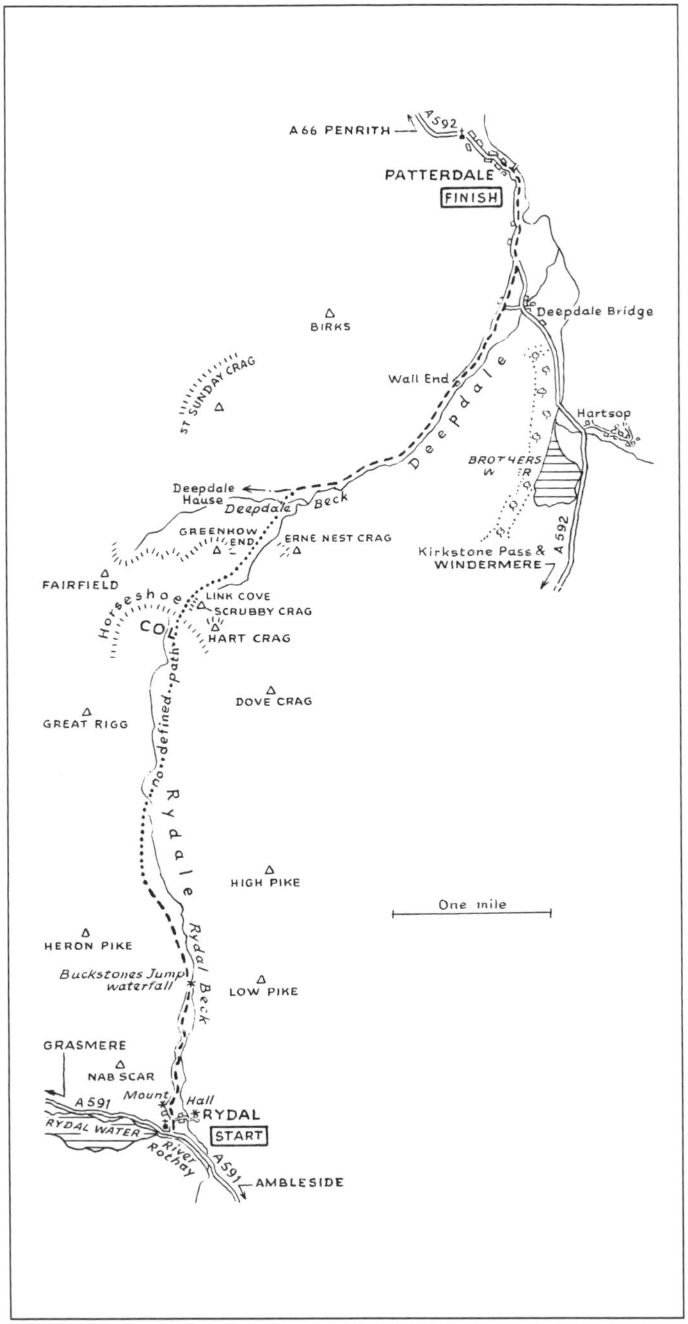
A66 PENRITH
A592
PATTERDALE
FINISH
Deepdale Bridge
BIRKS
ST SUNDAY CRAG
Wall End
Deepdale
Hartsop
BROTHERS W R
Deepdale Hause
Deepdale Beck
GREENHOW END
ERNE NEST CRAG
A592
Kirkstone Pass & WINDERMERE
FAIRFIELD
Horseshoe
LINK COVE
SCRUBBY CRAG
COL
HART CRAG
no defined path
DOVE CRAG
GREAT RIGG
Rydale
HIGH PIKE
One mile
HERON PIKE
Rydal Beck
Buckstones Jump waterfall
LOW PIKE
GRASMERE
NAB SCAR
A591
Mount
Hall
RYDAL
START
RYDAL WATER
River Rothay
A591
AMBLESIDE

AN EXCEPTION to the general rule that the passes offer simple walking is provided by the abrupt gap, formerly known as The Step, on the ridge linking Hart Crag and Fairfield. It is not the actual crossing of the gap that is arduous, but the approaches to it, especially on the Rydale side, and walkers who like to preserve a dignified bearing will not enjoy the steep and stony scramble to reach the crest. It is, however, the most direct way across the high range dividing the Rothay valley at Rydal from Deepdale and Patterdale; it is the shortest in distance but not in time. The route has other merits, too, being unfrequented, remote from traffic, and pleasantly approached from either side on easy paths, only the middle mile calling for strenuous effort.

Opposite *Fairfield*
Below *Head of Rydale*

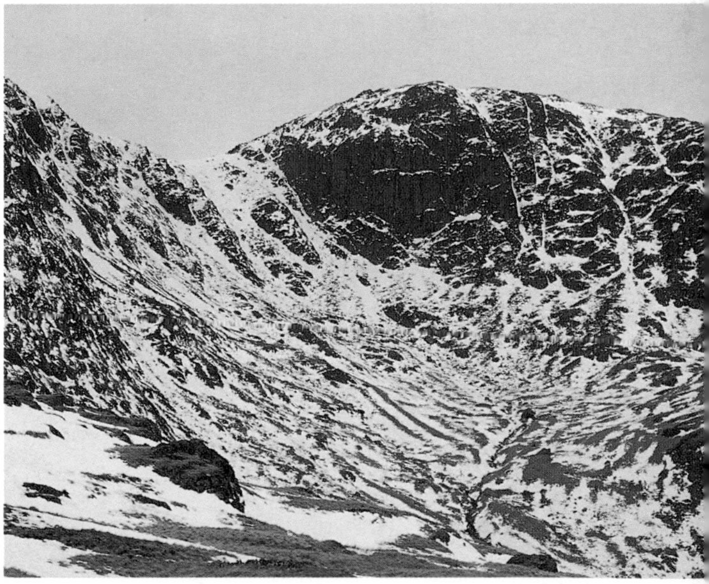

RYDAL IS LEFT by a side road from the A591, passing between the church and Rydal Mount on the left and Rydal Hall on the right, initially negotiable by cars. This soon degenerates into a rough lane and then a path; when clear of trees, there is a comprehensive view of the Fairfield Horseshoe ahead. The long valley opening in front is conveniently but unofficially known as Rydale. The surroundings are impressive and become more so as the walk proceeds up the valley alongside a wall, with Rydal Beck flowing nearby; there is a minor interruption at the small waterfall of Buckstones Jump. The dominant height in a lofty skyline is Great Rigg, falling in a rough declivity, and beyond this the valley is terminated by the high barrier of Fairfield and Hart Crag, the gap between them being the next objective. The hard work starts when the wall turns away and the path fades to nothing. The ground rises ahead and soon becomes unremittingly steep, upward progress not being helped by the absence of a path. The only guidance is given by the infant Rydal Beck which should be crossed and kept on the left during the final ascent. After a long and arduous struggle against gravity, the col is gained suddenly and with profound relief.

Rydale

Deepdale from the col

Although both sides of Hart Crag Col are virgin, untrodden and silent, the narrow crest has been blazed white by thousands of boots each year engaged on the very popular Fairfield Horseshoe walk, this spot being the only place where deviations are ruled out by the ruggedness of the terrain. It is also the most spectacular. The Rydal side has no terrors other than steepness and indeed has a tranquil view, but the Deepdale side has a fearsome aspect of wild country flanked by crags.

This is a true col, a narrow causeway poised above steep and inhospitable acclivities. The walk continues down a bouldery slope without the help of a foot-track, but the gradient eases as a way is made below the impending cliffs of Scrubby Crag. A stream joins the route of descent as it issues from the hanging valley of Link Cove, and takes over as guide on the next part of the walk.

Again the ground steepens as the stream plunges in cascades to the floor of the valley, passing below the tremendous buttress of Greenhow End in the shadow of Erne Nest Crag to join Deepdale Beck as it emerges from the wild recesses of Fairfield. This is a lonely place indeed: a silent sanctuary almost encircled by steep fellsides and dark crags with only the stream to point a way of escape. The vast sprawling slopes of St Sunday Crag fill the background as the waters of the beck are forded to gain the comfort of a path running above the far bank. Looking back from this point, the great tower of Greenhow End is seen as the impressive termination of the northern precipices of Fairfield.

Greenhow End

The rest is easy. The path curves around the base of St Sunday Crag and gradually the scene becomes less confined as trees, walls and cultivated fields mark the final stages of Deepdale. Across the beck flowing alongside rises the high but declining ridge of Hartsop above How, ending in woodlands above Brothers Water; on the left the steep and craggy slopes of St Sunday Crag and Birks rise to heaven. At the first farm of Wall End, the path merges into a lane with a few scattered houses, reaching the A592 near Deepdale Bridge. Patterdale village is a mile along the road to the left; a beautiful finish.

Above *View down Deepdale to Bridge End*   *Deepdale Bridge*

19 HAUSE GATE, 1150'
Newlands – Manesty

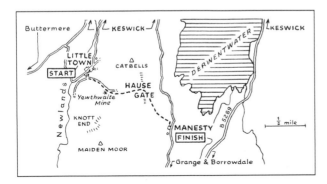

HAUSE GATE is a favourite objective although not well known by name. It is easily reached on a summer evening's stroll, rewarding the small effort with views of surpassing beauty. Everybody knows Catbells. The Hause (there is no gate, the word here meaning an open passage) is the grassy saddle on the ridge south of this popular summit, and is a place to halt awhile and try to memorise a scene to relive during moments of urban depression.

NEWLANDS IS LEFT at the hamlet of Little Town where an old mine road branches left and rises below the cliffs of Knott End to an area despoiled by the disused Yewthwaite Mine where there are still dangerous shafts and levels that call for caution if being explored, having already accounted for a fatal casualty. Beyond, the path rises in bracken to the top of the ridge at Hawes Gate, revealing a ravishing view of Derwentwater and its environs: a picture to bring tears of joy. A delectable grass path descends the fellside, every step a pleasure to tread, but there is such an eye-catching view ahead that it is advisable to halt on the uneven path when surveying the glorious scene.

At Manesty, the west Derwentwater road is joined and can be followed on to Grange in Borrowdale and its bus service.

Opposite *Derwentwater from Hause Gate*   Below *Borrowdale from Hause Gate*

20 HIGH TOVE, 1665'
Thirlmere – Borrowdale

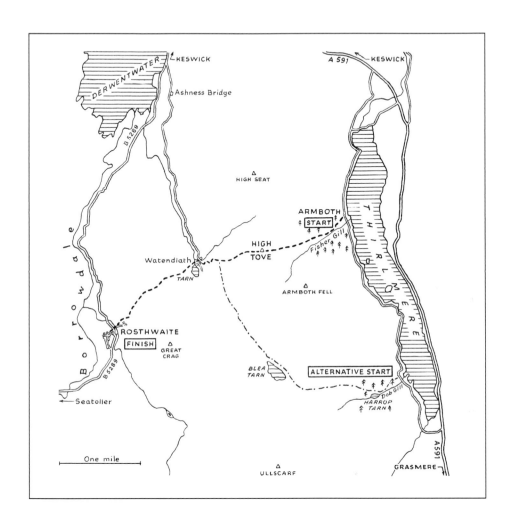

THERE ARE TWO paths along which walkers may cross the long central ridge that divides the Thirlmere valley and Borrowdale. One, giving a fine walk, leaves the west side of Thirlmere at Dob Gill near the south end of the reservoir, passes through the plantations around Harrop Tarn and crosses the indefinite ridge to descend to Watendlath by way of Blea Tarn. But this route is more in the nature of a cross-country walk than a pass.

The other path leaves the west side of Thirlmere near the north end of the reservoir and makes a beeline across the moorland of High Tove, actually visiting the summit, before descending to Watendlath. This route also hardly qualifies as a pass, traversing a low summit and not a depression, but passes over a watershed, being the most direct way, and has long been in use.

Opposite *Watendlath*

BEFORE MANCHESTER CORPORATION acquired rights to convert the natural lake of Thirlmere into a reservoir, Armboth House was the principal residence on the west shore, the centre of a small community connected to the east side by a picturesque wooden footbridge across the narrowest part of the lake. The house, other buildings and footbridge were all casualties of the reservoir and nothing was left of Armboth except its name, which curiously has survived on signposts. The slopes falling from the ridge have since been tightly afforested but directly above the site at Armboth a wide breach in the trees has been left unplanted to accommodate the old path over to Borrowdale. This climbs a bouldery slope alongside the plantation with outcropping rocks nearby and Fisher Gill in close attendance, and reaches a wall marking the upper limit of the plantations. The path passes through a gate and emerges on a wide moorland of heather and marsh, where it ascends more gradually to the cairned summit of High Tove, a place with no pretensions to interest or beauty, its one redeeming feature being as a viewpoint.

High Tove is a minor undulation on the long ridge forming the spine of central Lakeland. To the north, after a slight descent, the ground rises to High Seat; southwards, the nearest neighbour of note is Ullscarf, seen in the distance over the soggy morass of Armboth Fell. Over the watershed, the path descends gradually at first, and then, when Watendlath comes into sight ahead, much more steeply between two ravines, the gradient being eased by zigzags.

Watendlath is delightful and its qualities unique. There is no other place like it. A tiny cluster of white cottages and stone barns set at odd angles without pattern, a tarn, a stream and a bridge, all deeply inurned amongst surrounding fells and hidden from outside gaze: here are all the attributes of a perfect picture, a scene to enrapture artists and photographers. Apart from the intrinsic joys of this little hamlet in a fold of the hills, there are literary associations to attract visitors since this was the home of Judith Paris in the Herries novels by Hugh Walpole. Watendlath's link with the world outside is a narrow ribbon of tarmac branching from the Borrowdale road above Ashness Bridge, a three-mile journey of enchantment which, unfortunately, has been discovered by the touring motorist who often causes severe congestion. Watendlath should always be approached on foot; noise is sacrilege here. This is hallowed ground.

Watendlath Bridge

Watendlath is always left with regret and many a lingering look back. Sparing a crumb for the ducks, the walk is continued on a path that gets no rest from boots, and steadily climbs to the ridge that still hides Borrowdale; there are superb retrospective views of the hamlet and tarn on the way. This, if a census were taken, would be proved to be one of the most populated footpaths in Lakeland and, after topping the low ridge and starting the descent into Borrowdale, the reason for its popularity is clear. The upper reaches of this most beautiful of valleys unfold in a lovely pageant of colour and charm, the green strath and shaggy fells making a perfect canvas. With dragging steps, Rosthwaite is entered and the magic dispelled by tourist traffic.

Borrowdale

Below View towards Grisedale Pike from High Tove

21 HONISTER PASS, 1190'
Borrowdale – Buttermere

UNTIL THE MID-NINETEENTH century, when the turnpikes were improved for stagecoach traffic, and the railways came to Windermere and Keswick, the Lake District was a world apart, rarely visited by people from outside the area but, as early adventurers and the Lake Poets extolled its unique beauties, more were attracted to see for themselves. These were mainly professional gentlemen and their ladies.

In Victorian times, these visitors were conveyed in horse-drawn wagonettes on sightseeing tours along the few dusty and roughly metalled roads negotiable by wheeled vehicles, a romantic form of travel that vanished with the coming of tarmacadam and motor cars and omnibuses. Of these early tours, the great adventure, enjoyed on payment of a toll, was provided by the crossing of Honister Pass, a fearsome and exciting journey. Today the romance has been savaged out of existence by the procession of cars using this popular route linking Borrowdale and Buttermere, but the scenic grandeur of the past remains.

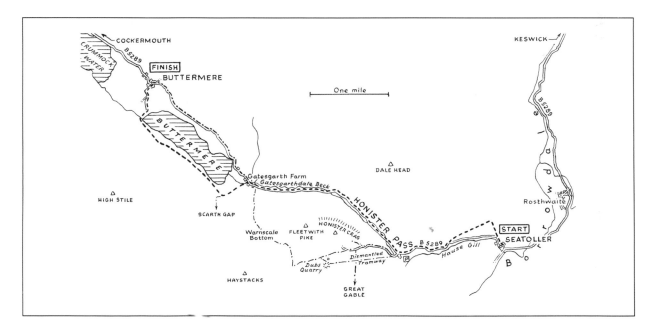

SEATOLLER IS THE bus terminus at the head of Borrowdale and from this attractive group of buildings the ascent to the pass starts at once and in earnest, the initial steepness being relieved by the sparkling cascades of Hause Gill alongside in a bower of trees, after which a bare landscape is entered as the unenclosed road rises more gently to the summit. Walkers can avoid most of the hard road to the top and the hazard of speeding cars by preferring the old toll road which is grassy, abandoned and much kinder to the feet: this branches off the road on the right after leaving Seatoller, and after a sharp turn heads directly for the pass at a higher level, joining the motor road below the top.

Opposite *Honister Pass*

Seatoller

Below *The cutting sheds, Honister Quarry*

Honister Pass is extremely impressive. The great feature is Honister Crag, a towering cliff honeycombed with quarries and a network of steep tracks used for bringing down the handsome slate that for colour, texture and durability has earned international renown. In the formative years of the industry, horse-drawn sleds were used to convey the blocks of slate to the cutting sheds; later a tramway served this purpose; this in turn was superseded by lorries making the perilous descent. Now all is silent: the centuries-old workings were closed recently and activity has come to an end. Honister Crag has had the heart torn out of it but has not been tamed.

There is a Youth Hostel on the top of the pass in addition to the quarry buildings, and limited space for the parking of cars; there is always activity here. It is a starting point for the ascent of Great Gable, using the old tramway, and on the north side an easy ridge can be climbed to the summit of Dale Head, where there is a classic view of Newlands and the Vale of Keswick backed by Skiddaw.

The High Stile range from Gatesgarth

Over the pass, the road descends steeply under a bridge built to carry a private cart-track from quarries on the side of Dale Head, and then winds down into a boulder-strewn defile. The gradient eases as Gatesgarthdale Beck comes alongside and a splendid view of the High Stile range unfolds ahead. The soaring slopes on the left gradually decline to valley level; a white cross on the lower rocks is a memorial to a girl accidentally killed here in 1887. The rugged crest of Haystacks appears in a wider landscape, and trees, welcome after the sterile crossing, enhance the majestic scene as the first habitation of Gatesgarth Farm is reached.

From Gatesgarth, the road continues for two lovely miles to Buttermere village with glimpses of the lake seen below. Walkers have a charming alternative on this final stage by following a lakeside path on the north-east side.

Fellwalkers who have a rooted objection to travelling along hard roads may follow a parallel course from the top of the pass by climbing up the old tramway on the left side and continuing on a good path skirting Dubs Quarry and descending to Gatesgarth along an old quarry road through Warnscale Bottom. This route is more arduous but in the matter of views better by far.

Kirkstone Pass looking north and (below) *south*

22 KIRKSTONE PASS, 1489′
Ambleside – Patterdale

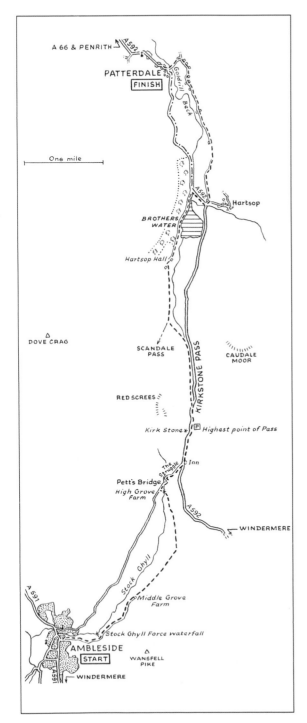

KIRKSTONE PASS is the high crossing that most excites the tourists who inspect the Lake District from the comfort of a car or coach. The environs of the pass are spectacular, a narrow road winding through a gap between the rugged downfall of Red Screes and the scree slopes of Caudale Moor. It is a wild defile of tumbled rocks and mountain debris, but the loneliness that characterised it a century ago, when horse-drawn carriages braved the rigours of the journey carrying parties of awestruck Victorians, has been dispelled by the procession of motorists who today throng the limited confines of the road. The atmosphere of frightening solitude has been lost and is fleetingly regained only when winter snowfalls block the pass.

A road climbs steeply to the summit from Ambleside, there joining the busy A592 from Windermere for the long descent to the Patterdale Valley. The weight of traffic on most days of the year makes this a route to be avoided by travellers on foot who would do well to favour instead the quiet and unfrequented track over Scandale Pass although this alternative bypasses Kirkstone's exciting scenery. However, the route described in this chapter enables walkers to make acquaintance with the pass on footpaths that avoid the motor road except for a long mile across the highest part. Even so, Kirkstone Pass is best appreciated when the summer visitors have departed.

LEAVE AMBLESIDE along the signposted road to Stock Ghyll Force, this delightful waterfall being seen by a walk through the woods alongside Stock Ghyll. In former days, an admission charge was made for the privilege of entry, but today access is free and a well-worn path leads up to the impressive plunge of the stream in a bower of foliage. It is a charming scene for Stock Ghyll Force is the most beautiful waterfall in the Lake District.

Near Middle Grove

The ruins near High Grove
Right *Red Screes*

A path above the fall leads back to the road which continues upstream to Middle Grove Farm along the lower flanks of Wansfell with Kirkstone Pass in sight ahead. Beyond the farm, a cart-track goes on to the ruins of High Grove Farm, from which a path crosses to join the motor road from Ambleside at Pett's Bridge. Originally the track went directly forward, climbing to join the A592. It is likely that this route by the Grove farms was the usual way to Kirkstone Pass before the road from Ambleside was constructed.

From Pett's Bridge, the motor road rises very steeply to the summit of the pass, this section being known as The Struggle for reasons that must have been very obvious when wheeled traffic was horse-drawn. At the top of this incline, the road meets the A592 at the Kirkstone Pass Inn, once known as the Travellers' Rest where there is an ample and well-patronised car park. This is a popular halt for refreshment or for gazing up at the formidable ramparts of Red Screes, up which there is a steep and arduous track from this point. The gentle slopes behind the inn provide simple ski runs when snow has been cleared from the road and cars can reach the inn. On a high shoulder of Caudale Moor overlooking the pass is a memorial cairn to Mark Atkinson, mine host at the inn for many years until his death in 1930.

The highest point of the pass is a short distance beyond the inn, and here a dramatic view forward is revealed, the long descent into Patterdale commences, the road being tightly enclosed between stone walls. A car park has been provided to discourage motorists from stopping on the edge of the road to admire the scene. Nearby is a massive fallen boulder, the Kirk Stone, from which the pass was named; its appearance on the skyline when approaching from the north resembles the steeple of a church tower. All around is chaotic convulsion of nature, a primeval desolation.

Opposite *The north side of Kirkstone Pass*   Above *Patterdale*

A signpost on the roadside lower down indicates a footpath along which pedestrians can escape from the hazards of speeding cars, this leading pleasantly down to valley level; there the path from Scandale Pass joins in. The walk proceeds, with views of Dove Crag, to Hartsop Hall, a farmhouse unusually distinguished by having a public right of way through the building as a result of the erection of an extension over a bridleway that formerly passed alongside.

A wooded lane continues the walk along the shore of Brothers Water, which was named Broad Water until two brothers lost their lives here by drowning on separate occasions early in the nineteenth century. The A592 is rejoined at the end of the lane and may be followed for two lovely miles to Patterdale village, but if traffic is heavy it is advisable to go back about 200 yards to the Hartsop junction, there taking a parallel and pleasant by-road where there is less danger of being annihilated by a car.

Thus ends an enjoyable ten-mile walk in contrasting surroundings, nature being displayed both in the raw and at its supreme best. For walkers already familiar with Kirkstone Pass, however, it is preferable to make the journey by way of Scandale Pass, which is innocent of wheels, rather shorter in distance, requires little more effort and is blessed with a profound solitude: *see* page 161.

23 THE LOFT BECK CROSSING, 1900'
Ennerdale – Borrowdale

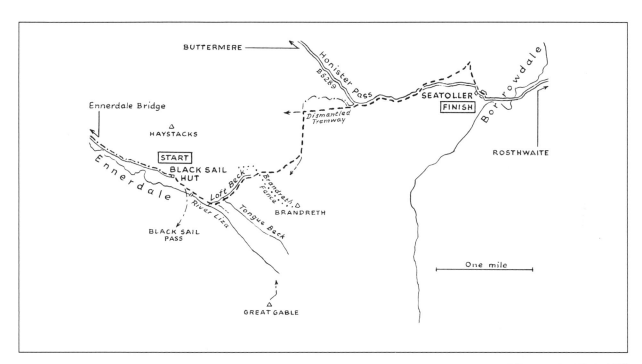

A USEFUL TIME-SAVING route between the Black Sail Hut in Ennerdale and Honister Pass is available by climbing up to the grassy plateau crossed by the Brandreth fence: this is a route not generally recognised as a pass but has the attributes if not the appearance of one. There is now a distinct track and this should be kept strictly underfoot in misty conditions, the highest part of the crossing being without landmarks. The track joins the broad path coming down from Great Gable for the descent to Honister Pass, from which the well-known delights of Borrowdale can be reached by an easy hour's march.

Left *Loft Beck*
Opposite *Great Gable from the River Liza*

A PATH FROM the Black Sail Hut goes up the valley of the River Liza towards Great Gable, ignoring the footbridge, to the point where the tributary of Loft Beck comes down steeply on the left. Loft Beck is the key to the route: it is followed up closely on a steep and rough track, passing a confluence of waters where Tongue Beck joins in, until the climbing ends on an extensive upland prairie. With Ennerdale now lost to sight behind, the path trends to the right across a grassy expanse with no distinctive features other than the old Brandreth fence, which is crossed to join the Great Gable path at a large cairn. Although the immediate environs are dreary and without interest, the views of the Buttermere fells and valley are of classical beauty.

Left *The Brandreth fence*
Below *The Buttermere fells*

Honister Pass

There are no problems of route finding when the Great Gable path is reached, this having been worn to the dimensions of a road, albeit a rough one, as the result of daily flagellation by countless boots. It goes easily down to the top of the old quarry tramway above Honister Pass and this is descended to the motor road on the summit of the pass.

Here, if continuing to Borrowdale, the road to the right leads down to Seatoller, and the bus terminus, but travellers on foot should, for the comfort of their feet, branch left along the old toll road, now no more than a grass cart-track, which reaches Seatoller much more pleasantly.

24 THE MARDALE CORPSE ROAD, 1670'
Mardale Head – Swindale

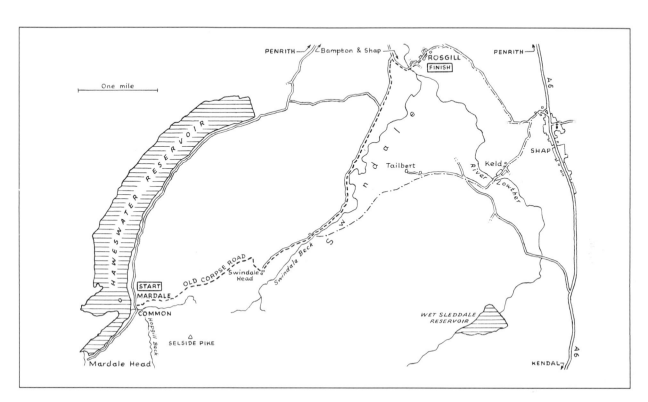

THE EARLY SETTLERS in the Lake District, living in isolated communities amongst the fells, faced many problems, one of them being the disposal of their dead. Some had a church with burial rights nearby, but others had to devise routes across high country to the nearest consecrated ground. Such a community lived at Mardale Green, a lonely hamlet later to be drowned beneath Haweswater Reservoir in 1937. Before a church was built here in the seventeenth century, bodies were conveyed to Shap, eight miles distant, the coffins strapped to the backs of horses. The shortest way was due east, over Mardale Common, and is still known today as the Old Corpse Road.

Opposite *Mardale Head from the Old Corpse Road*
Right *The road around Haweswater Reservoir*

A STEEP PATH, rising in zigzags to ease the gradient, climbed directly from the little group of buildings at Mardale Green. It is probable that this path was engineered primarily as a sledgate for bringing peat down from Mardale Common, peat then being the main source of fuel, but it served the funeral corteges also and is best remembered for this purpose. The lower section of this path was engulfed and submerged by the reservoir, and a little higher is interrupted by the new road to Mardale Head which cuts across it, a signpost indicating the path's continuation up the fellside; this is the point at which modern walkers start the crossing to Swindale.

For several hundred feet the ascent is unremittingly steep, a series of delightful turns and twists, on a distinct path. Hopgill Beck nearby displays a long white ribbon of cascading waters: a pretty sight. Two roofless stone huts, built for the drying and storing of peat, are reached and then another.

The retrospective view of Mardale Head is superb, the encircling mountains appearing in fine array around the deep valley and presenting a scene that, in my opinion, is unrivalled in Lakeland. Above the huts, the steepness abates and the path continues as a narrow track across a wide grassy upland, reaching its highest point amidst undulating moors overtopped by Selside Pike. Then the path trends easily downhill into Swindale, reaching a road terminus at the farm buildings of Swindale Head.

Opposite *Swindale*
Below *Hopgill Beck*

This road goes down the valley, breasts a small hill where it is crossed by the Haweswater access road and descends to Rosgill, between Bampton and Shap. This is the end of the Mardale Head-Swindale pass but for the early mourners was only the first stage of their sad journey, Shap being still six miles distant, their route crossing Swindale and contouring around the facing fells to the last resting place at Shap.

It is interesting to note that when the church at Mardale Green was dismantled and demolished in 1936 as a casualty of the reservoir, the graves in the churchyard were exhumed and the coffins taken by an easier mode of transport to Shap for re-interment, thus reuniting the remains of the more recent dead with those of their ancestors who came the hard way along the Old Corpse Road.

This walk serves also as an introduction to Swindale, a quiet and lovely valley rarely visited by tourists and quite unspoilt. Swindale Beck did not escape the eyes of Manchester Corporation and its waters have been plundered, but thankfully unobtrusively and with little disturbance to the environment, being taken through a tunnel to augment Haweswater Reservoir.

25 MICKLEDORE, 2650'
Eskdale – Wasdale

MICKLEDORE IS the well-defined gap between Scafell and Scafell Pike crossed by a narrow ridge linking the two in a situation of awesome grandeur and amidst highly exciting rock scenery. I consider Mickledore to be the most impressive place in Lakeland: it compels attention to the exclusion of all else. Here is nature in the raw – savage, primeval, immense. In such surroundings man is a speck, insignificant and unimportant.

The ridge across the gap is short, the crest is narrow and the sides steep, and no deviations are possible from the blazed path along it. With towering crags at both ends, the gap is a natural pass yet the ridge is rarely used as such. The crossing from Eskdale to Wasdale Head is arduous. Why suffer all this effort when a simple walk by Burnmoor Tarn connects the two valleys? Almost invariably the Mickledore ridge is traversed by walkers passing between Scafell and Scafell Pike, this being the only feasible way from one to the other, and not as a pass between valleys, although in appearance it is the grandest pass of all.

Mickledore is high drama.

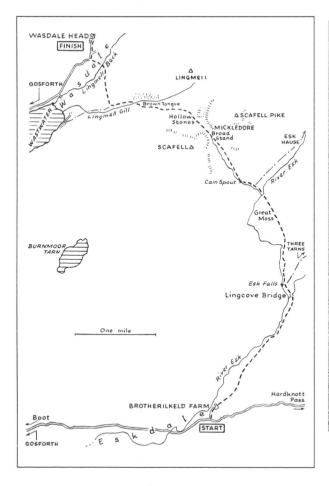

Cam Spout
Opposite *Mickledore*

WITH A FULL DAY ahead and emergency rations in the rucksack, the road along Eskdale is left near the foot of Hardknott Pass and the Esk followed upriver from Brotherilkeld Farm for two miles to Lingcove Bridge, spanning a tributary just above the confluence of waters. The main river here comes round a bend on the left, emerging from a deep gorge in which are the Esk Falls, a series of spectacular waterfalls and cataracts defying close access. The bridge is crossed to a path rising at a higher level in the same direction. The Scafells soon appear ahead, with Mickledore seen as a high gap on the skyline between the two giants in the range. The path continues easily to the foot of the tremendous mountain wall, crossing the flat and marshy expanse of Great Moss. The next objective is the slender waterfall of Cam Spout, this being reached after fording the Esk which is seen winding down from its headwaters below Esk Hause but is left behind at this point.

The ascent now starts in earnest up a steep path alongside Cam Spout. The stream pouring over the lip of the waterfall comes down from Mickledore and, ignoring tributaries joining from the left, gives direction to the remainder of the climb. Easier ground is reached above the waterfall, but the uphill trudge is relentless, flanked by the lower crags of Scafell and the stony slopes of Scafell Pike and in surroundings of extreme wildness and desolation. Timid pedestrians may well suffer apprehension as the track mounts higher towards even grimmer fastnesses ahead. An obvious gully opening on the left offers a scrambling route to the summit of Scafell by way of Foxes Tarn, but for Mickledore the route is directly ahead. It passes into the shadow of the vertical cliffs of Scafell's East Buttress and, beyond, the gaping mouth of Mickledore Chimney which, mercifully, does not have to be entered. Now on a treadmill of scree, with the gap of Mickledore close ahead, the final scramble is alongside a wall of crags split by two vertical cracks; the second, Fat Man's Agony, gives access to the notorious Broad Stand, a rockclimbers' short cut to Scafell but definitely not for lesser fry. After a few more slithering steps, the ridge is reached for a deserved halt.

I always find it difficult to tear myself away from Mickledore, always feel it a great privilege to be allowed admittance to such a wonderful place. Not because there is beauty here. The scene is brutal, uncompromising, yet fascinating and a little frightening. Massive towers of naked rock soar majestically into the sky on all sides. Here is nature's architecture, and it is overwhelming, reducing man to insignificance and a reverent humility. These vertical precipices are repelling: surely they could never be scaled? 'Nobbut a fleeing thing could get up theer,' said old Will Ritson a hundred years ago, yet since that time a network of climbing routes has been forged by expert pioneers on Scafell Crag and the neighbouring cliffs. Legs turn to jelly at the merest thought. Brave men, these, and I am not amongst them.

The Mickledore ridge is not razor-sharp nor a tightrope but is extremely narrow. Within two paces of reaching the crest, steps are immediately downhill on a funnel of scree, descending into a wild hollow below Scafell Crag, the most magnificent of Lakeland's cliffs, rising vertically on the left and far above. On the right, Pulpit Rock and Pikes Crag, outliers of Scafell Pike, enclose the amphitheatre effectively. There is grass here and many huge boulders, some of which offer crude shelter. This sanctuary is known as Hollow Stones.

Opposite *Scafell East Buttress from Mickledore*

Above *Hollow Stones*   *Lingmell Beck and Wastwater*

Wastwater

A night's bivouac in Hollow Stones is an experience long remembered. The hours of darkness are distinctly eerie, the impending crags around appearing as black silhouettes and the silence being that of the grave. Dawn brings a rich reward, the gloom gradually being dispelld as the first rays of the sun touch the uppermost tips of Scafell Crag and then very slowly diffuse the whole rock face in a rosy pink glow.

But those who prefer a comfortable bed will continue easily down towards Wasdale, now in sight, passing the long fans of scree brought down from Scafell Pinnacle during a tremendous electric storm in 1958, overlaying earlier stonefalls. A path forms at the top of a long descending spur, Brown Tongue, this emerging from the claustrophobia of the crags and enjoying the wider landscape ahead.

At the foot of Brown Tongue, Lingmell Gill is forded, this also carrying the debris of a violent cloudburst, and the path rounds a corner to reveal splendid views of Wastwater and the patchwork fields of Wasdale Head backed by the Pillar range. With the latter prospect in view, the path descends to the valley, slanting down the breast of Lingmell End, a delightful finish to the day. Those who use Mickledore as a pass will never regret their choice over the soft option of Burnmoor. This has been a walk to remember and its memories will be evergreen.

26 MOOR DIVOCK, 1000′
Pooley Bridge – Helton

THE EASY CROSSING of Moor Divock would appeal not only to sedate walkers but also to those with archaeological and geological interests. The Moor is a wide grassy upland forming a broad saddle between Heughscar Hill where limestone is much in evidence, and the greater bulk of Loadpot Hill at the north end of the High Street range. At first sight, the moor seems to be a featureless expanse without

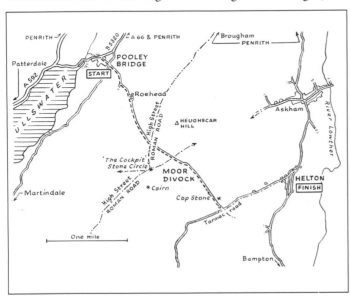

landmarks, but appearances deceive. The bland surface of the ground abounds in surprises, but they are not obvious and need searching out. Moor Divock is in fact a rich field of exploration and discovery, a graveyard of relics of prehistoric occupation: stone circles, ancient cairns, burial mounds, settlements, standing stones and avenues. Here too is the famous Roman road, High Street, and even earlier than this is the wide path across the moor that probably originated in neolithic times. For the geologist, there are shakeholes and sinkholes galore, indicating a limestone bedrock, and for the simple walker a pleasant stroll amongst ghosts of the past. Moor Divock is history.

Opposite *Moor Divock*   *The Roman Road*

The stone circle

A LANE RISES south-east from Pooley Bridge, passing Roehead and reaching open country beyond, its continuation being a wide track, with branches to the left used by pony trekkers. The track ascends gently to a large cairn where it is crossed by the Roman road coming down from High Street on its way to Brougham. At this point, a recommended diversion follows the Roman road to the right, reaching a large stone circle alongside; about thirty yards in diameter and named on Ordnance maps as The Cockpit, it is worthy of leisurely inspection.

Returning to the main path, preferably by retracing steps to avoid the bogs met on short cuts, the walk is resumed, still ascending slightly and passing a line of shakeholes on the right. Near an old boundary stone, a path branches left for Askham. Ignoring this, the path goes on, in places as wide as a motor road. Across the moor on the right are the Pulpit Holes, a group of shakeholes which, on my first and only visit, were depositories for the carcasses and skeletons of sheep: this is not a diversion to be recommended! On the left side of the path reached by short detours is a series of small circles, cairns and burial mounds some of which have obviously been excavated or disturbed. These remains are not as complete as reported by nineteenth-century investigators, and it seems likely that some of the stones have been removed for use in the construction of shooting butts nearby: a double sacrilege.

Ahead on the skyline is a prominent upright boulder, the Cap Stone, thought to be a survivor of a former avenue of stones akin to the one at Shap and possibly a continuation of it. Just beyond, the path debouches on an unenclosed tarmac road, with wide verges often occupied by parked cars and this, followed to the left, leads down to the village of Helton, in the valley of the River Lowther.

This walk across Moor Divock, however, is so effortless and the path so pleasant that, on arrival at the tarmac, most walkers will simply turn round and return to Pooley Bridge the same way with the extra bonus of lovely views of Ullswater on the descent.

Above *A burial mound*

Above right *The Cap Stone* and below *Ullswater*

27 THE MOSEDALE WATERSHED, 1600'
Longsleddale – Swindale or Wet Sleddale

THERE ARE FIVE Mosedales in the Lake District, all of them justifying the interpretation of the name as 'Dreary Valley', and this one, the highest of them, is not merely dreary, but wild and lonely. It provides a crossing out of Longsleddale to Swindale or Wet Sleddale, passing between the high fells of Tarn Crag and Branstree, and was once in regular use but today is unfrequented and the path in parts has gone to seed.

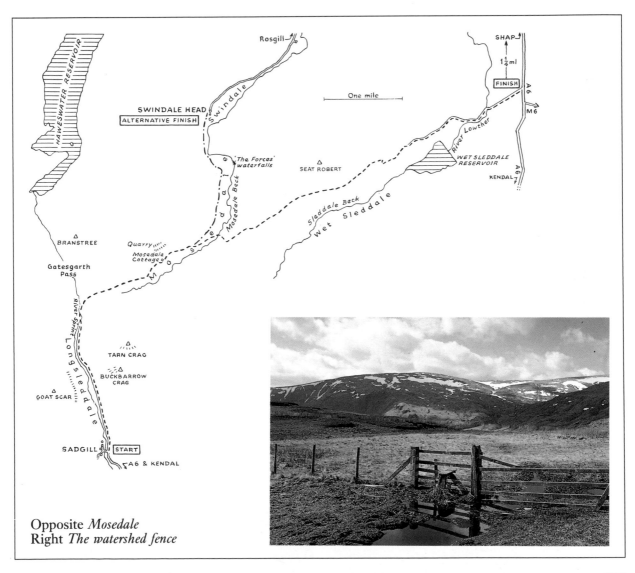

Opposite *Mosedale*
Right *The watershed fence*

FROM SADGILL BRIDGE in Longsleddale, where the motor road ends, a continuing cart-track goes forward into the head of the valley through a rocky portal formed by the cliffs of Goat Scar and Buckbarrow Crag. This section has many features of interest (described in the chapter on Gatescarth Pass, page 61). When the track escapes from its confining walls at a gate at the top of a steep rise, a path soon branches to the right from the Gatescarth route and aims for a wide depression in the skyline between the declining slopes of Tarn Crag and Branstree. The ascent to it is gentle; however, the original path, once of commercial use but now abandoned and taken over by nature, is obscure and interrupted by marshes as it rises to a gate in a wire fence crossing the depression. This is now seen to be a watershed as the ground beyond slowly declines and a new landscape appears ahead. The path goes on, indistinctly, across a vast grassy prairie for a further mile, maintaining a level contour. Mosedale Beck forms nearby, sluggishly confirming, against the visual evidence, that the watershed has indeed been crossed and the ground trending down. The path becomes clearer when a solitary building comes in sight: this is Mosedale Cottage, an overnight refuge for shepherds. On the fellside behind is the large disused Mosedale Quarry. These names confirm that we are now in Mosedale, although the bare and featureless terrain at such a high altitude bears little resemblance to a dale.

Mosedale Cottage and Quarry   *The Forces*

Wet Sleddale

Beyond the cottage, which is surely the loneliest in Lakeland, the path divides, the left branch contouring the slope and turning north with Mosedale Beck into Swindale. In the later stages of the descent, the beck provides a display of waterfalls known as The Forces before the road terminus is reached at the farm buildings of Swindale Head.

The main branch goes ahead to cross Mosedale Beck at a primitive bridge as its waters drain north into Swindale. The facing slope is rounded and then follows a long and gradual descent into Wet Sleddale on a distinct track, once a cart road but later reduced to the status of a bridleway. Wet Sleddale is a long deep valley flanked by lesser fells and its details are well seen from the track which maintains a high level above it. Down in the bottom of the valley may be discerned the stone walls, 12 feet high, of a medieval deer trap, unique in the district. Further on is the new Wet Sleddale Reservoir, Manchester's latest and hopefully last, with its attendant casualties of ruined buildings and broken walls.

The track slants down to valley level, becoming tarred to serve the remaining active farms; it passes a Victorian postbox set in a wall before crossing the River Lowther to join the A6 a mile south of Shap.

Nobody will rank the crossing of this Mosedale amongst the best of Lakeland passes, much of it being dull and unexciting, and Wet Sleddale has an atmosphere of forlorn sadness, but on a day of fine weather it provides a satisfactory nine-mile walk.

28 MOUSTHWAITE COMB, 1350'
Scales – Mungrisdale

A SHORT AND simple pass walk is available on the eastern fringe of the Northern Fells, crossing a low col to enter the little-known valley of the River Glenderamackin and passing below the long escarpment of Bannerdale Crags before reaching the village of Mungrisdale. It is a pleasant expedition in unfrequented terrain, requiring little effort and suitable for a short half-day after a morning's rain.

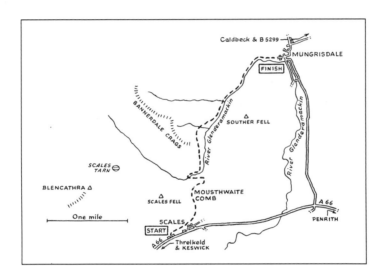

FROM THE HAMLET of Scales on the A66 east of Threlkeld starts a popular path over Scales Fell to Blencathra, skirting a hollow in the fells known as Mousthwaite Comb.

Crossing this hollow and ignoring the well-trodden path up Scales Fell and another branching left to Scales Tarn, the head of the hollow is reached at a col on the east side, whence a descending path slants down to a bridge over the River Glenderamackin and joins another path on the far bank.

The course of the Glenderamackin is interesting, suggesting an early problem in deciding the direction of flow. From its source, it heads south-east, turns east on finding its way barred by Mousthwaite Comb, is then turned north by Souther Fell and when the latter declines to valley level flows east through Mungrisdale and then due south and finally west to join the River Greta, almost completing a circuit of Souther Fell.

Across the river rises the long southern slope of Bannerdale Crags, and the path on the far bank contours round its base, following the river as it turns north and soon bringing into view the mile-long escarpment of Bannerdale Crags. These are palpably inaccessible except at one point where a steep ridge comes down to the valley, yet has ruins of old mines high amongst the cliffs. When the river turns east, a tributary beck is forded and an improving path, becoming a lane, leads into the attractive small village of Mungrisdale, two miles by road from the A66 and its bus service.

Opposite *Blencathra from Mousthwaite Comb*

29 NAN BIELD, 2100'
Kentmere – Mardale

OF ALL THE Lakeland passes, I rank Nan Bield amongst the finest. It conforms most to my concept of a true mountain pass or col, being delicately sculptured, narrow at its crest and steeply descending on both sides. It is poised high, a lonely gap between lofty fells, and retains features from long ago when it served as a trade route for packhorses. Unmarred by wheeled traffic, this is a way only for travellers on foot and wearing stout boots.

Nan Bield provides a direct link between the Kentmere valley and Mardale, and six miles of rough and in places steep ground separate their road termini. The road to Kentmere leaves the A591 at Staveley, midway between Kendal and Windermere: the A591 is the usual approach to the Lake District from the south and the turn to Kentmere is often overlooked or, being a dead end, ignored by motorists hurrying to reach Windermere which, for many of them, marks the start of Lakeland. The four miles to the little community of Kentmere are consequently relatively quiet and mainly used by local traffic and the discerning few who disagree that Lakeland starts at Windermere. These four miles along a winding valley are lovely, the River Kent pursuing a rapid course through pleasant pastures and woodlands where daffodils and bluebells are a springtime delight. Of course Lakeland doesn't start at Windermere; here in the Kentmere valley, natural charm typical of the district is all around and no less enchanting. Here romance is allied to beauty.

Opposite *Nan Bield*

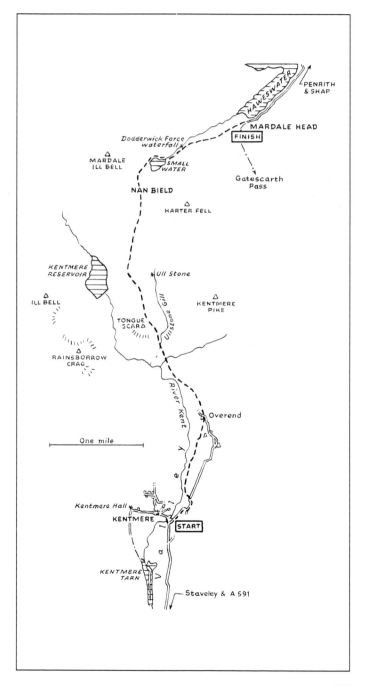

Unlike the neighbouring Longsleddale, the Kentmere valley curves, revealing a succession of fresh scenes and occasional sightings of the mountains ahead. After passing a former asbestos works, open ground is reached and there is a distant view of the church on a hill. Across fields is the new Kent Mere. On the flat strath south of the church was formerly a shallow lake, the Kent Mere that gave its name to the valley and village. This was drained in 1840 to provide more land for cultivation – a purpose not entirely achieved, much of the reclaimed ground remaining too marshy for the plough and for grazing. Analysis of the former bed of the lake in the present century disclosed the presence of rich deposits of diatomaceous earth which, when extracted and processed, proved a valuable insulation material and led to the establishment of a works on the site. During these operations, the remains of two primitive boats in the form of dugout canoes, believed to be of the Viking period, were discovered; the better of the two specimens is now at the National Maritime Museum. The draining of the lake in 1840 was probably a factor in the erratic flow of the river that led to the promotion of an Act of Parliament to create a reservoir in the upper reaches of the valley. Today, with supplies of diatomaceous earth exhausted and the industry closed, a new Kent Mere has come into being on the same site: a narrow sheet of water half a mile in length.

Nearby is the site of an ancient British village settlement and the valley has other evidences of prehistoric occupation. Not far from the church is Kentmere Hall, with a ruined fourteenth-century pele tower: this was the birthplace in 1517 of Bernard Gilpin, who had a distinguished career in the Church and became known as 'The Apostle of the North'.

Rainsborrow Crag

Ill Bell and Kentmere Reservoir

Southern approach to Nan Bield

THE ROADS in the village are narrow and unsuitable for the parking of cars: it is usual to take advantage of an open space alongside the church. The way to Nan Bield, now on foot, starts from the bridge where the Low Bridge Inn was formerly. Here turn up a side road heading north until a signpost (to Mardale) indicates a path with the River Kent nearby rushing through a tree-lined gorge in a series of cataracts and waterfalls. The footpath leads to the farm buildings of Overend, the last outpost of civilisation, and continues beyond, passing a quaint bridge used for access to fields across the river. The scenery now is very impressive, the dominant feature being Rainsborrow Crag on the other side of the valley, backed by Ill Bell and its satellites. On the right, colourful slopes rise to Kentmere Pike, 1600 feet above. Ahead, blocking the valley, is Tongue Scar, a craggy upthrust at the foot of which are long-established badger setts. The river curves to the left amongst many disused quarries to the outflow from Kentmere Reservoir, but the path to Nan Bield goes ahead.

A tributary beck is crossed in a pretty dell, and the path then climbs the east slope of the Tongue, the route being indicated by a line of cairns erected by Kendal schoolboys. At one point, where a quarry road branches to the right, is an upright stone slab bearing the inscription 'To Mardale': a relic of packhorse days. On the fellside to the right, across Ullstone Gill, is a disused quarry and below it a huge boulder, the Ull Stone, provides shelter for sheep.

When abreast of the top of the Tongue, the gradient eases and a splendid view unfolds of the mountains around the head of the valley, and Kentmere Reservoir comes into sight down below on the left. Nan Bield is seen a mile ahead as a lofty gap between Mardale Ill Bell, left, and Harter Fell, right; the path aims directly towards it and becomes a narrow track over open grassland. The ground steepens on the final rise to the pass, upward progress being helped by a series of zigzags, skilfully engineered not for the benefit of pedestrians but for the comfort of laden packhorses. At the top of the slope, the crest of Nan Bield is reached, adorned with a large wind shelter of stones, its back to the prevailing wind. A crude shelter that many a stormbound traveller has been glad to enter.

On a day of clear visibility the view northwards from Nan Bield is excellent. Mardale is seen ahead and below, and the long line of the Pennines closes the distant horizon. Retrospectively, the Kentmere valley is well displayed, the Tongue dwarfed to insignificance by the enclosing mountains.

The descent into Mardale commences at once, and after only a few paces Small Water and Haweswater come into sight far below: an arresting picture for the camera.

The path on the Mardale side of the pass, originally in the form of well-graded bends and twists to ease the descent, has unfortunately been cut to ribbons by the tread of impatient boots, the way down being a river of sliding stones where there is a need to walk circumspectly with regard to the placing of every step as the eye searches for firm footing; this is a bad case of erosion by careless walkers. The fine view ahead demands attention but should be observed only by halting; here the scenery should not be viewed while in motion or mishaps will occur.

At the foot of this unpleasant descent, the shores of Small Water are reached. This is one of the finest mountain tarns, deep-set in a wild surround of craggy heights, a gem of its kind, best appreciated when you are not in the company of others.

Small Water and Haweswater

Small Water   Below *Shelters by Small Water*

The path skirts the edge of the tarn, passing three stone shelters, these presumably being constructed long ago for the benefit of travellers overtaken by storm or darkness; they are still serviceable and can be entered by crawling, to the consternation of the resident spiders.

The path fords the outlet of the tarn and descends along a pony route by which early visitors were taken to Small Water. The issuing stream leaps alongside and, lower down in a hidden gorge, makes a final plunge at Dodderwick Force before proceeding quietly to enter Haweswater. The path crosses a declining moorland below the crags of Harter Fell and joins a track coming down from Gatescarth Pass for the last 100 yards to the road terminus and car park at Mardale Head.

A strong walker may return to Kentmere by way of Gatescarth Pass and Sadgill in Longsleddale. But not many will. For the weary, the temptation of a soft seat in a car and an effortless drive alongside Haweswater will be too great to resist. Nan Bield is enough for one day.

30 NEWLANDS HAUSE, 1096'
Newlands – Buttermere

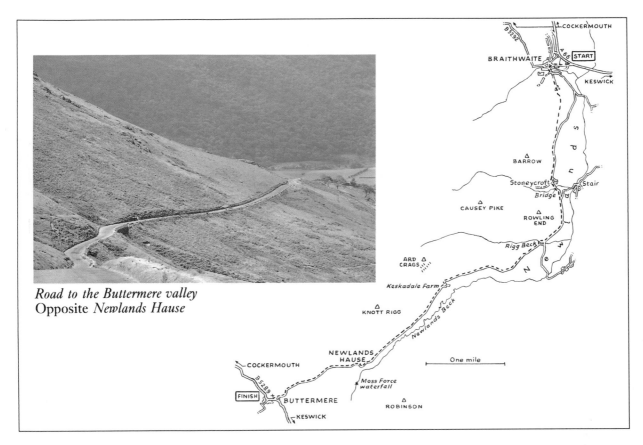

Road to the Buttermere valley
Opposite *Newlands Hause*

NEWLANDS HAUSE, often wrongly referred to as Buttermere Hause, carries a narrow motor road, non-commercial and normally quiet but much used by summer and weekend visitors to the district. The lovely valley of Newlands is patterned with country roads, any of which may be taken at the start of the journey. The most direct leaves the village of Braithwaite, then rounds the abrupt hill of Barrow which still bears the scars of disused lead mines, crosses Stonycroft Bridge over a stream where relics of mining activity can be seen in the form of a watercut, now dry, and passes along the base of Rowling End, elevated above the valley pastures. At Keskadale the road, fairly straight thus far, escapes from an impasse by steep curves to resume a direct ascending course to the hause rising along the flanks of Knott Rigg. Across the narrowing valley is the massive bulk of Robinson Fell. On the hause is ample space for parking cars from where Knott Rigg may be climbed or a waterfall, seen on the left, visited. Around the corner, the Buttermere valley comes into view with its attendant heights, a prospect full of promise; then the road starts a long decline to the village, allowing a more intimate appraisal of the delightful environs.

The road is not exclusively the preserve of motorists, and walkers can and often do use it but there is little opportunity to escape from the hard surface and at busy times it is best left to those who travel on wheels. Fortunately there is a direct alternative for walkers avoiding the hause, which is free from noise other than the tinkling of streams. This is the route alongside Rigg Beck (*see* page 151).

31

ORE GAP, 2575'
Eskdale – Borrowdale

THERE IS A splendid alternative route between Eskdale and Borrowdale, less spectacular than that over Esk Hause and having a considerable amount of rough and pathless walking, but because the way is guided by streams, there is little danger of going astray. This is a walk rarely undertaken, the adjoining mountains having the greater appeal, but in misty conditions when the tops are obscured it has merit as a foolproof route. However, it should not be underestimated; for most walkers it will prove a full day's expedition. Novice fellwalkers should not attempt the journey. In bad weather, it is safer to go from Boot to Wasdale Head by way of Burnmoor Tarn and thence over Sty Head to Borrowdale.

The route aims for the narrow col between Esk Pike and Bowfell, named Ore Gap and identifiable when reached by the red subsoil of a vein of hematite that gives the place its name which, occasionally and obviously wrongly, is spelt Ewer Gap.

View up Esk Valley to Bowfell
Opposite *View to Eskdale from Ore Gap*

THE ESKDALE ROAD is left at the foot of Hardknott Pass, passing the farm of Brotherilkeld and continuing up the valley of the River Esk on a distinct path with an exciting mountain prospect ahead. The walking here is pleasant and the Esk a delightful companion, but after passing below the formidable cliff of Heron Crag, high on the left, the terrain becomes rougher as a confluence of waters is reached at the picturesque arch of Lingcove Bridge. Here the Esk changes direction, coming down a deep gorge on the left, the bridge spanning a tributary, Lingcove Beck. The way to Ore Gap does not cross the bridge, but proceeds on a path climbing alongside the beck, which here displays a series of waterfalls. Bowfell and Crinkle Crags rear up massively in front, and after passing the opening of another Mosedale on the right, in surroundings of wild and chaotic desolation, the path goes forward to a grassy basin on the left. This is Green Hole and here the hard work starts.

The valley of the River Esk

Yeastyrigg Gill

Ore Gap looking up to Esk Pike

Abreast of Green Hole, the path thus far followed from Lingcove Bridge heads purposefully north-east, bound for the depression of Three Tarns between Bowfell and Crinkle Crags, but here is left in favour of a pathless crossing of Green Hole alongside the principal watercourse, Lingcove Beck. This stream emerges from a long and stony ravine, Yeastyrigg Gill, an uninviting chasm with the sole merit of pointing the way exactly to Ore Gap, not yet in view. The scramble up the bed of the stream is arduous, and better progress will be made on the adjoining slopes of Bowfell, which now appears as a massive pyramid of stones. At length, after an exhausting ascent, the ravine ends on an open fellside, the stream becomes a trickle, and Ore Gap is now clearly in sight ahead and reached with mute cheers. This is the end of uphill walking for the day.

Langstrath

A much-trodden path crosses Ore Gap, linking Bowfell and Esk Pike, and a distant view to the north opens up, revealing a kinder landscape with the promise of easier travel. Over the crest of the col, the way down starts immediately on a thin track aiming for Angle Tarn, seen as a dark circular pool in a green hollow below, and comes alongside it after a rough descent.

At the outlet of the tarn, the popular pedestrian highway coming over Rossett Pass and bound for Wasdale Head is met. The comfort of a well-trodden path is short-lived, the stream issuing from the tarn being followed down into the great hollow of Langstrath immediately in front and appearing verdant and restful after the arid wastes so far traversed. Ahead is a green and refreshing landscape, a valley set deep amongst enclosing fells: Allen Crags and Glaramara on the left and Rossett Pike on the right. The way down, on grass, does not have the advantage of a good path, but it is a pleasure to accompany the lively stream, here named Angletarn Gill and in maturity Langstrath Beck. Lower down a thin track forms and after two miles of walking from the tarn a distinct path is joined, this coming over Stake Pass from Great Langdale. Langstrath is now seen stretching far ahead, and tired feet will testify to the interpretation of its name as 'Long Valley'. But even tired feet will find the remainder of the walk a joy to tread.

Special delights of Langstrath are related to its charming beck, which flows along an alluring channel in a succession of bathing pools and cataracts and waterfalls. The enclosing heights, too, become more impressive, Sergeant's Crag and Eagle Crag rising very steeply to a rim of cliffs. Adding to the beauty of the lower reaches of the valley, trees appear in profusion and extend up fellsides which are coloured by heather and bracken.

Langstrath terminates at a delightful meeting of waters where a stream joins from Greenup Edge, the combined waters turning left into the Stonethwaite valley.

A bridge across the beck before the watersmeet and a path therefrom enters a rural lane that leads very pleasantly into the unspoilt hamlet of Stonethwaite, the cottages here being the first habitations seen since leaving Brotherilkeld.

This is a lovely corner of the district, typical of the romantic natural beauty of Lakeland and here still defended against modern intrusions.

A motor road connects with the nearby valley of Borrowdale at Rosthwaite. A pleasanter option, however, is to take the path alongside the beck for the final stage of the walk.

The Stonethwaite valley

Above *Langstrath Beck*

32 RIGG BECK, 1200'
Newlands – Buttermere

THE RIGG BECK route provides a direct way between Newlands and Buttermere exclusively for travellers on foot: it is not so much a pass as a deep cutting through mountainous terrain, rising gently to a low watershed from which streams descend on both sides. So confined and clearly defined is this crossing that only a genius could possibly go astray.

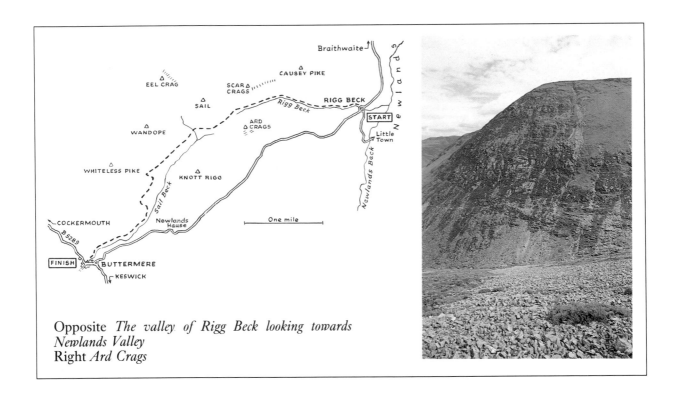

Opposite *The valley of Rigg Beck looking towards Newlands Valley*
Right *Ard Crags*

A GOOD PATH leaves the Newlands Hause road at the point where Rigg Beck comes down a pleasant valley from the west; there is limited parking for cars on the verges near the bridge. The path rounds a curve to enter a long straight furrow through the steepening fellsides of Ard Crags and Causey Pike. With Rigg Beck gurgling alongside, the path proceeds to its head waters; Ard Crags give place to Knott Rigg and Causey Pike is succeeded by Scar Crags, Sail and Eel Crags without any noticeable variation in the high skyline. These lofty enclosing walls effectively shut out distant views, but when the slight watershed is reached, the Buttermere Fells are seen in their full glory ahead. Past the divide, the role of guide is taken over by Sail Beck, the path following faithfully all the way down to the village of Buttermere in an environment of increasing beauty, being joined in its final stages by the path coming down from Whiteless Pike. Thus ends a walk greatly to be preferred to the hard road over Newlands Hause (*see* page 143).

33 ROSSETT PASS, 2000'
Great Langdale – Wasdale Head

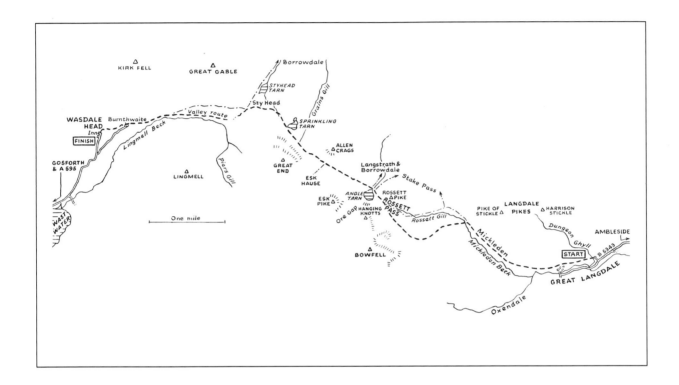

PASS WALKING has not the exhilaration and excitement of fellwalking, nor are the views as extensive as those seen from the ridges and summits. Lacking too is the interest of route planning and route findings: most passes have no easy variations from the well-trodden paths and there is no fear of going astray. For newcomers to the fells, walking the passes is a good apprenticeship for walking on the tops.

But there is one popular pass in Lakeland that comes near to the excellence of a high-level fell walk, one that affords intimate acquaintanceship with grand mountains, winds through contrasting and impressive landscapes, climbs to a considerable altitude and is exposed to the elements: in short, it deserves to rank as a first-class mountain expedition. This is the crossing between Great Langdale and Wasdale Head, generally and indeed almost always referred to as the Esk Hause route although this is a misnomer because the path does not reach or cross the true Esk Hause. It may perhaps be more accurate to refer to the route as Rossett Pass which is certainly crossed on the walk from Great Langdale although succeeded by higher ground before the descent to Wasdale Head commences. Two sections of the walk are uncomfortably rough and stony but can be avoided by grass alternatives mentioned in the chapter.

For full appreciation a whole day should be allowed for the journey.

Opposite *Rossett Pass*

BEYOND DUNGEON GHYLL, Great Langdale divides into two valleys, Oxendale and Mickleden. The path travels the two easy miles of Mickleden below the towering skyline of the Langdale Pikes, with the Band of Bowfell rising on the left. The valley terminates abruptly at the base of Rossett Pike, where a path branches right to climb to Stake Pass, the main path trending left and arriving at the foot of Rossett Gill. Nobody ever said a kind word about Rossett Gill. The direct climb is abominably rough, up a river of sliding stones through a height of a thousand feet; a torment of the flesh that only hardened masochists will enjoy. I had toiled up this ladder of loose stones dozens of times before discovering on an old map that there was formerly a pony track that made the ascent by a circuitous route across the lower slopes of Bowfell. I traced this old way on the ground without difficulty, finding it quiet, well graded and pleasant, and never again did I suffer the discomforts of the direct route. This alternative I recommend.

Langdale Pikes and Mickleden from Rossett Gill

It leaves the floor of Mickleden short of the head of the valley, fording the beck at a point I've never been able to identify exactly but no matter; the stream may be crossed at any convenient place and the pathless fellside beyond climbed half-right and across a landslide to a line of ancient cairns. The route thus far has been indistinct underfoot although, like many old tracks, plainly seen from a distance. Once found, with the help of the cairns, the path is a joy to follow, quite easy and within sight of the crowds struggling up Rossett Gill. It rises more steeply to a hollow threaded by many waterslides coming off Bowfell and crosses a causeway at a pool. Nearby is an old sheepfold, screened from sight of the valley below where, I was told by a Langdale historian, the dalesmen hid their sheep during the border raids. Within easy reach on a grassy mound, is a cross of stones laid on the ground, marking the grave of a packwoman who used to call at the Langdale farms carrying articles for sale and whose remains were found at this spot 200 years ago.

Angle Tarn

The pony route then heads directly to the top of Rossett Pass, appearing as a straight groove in its later sections, and here joining the direct climb up the gill. Some pony routes were devised for the pleasure of visitors and others, like this, were trade routes in the days of packhorses.

Rossett Pass, with grass succeeding stones, is a welcome relief to the feet, but a wild and inhospitable landscape meets the eyes. High on the left, the Hanging Knotts of Bowfell plunge into the waters of Angle Tarn; the tarn has been variously described as dark and sinister or as calm and lovely in its solitude. There is a short descent to the outlet of the tarn, and here you can see that the issuing stream crosses the path and descends into the valley of Langstrath, a vast hollow on the right leading down into Borrowdale. Indeed, beyond Rossett Pass, all the ground in sight is within the Borrowdale watershed, and the path over the so-called Esk Hause, straight ahead and much higher, is for some miles, until the descent of Wasdale Head from Sty Head, the catchment area of Borrowdale's rivers.

Esk Pike

From Angle Tarn the path goes ahead, climbing gradually to a wall shelter of stones, the highest point of the journey and commonly known as Esk Hause, although the true Esk Hause – i.e. the pass from Eskdale – is the higher ridge seen on the left between Esk Pike and Great End. The site of the shelter, at 2386ft, qualifies as a pass but only a minor one. The main watershed, at 2490ft, divides the gathering grounds of Eskdale and Borrowdale at Esk Hause proper and is not visited on this walk.

The journey becomes more exciting as the path leaves the shelter and descends gently, coming alongside Ruddy Gill where the vein of hematite seen at Ore Gap is again in evidence; this colourful ravine curves to the right, heading for Borrowdale via Grains Gill and a path accompanies it. The main path continues forward below the massive cliff of Great End, riven by gullies and dominating all else. Soon the shore of Sprinkling Tarn is reached: a lovely sheet of water that cries out for a halt; invariably rucksacks are cast off here for a rest while those walkers with cameras inevitably take the classic picture of Great End seen soaring above the indented shore.

Resuming the walk, the feature that compels attention is the immense pyramid of Great Gable directly ahead and increasing in stature as the path descends gradually towards it to arrive at Sty Head, a walkers' crossroads known to all who frequent the fells and from which tracks radiate in all directions. Away to the right is the inky pool of Styhead Tarn.

Great End from Sprinkling Tarn

Below *Great Gable*

From Sty Head, the path for Wasdale Head turns a corner on the left, a fine viewpoint and, with the promised land of Wasdale coming into sight as an inviting green oasis, makes a beeline for it. But over-use has turned the surface of the path into an uncomfortable channel of loose stones. Much better is the original path, now rarely used, known as the Valley Route, reached by descending at once from Sty Head into the grassy depths on the left to join the stream there: this, augmented by the flow from Piers Gill, becomes Lingmell Beck. The path follows it closely, arriving at the cultivated fields of Burnthwaite, from which a short lane leads to the inn at Wasdale Head and journey's end.

There are few, if any, grander cross-country walks than this. It will remain an evergreen memory.

Looking towards Newlands

Below *The summit of Sail Pass*

34 SAIL PASS, 2050'
Newlands – Buttermere

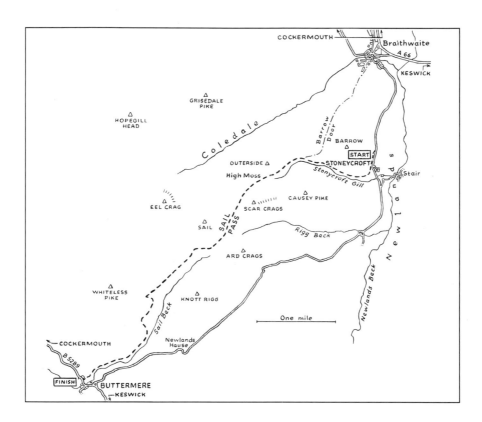

IN ADDITION TO the two crossings between Newlands and Buttermere by way of Newlands Hause (No.30) and Rigg Beck (No.32), there is another, rather more arduous, that takes advantage of an old mine road and gives much grander mountain views. This leads to a former cobalt mine of which a few traces remain, crosses a ridge beyond and descends to join the Rigg Beck route to reach Buttermere.

THE MAIN ROAD leaves Newlands at Stoneycroft, branching off at the valley road from Braithwaite, and soon starts to climb steadily up the side valley of the Stonycroft Gill overlooked by the imposing peak of Causey Pike and the heathery slopes of Barrow. It is joined after a mile by an alternative route from Braithwaite through Barrow Door, itself a pass, and becomes less distinct as it crosses the marshy plateau of High Moss before finally rising to the site of the old mine. There's a striking view hereabouts of the head of Coledale down below on the right and closely confined by the impending heights of Eel Crag, Hopegill Head and Grisedale Pike. Beyond the mine, the route, now reduced to a thin track, reaches a depression in the ridge above. This is Sail Pass, carrying a ridge path in popular use. Over the pass is the deep valley of Rigg Beck and a slender track, probably used by miners but little used today, slants down across the breast of Sail to the watershed of Rigg Beck and Sail Beck, the latter then being followed down on a good path to enter the village of Buttermere, arriving there in sylvan surroundings on a parallel course with the motor road over Newlands Hause.

35

SCANDALE PASS, 1680'
Ambleside – Patterdale

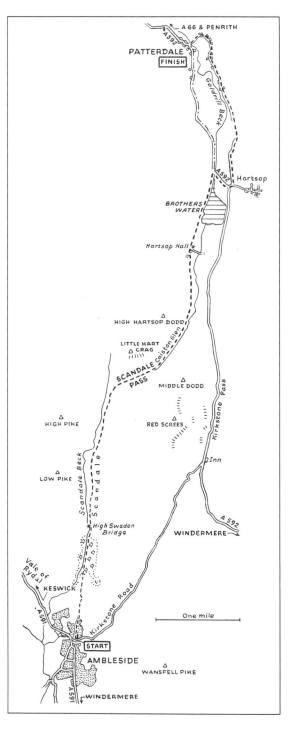

A CENSUS OF the travellers making the journey between Ambleside and Patterdale via (a) Kirkstone Pass and (b) Scandale Pass, would show the former route to be used almost exclusively and the latter, having no motor road, hardly at all. Even those who travel on foot seem to prefer the animation of Kirkstone to the loneliness of Scandale. Scenically, Kirkstone is the grander of the two by far, its untamed wildness being very impressive despite the tourist traffic it attracts. Scandale cannot compete in the matter of scenery, being tedious and dull by comparison, and its more limited appeal is due to its quietness and solitude.

AMBLESIDE IS LEFT by way of Sweden Bridge Lane, branching from the Kirkstone road near the old church. The lane climbs into an enviable suburbia, but when the residences and tarmac are left behind at a gate it becomes a rough cart-track. The next mile is perfect bliss, the rising lane affording exquisite views of the Vale of Rydal and the surrounding fells, while nearby Wansfell Pike assumes a stature that belies its rather modest altitude.

Opposite *The head of Scandale in summer Red Screes' summit rocks*

High Sweden Bridge in Scandale

The lane enters a woodland glade and here is an avenue of loveliness, especially when dappled by sunlight; a musical accompaniment to the scene is provided by the rushing waters of Scandale Beck, hidden in a gorge down on the left. The lane is another of Ambleside's many treasures and is well patronised by visitors, their objective coming into sight at the end of the trees. Here is the picturesque High Sweden Bridge, a gem of its kind, its one simple arch spanning the stream. Everybody with a camera takes photographs at this romantic spot.

The bridge is the great attraction for the many people who walk the two miles from Ambleside, the prize they seek, and few aspire further along the valley to its head at Scandale Pass. This is not surprising; it must be conceded that the scenery beyond the bridge compares unfavourably with the beauty of the approach to it.

The higher reaches of Scandale are therefore likely to be of interest only to walkers bound for Patterdale. The cart-track continues upstream, not crossing the bridge, and rises gently, enclosed by walls, to reveal a different landscape, a barren wilderness where the many stone walls are the only signs of human intervention in the dreary scene. The track descends to a marshy amphitheatre hemmed in by the high ridge of Low Pike and High Pike on the left and flanked by the featureless slopes of Red Screes which reserves its interest for the savage Kirkstone face. Ahead is the pass, overtopped by the twin peaks of Little Hart Crag. The hollow is crossed and the ground rises steeply, trending to the right to gain the top of Scandale Pass, crossed by a sturdy stone wall.

The ascent of Red Screes may be made from the top of the pass, the wall serving as guide, but this side of the mountain exhibits nothing of the ruggedness displayed to the crowds at the Kirkstone Pass Inn.

The descent from the pass starts at once along the steeply declining valley of Caiston Glen, equally dreary and even more shut in by fells but having a vista of verdant greenery in front framed by the slopes of High Hartsop Dodd and Middle Dodd, the former terminating in a downfall of crags and scree where, in 1948, the efforts of the local dalesmen to rescue two trapped terriers won headlines in national newspapers for several days until the dogs were finally released.

With the high ground falling away sharply alongside, the surroundings become more open, trees making a welcome appearance, and then the path from Kirkstone Pass joins for the pleasant walk down the Patterdale Valley to the farm of Hartsop Hall, whence a lane continues the route along the shores of Brothers Water and to the A592. The village of Patterdale is two miles further or, if the road is busy, a parallel by-road from the Hartsop junction is to be preferred.

There is rural loveliness and quiet serenity at both ends of the Scandale Pass, but only drab desolation in its middle section. For walkers who choose not to be in close proximity to cars and enjoy solitude, this route is greatly to be preferred to the popular Kirkstone Pass with its endless traffic and noise. You will never see a buzzard or an eagle in the sky above Kirkstone; over Scandale you might.

The head of Scandale in winter

36 SCARTH GAP, 1400'
Buttermere – Ennerdale

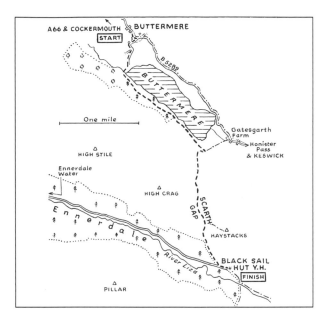

THERE IS NO WAY across the mountain barrier separating Buttermere and Ennerdale that does not call for serious fellwalking at a high level, and those who wish to travel from one valley to the other with minimum output of energy must have recourse to the Scarth Gap path which skirts the range to the east. This is a splendid walk, not long in distance but endowed with magnificent views; the camera is as essential as boots. Scarth Gap, often referred to as Scarf Gap in earlier days, is the depression between High Crag, one of the trinity of peaks forming the High Stile range, and Haystacks which is a lesser summit. The path is distinct, without deviations, and poses no problems of route finding.

Opposite *The summit of Scarth Gap*
Buttermere

FROM BUTTERMERE VILLAGE, either side of its lake may be followed, the more direct way being along the south-west shore, reached by a bridge over the outflow. Then amongst trees, some natural and some planted, the charming lakeside path leads for a mile below the majestic presence of High Stile, almost to the head of the lake where a cairned path branches off and climbs the open fellside.

This point may be reached more quickly by crossing the pastures from Gatesgarth Farm, this alternative saving a mile of walking but missing the delights of the lakeside.

The path rises steadily over grass slopes in the direction of Haystacks. Halts are justified by the excellence of the retrospective view over the Buttermere valley to Grasmoor. Scarth Gap is obvious in front, and the path leads unerringly to a large cairn marking the summit of the path.

There are signs at Scarth Gap that men have been at work recently trying to combat erosion caused by boots; in particular, steps have been made in the scree slope leading up to Haystacks. Early guide-books dismissed Haystacks as of little consequence and barely worth a mention, but in recent years it has deservedly become a popular objective of fellwalkers. I cannot agree, however, that steps should be provided to ease the ascent. Erosion of paths by over-use is a growing problem, but steps are not the answer. Steps up a mountain are incongruous, out of place. Steps are for going upstairs to bed, not for climbing mountains. Unfortunately, there are now many examples: there are flights of steps on Loughrigg and Nab Scar, and worst of all a stairway to the top of Mam Tor in Derbyshire – with hand rail provided. Heaven forbid, at least in Lakeland. No, the cure for erosion is for walkers to tread carefully and firmly on paths, not to kick them to bits.

A scene of grandeur greets the eyes on the descent into Ennerdale. Great Gable and Pillar rear up proudly across the gulf, Great Gable naked and unashamed, Pillar wearing an unbecoming skirt of foreign conifer plantations which have draped across the lower slopes for the last few decades. They reach all the way down Ennerdale and have no natural beauty. I saw Pillar before the trees came, in full stature, and it was a glorious sight. Now, its tears of lost pride and dignity swell the River Liza at its base. I weep with it. This should not have happened.

Gatesgarth Farm

Great Gable from Scarth Gap

The path from Scarth Gap goes stonily down to come alongside the dark cloak of a plantation, and reaches the cart-track now used as a forest road that follows the River Liza down-river for several miles to the scattered habitations near Ennerdale Water; there is a Youth Hostel midway. But at the point of arrival from Scarth Gap the only sign of civilisation is the solitary Black Sail Hut, most remote and isolated of Lakeland's Youth Hostels. Failing accommodation here, there is no alternative to the long trek down the valley with no respite from regimented avenues of battery-reared skeletons of trees. Where now is the beauty that was Ennerdale?

Pillar from Scarth Gap

The path to Skiddaw House   Below *Skiddaw Forest*

37 SKIDDAW FOREST, 1500'
Keswick – Orthwaite or Mosedale

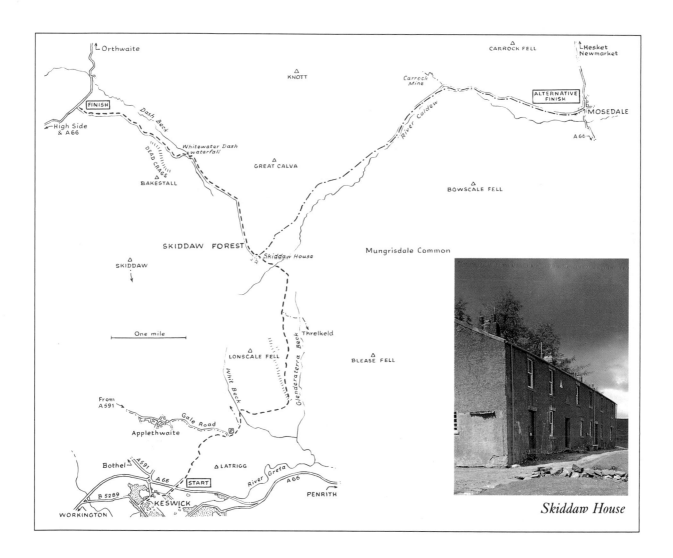

Skiddaw House

THE NORTHERN fells of Lakeland rise in complete isolation from the Vale of Keswick and extend to the coastal plain of Cumbria as a huge natural barrier topping 3000 ft in altitude. This high mass, roughly circular in plan, is dissected by watercourses to form a score of separate summits. They are individually named and closely linked and nowhere permit easy passage between them except by two low crossings which divide the area into three segments, each having its own group of fells. These crossings are remarkably easy considering the high ground they penetrate, and are even negotiable by cars in parts. They start as one from the Vale of Keswick, branching in the heart of Skiddaw Forest; the main route goes on to the farming communities north-west of Skiddaw, the other follows the River Caldew east to Mosedale.

Dead Crags

STARTING FROM KESWICK, the small hill of Latrigg, 'Skiddaw's cub', must be rounded after crossing the new A66, either by way of Spooney Green Lane on foot, or by motor road via Applethwaite to the terminus of Gale Road; here the two routes converge and there is parking for cars. Here commences the time-honoured path to Skiddaw, heading north for the mountain. Around the first bend, the path to Skiddaw Forest branches to the right, makes a wide sweep to cross Whit Beck and contours along the lower slopes of Lonscale Fell, a terrace walk with lovely views of the Greta valley. The path turns north abruptly, in places cut out of the living rock, above the deep watercourse of Glenderaterra Beck, and now having the immense slopes of Blease Fell opposite. With Lonscale Fell displaying its rugged eastern face, culminating in a fine tower of rock, the path aims directly forward, passing an area of abandoned lead mines of which a few relics remain, and being joined by a path from Threlkeld. Walls come alongside, a gate is reached on a minor watershed, and the path trends left to the lonely buildings of Skiddaw House, built as a gamekeeper's lodge and later occupied by shepherds. A small plantation behind serves as a windbreak.

   Here we are in Skiddaw Forest, a vast tract of open moorland extending into the far distance, a forest without trees, once a hunting ground and now a spacious pasture for sheep. Note that the sheepfolds hereabouts are circular, conforming to the Scottish pattern, and not rectangular as elsewhere in Lakeland. The forest is a wilderness, dreary under cloud, yet having a haunting beauty when sunlight dapples the landscape. The solitude is profound.

Skiddaw House is served by a rough access road, and if the objective is the pastoral countryside north-west of Skiddaw, this is followed below the shattered cliffs of Dead Crags into the valley of Dash Beck which has a spectacular but little-known waterfall called Whitewater Dash. Soon the fells are left behind and, amongst cultivated fields, a quiet motor road is reached between Orthwaite and High Side, the latter having a bus service.

The alternative route, for Mosedale: from Skiddaw House, the way slowly declines north-eastwards into the valley of the River Caldew; a thin track goes towards this pleasant watercourse and then comes alongside it. The track follows the river downstream on its north bank for three lonely but enjoyable miles as it develops bathing pools along its slaty bed. The track joins a tarred road below Carrock Mine, this leading into the hamlet of Mosedale along the base of the rugged declivities of Carrock Fell. From Mosedale a country road goes south for three miles to reach the A66 and its bus service.

Valley of the River Caldew

Above *Whitewater Dash*

38 STAKE PASS, 1576'
Great Langdale – Borrowdale

THE LAKE DISTRICT was not designed for motorists who, to pass from one valley to the next, must in many cases travel up to ten times further than the crow can fly because of intervening high ground. Walkers are better favoured although, even with greater mobility, they can rarely make crowlines or beelines and must seek the easiest contours. Nature obviously never intended Lakeland to be overrun by men on wheels, nor by timid pedestrians; it was fashioned as a rugged wilderness to be enjoyed only by lovers of solitude and primitive landscapes. One should be thankful for this.

Thus the two valleys most populated by modern tourists, Great Langdale and Borrowdale, have no linking road and cars must make a wide detour around Keswick to pass from one to the other. But walkers have one possible route that avoids rough climbing and reveals glories that motorists never see.

This is the Stake Pass.

Opposite *Mickleden Stake Pass*

Langstrath

BEYOND DUNGEON GHYLL at the head of Great Langdale a much-used level path proceeds along the branching valley of Mickleden, set deep between the ramparts of the Langdale Pikes on one side and the rising shoulder of Bowfell on the other. After two miles of easy walking, Rossett Pike presents an insuperable impasse directly ahead and the path bifurcates, the main branch trending left to Rossett Pass and the other ascending grassy slopes on the right to the skyline depression formed by Stake Pass. The climb is unremitting and the original well-engineered zigzags have unfortunately been abused by impatient walkers who have yet to learn that a staggered path following the easiest slopes gives by far the most enjoyable mode of progression: these untidy short cuts are invariably made, not in ascent but by clumsy walkers descending at speed, and are inexcusable. All mountain paths should be savoured slowly and treated with respect even in bad weather or when there's a bus to catch. They are the walker's greatest help in his wanderings amongst the fells and should be preserved with care, not kicked into unsightly ribbons of loose stones which can also cause accidents. I love zigzag paths and it pains me to see them wrecked unmercifully by walkers who do not appreciate their worth and do not deserve the privilege of freedom on the fells.

The ascent is dull, relieved only by the growing stature of Bowfell behind, but when the top of the pass is reached and crossed, a glorious prospect unfolds ahead as the environs of Borrowdale come into sight. On the right, the Langdale Pikes assume an unfamiliar outline, appearing insignificant over a wide moorland.

Gradually the path leads down into the long valley of Langstrath, promising a few miles of pleasant travel as a prelude to Borrowdale. And so it proves. Langstrath is lovely.

Down in the valley acquaintance is made with Langstrath Beck, an exuberant rushing of waters attractively endowed in its lower reaches with waterfalls and rocky pools. The path accompanies it along the valley, passing Gash Rock, a huge fallen boulder providing a few rock climbs. Across the beck rises the massive whaleback of Glaramara, and soaring above the pass are the unassailable heights of Sergeant's Crag and, further, Eagle Crag, both falling in scree slopes from dark towers of rock.

Langstrath has many temptations to linger over, but in due course a bridge spans the beck and admits to a lane in surroundings more akin to heaven than earth; rich carpeted fellside and woodland glades and the sparkling beck make the turn into the Stonethwaite valley a sylvan delight.

The unspoilt hamlet of Stonethwaite is reached with envy of those who live in this secluded community where little has changed since men first settled here and which still has an aura of seventeenth-century Lakeland. A tarred road shatters the illusion, reminding us that the days of horses and carts are over; this leads into the main valley road of Borrowdale, half a mile distant.

If Rosthwaite is the objective, a bridge over the beck can be crossed and a pleasant path followed to this hospitable village amongst trees and pastures; a most fitting finish to the walk that emphasises again that travelling on foot is so greatly preferable to motoring.

One is poetry, the other prose.

Gash Rock

Langstrath Beck

39 STICKS PASS, 2420'
Stanah (Thirlmere) – Glenridding

ONLY ONCE HAVE I walked from one end of Sticks Pass to the other (once being enough), although perforce having to use sections of it on many occasions subsequently. It is almost sacrilege to describe any of Lakeland's paths as unattractive, but this high crossing of the Helvellyn range has little to commend it except as an exercise for the legs; it is tedious and drab and in places badly scarred by abandoned lead-mining activities. Sticks Pass is the only crossing between Thirlmere and Ullswater served by a continuous path, its one distinction being that it is the highest pass in the district in regular use. Formerly the highest part of the path was marked by a line of wooden posts, hence the name, but these have vanished.

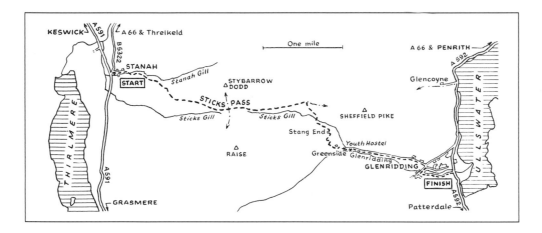

Opposite *The summit of Sticks Pass*   *Looking west from Sticks Pass*

STANAH IS A little group of buildings reached by a short lane from the A591 at the point where a road branches to St John's in the Vale. A path leaves here, crosses a small bridge, and climbs very steeply above the deep ravine of Stanah Gill, a gloomy chasm with many waterfalls.

The gradient eases when a sheepfold is reached, the cairned path then slanting across an open moor, the sprawling west slope of Stybarrow Dodd, to overlook the valley of Sticks Gill which is followed up to the source of the stream. Across it are the bare slopes of Raise which are normally unfrequented except when presenting animated scenes in snowy winters, being much favoured by skiers.

The final rise to the summit of the pass is steep. At the top the ascents of Stybarrow Dodd, left, and Raise, right, may be made.

The prospect ahead is not one to inspire enthusiasm. It is a scene without beauty, an arid and sterile landscape.

Stanah Gill
Stybarrow Dodd

The path starts a long descent and is soon joined by another Sticks Gill. This is the only instance of streams descending from a watershed in opposite directions having the same name. At length a small reservoir constructed to serve the Glenridding lead mine is reached: this, having outlived its usefulness, has been abandoned and now appears as an unlovely muddy waste, and has been removed from the latest Ordnance maps. Beyond the bed of the old reservoir, a path goes forward and descends to Glencoyne but the main route, now faced by the slopes of Sheffield Pike, turns to the right and enters an area of industrial devastation at Stang End where there are many traces of departed enterprise, notably a long flue that discharged at a chimney, now derelict, on the lower slopes of Raise.

With the Glenridding valley and Ullswater coming into sight, the path drops sharply in zigzags to the site of the Greenside lead mine, its scars grassed over and some of the buildings converted to other uses including a Youth Hostel. From here a road goes down to the lakeside village of Glenridding, its economy no longer based on mining but on catering for the many visitors to Ullswater. Here arc hotels, guest houses, shops, a bus service and facilities for sailing on the lake.

Mining relics
The valley of Glenridding from Stang End

40 STILE END, 1100′
Kentmere – Longsleddale

IF, AS IS SUPPOSED, Garburn Pass was the first section of an old road across the south-eastern corner of Lakeland, its logical continuation from Kentmere must have been the cart-track into Longsleddale, referred to here in the absence of a name as the Stile End crossing. The way is distinct underfoot but happily sufficiently rough to break the springs of a car and is now classed as a bridleway.

Incredibly, an insensitive county council some years ago planned to transform this pleasant path into a modern road for the benefit of tourists but the scheme was quite rightly howled down by public outrage.

Kentmere village is left by the rising no-through road to Hallow Bank, this being departed from short of the hamlet where a signposted lane turns off to the right and climbs gently to Stile End; here two stone barns make a good foreground to the classic view of the head of Kentmere beyond. Through a gate, the track continues easily across open grassland to its highest point and then descends to Longsleddale ahead. In one steep section, the track has been badly eroded, an effective barrier to wheels, but is followed by a better surface as the track turns north below Sadgill Wood with a splendid view of the head of Longsleddale in front. It ends at Sadgill Bridge at the terminus of a motor road to the A6 and Kendal.

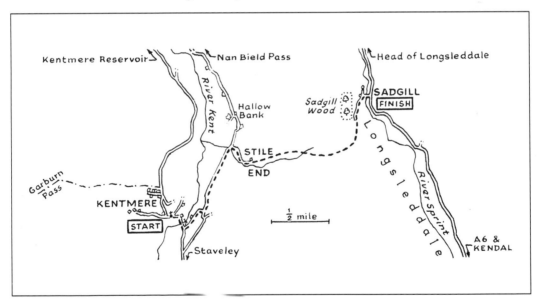

HAVING COME THUS far, which route would the old road take beyond Sadgill? Here it would be faced by an insuperable obstacle, high fells barring a straight continuation. The only feasible way for horse-drawn traffic was to ascend to the head of Longsleddale by cart-track (later used as the Wrengill Quarry road) thence heading across Mosedale and down Wet Sleddale to join the Great North Road (now the A6) at Shap.

This is amateur conjecture only.

Opposite *The head of Kentmere from Stile End*

41 THE STRAITS OF RIGGINDALE

WHEN IS A PASS not a pass? The essential requirement of a mountain pass is that it must permit access from either side, allowing a crossing from one valley to the next.

Seen from a distance, or on a map, the Straits of Riggindale would seem to qualify, appearing as a pronounced dip in a high skyline where the declining ridge of High Street falls briefly before rising sharply to Rampsgill Head; the name too (Straits = a narrow passage) promises a through route – but this is not so.

A footpath from Patterdale by way of Boardale Hause and Angle Tarn crosses an extensive area of foothills before rounding The Knott and slanting upwards to the Straits where it meets the Roman road traversing the ridge. Here one arrives at the brink of the yawning gulf of Riggindale, the way forward being abruptly stopped by a very steep downfall of rocks and scree with no possibility of continuing the line of approach by direct descent into Riggindale although this valley is soon to lead straight to Mardale. True, an adventurous walker may pick his way carefully down the crags and stone gullies but I write for ordinary mortals.

Riggindale is inexpressibly wild and has become a sanctuary for deer and fell ponies, foxes and golden eagles since the only habitation was demolished during the construction of the Haweswater Reservoir and the hamlet at its foot, Mardale Green, has vanished beneath the engulfing waters.

Prudent walkers arriving at the Straits of Riggindale and bound for Mardale complete the journey by going over Kidsty Pike and descending the easy slopes beyond. The Straits form only half a pass, and therefore are no pass at all.

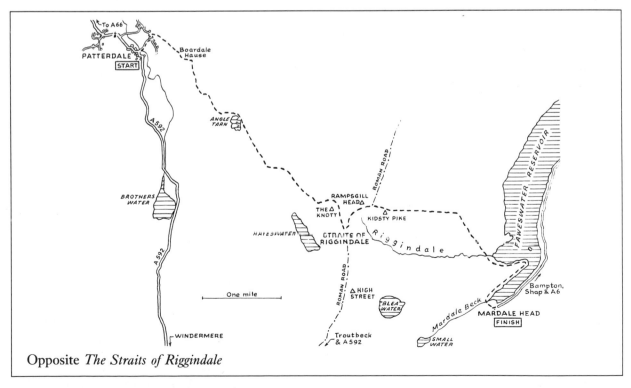

Opposite *The Straits of Riggindale*

42 STY HEAD, 1600'
Borrowdale – Wasdale Head

The top of Sty Head

SOONER OR LATER a very active walker in the Lake District arrives at Sty Head, usually on the crossing between Borrowdale and Wasdale, and most call here frequently during the course of their wanderings. It is a popular halt and there are few days in the year when walkers are absent from its well-trodden paths. The distance from one valley to the other is short, but the mountain barrier intervening is so impregnable that motorists wishing to make the journey must take a circuitous route of forty-five miles. This inconvenience led to an ill-fated proposal many years ago that a motor road be constructed over the pass; thankfully the proposal never got off the drawing board because of the weight of public opposition. Sty Head is a sanctuary of silence and peace amongst the grandest mountains in the country and should remain so. It is a place of outstanding scenic quality, staging a permanent exhibition of awesome impressiveness. This is a part of Lakeland that has never changed. Today's visitors see it as it has always been; to an old man it appears just as it was in the days of his youth, only the paths can show evidence of greater use and the cairns have grown in size.

Dalesmen have been familiar with the route for centuries, and there are signs that the steeper sections were originally skilfully graded and roughly metalled to ease the passage of laden horses.

'Sty Head' means 'The top of the ladder'. To many of us it also means Lakeland at its best.

Opposite *Sty Head and Great Gable*

Seathwaite   Below *Stockley Bridge*

THE WALK STARTS at the farmstead of Seathwaite at the terminus of the Borrowdale road where it is usual to find dozens of cars parked on the verges of the tarmac. Seathwaite is the wettest inhabited place in England, suffering an average annual rainfall of around 140 inches, and has been the scene of devastating floods; yet it offers a friendly welcome to the many visitors who pass through the farmyard all day long.

There is a choice of two routes. The original and usual path continues up the valley to Stockley Bridge, a picturesque stone arch above the rocky channel of Grains Gill. The path has been trodden to dust by endless processions of pedestrians most of whom, ill-shod and ill-equipped for rough walking, settle on the rocks by the bridge and go no further. Hardier souls bound for Sty Head cross the bridge and choose from a variety of tracks up the facing slope, which has been cut to shreds by the clumsy boots of those who see no virtue in following the well-engineered gradients of the original path and prefer short cuts. This section is a disgrace: verges have been trampled and vegetation stripped. Nature never gets a chance to heal the scars. On easier ground above, the path reverts to its old course by Styhead Gill, crossing it at a footbridge.

The alternative route from Seathwaite is quieter and more exciting. It was formerly little known and was late in appearing on Ordnance maps. This starts along a short lane from the farm buildings to a bridge across the Derwent, then following the river up the valley on the west bank through moist and rough pastures. The Derwent is formed by the meeting of Grains Gill and Styhead Gill, but before the confluence the path turns steeply up the fellside to enter the rocky confines of Taylorgill Force, a splendid waterfall. The path here is awkward in places as it hugs a wall of cliffs on the right before emerging into open country above the waterfall and continuing alongside Styhead Gill to join the usual and more frequented path at a footbridge.

A short distance further the shore of Styhead Tarn is reached.

Styhead Tarn

Above *Taylorgill Force*

Ahead is the massive dome of Great End and the giants of the Scafell range behind. On the left is Seathwaite Fell which, like the tarn, keeps its own rainfall records, and high on the right rise the vast slopes of Green Gable and Great Gable, split by the immense fissure of Aaron Slack. The wildness of the scene is accentuated rather than softened by the dark waters of Styhead Tarn.

The path proceeds to the highest point of the pass, a most important crossroads for walkers, furnished with a stretcher box for casualties.

From the large cairn, paths radiate in all directions. Here starts the popular Breast Route to the top of Great Gable, and a secondary and less obvious path contours to Kern Knotts and the Girdle Traverse of Gable. To the left goes the path to Esk Hause and Great Langdale, with the Corridor Route to the Scafells branching from it. The main path to Wasdale Head goes forward, turning a corner to face Lingmell's dark cliffs and the huge gash of Piers Gill.

Lingmell

Wasdale Head from Sty Head

The main path aims directly for Wasdale Head, slanting down across the flanks of Great Gable; through over-use it has become an uncomfortable channel of loose stones, appearing from afar as a great wound slashed by a giant knife across the mountainside. During the long descent, Wasdale Head comes into sight as a patchwork of small fields bordered by stone walls: a welcome green oasis enclosed by bare mountains.

An alternative way down from Sty Head is provided by the original path, known as the Valley Route, once long abandoned but recently restored to favour. This descends at once in the direction of Lingmell, easy grass slopes leading down to the stream flowing from Great End. A path accompanies this to the confluence with the waters of Piers Gill. High above is the long escarpment of Lingmell, and on the right Great Gable towers into the sky, seen foreshortened but imposing a majestic presence upon the landscape. The combined waters take the name of Lingmell Beck (on early Ordnance maps named as Cawfell Beck – a rare aberration) and a path continues alongside very pleasantly until it ends at a junction with the usual direct path. All that now remains is a stroll through cultivated fields to Burnthwaite Farm and a short lane to the little cluster of buildings at Wasdale Head.

There have been changes here since my early days. The primitive inn that was the Mecca of the pioneer rockclimbers has become a sophisticated hotel and cars have brought a new and growing clientele. Once all visitors wore heavy boots; today sightseers have introduced sandals. I liked it better as it was . . . But of course the mountain scene is unaffected by happenings in the valley and remains superb. Wasdale Head is wonderfully situated in a green hollow below an array of challenging peaks, Great Gable in particular rising starkly as a shapely pyramid. In this magnificent setting, minor irritations simply don't matter.

43 THREE TARNS, 2250'
Great Langdale – Eskdale

MOTORISTS WISHING TO travel between Great Langdale and Eskdale must make a roundabout and up and down journey over Wrynose and Hardknott Passes, but others unencumbered by wheels have available a splendid direct cross-country route with a single ascent and descent which, moreover, leads through impressive mountain scenery.

This is the Three Tarns route, taking advantage of a pronounced depression in the Crinkle Crags–Bowfell skyline, occupied by small tarns, usually considered to be three in number although there is a lesser fourth.

Coming up from Great Langdale, there is invariably the company of others engaged on the ascent of Bowfell, but beyond the tarns the way is unfrequented and rough underfoot as it threads a passage through a barren waste of rocks and stones undisturbed down the ages. The scene is primeval, but softens as Eskdale opens in front, waterfalls giving a foretaste of the manifold delights to come.

Opposite *The Links of Bowfell and Three Tarns*

Bowfell

FROM DUNGEON GHYLL at the head of Great Langdale, a level strath is crossed on a farm road to Stool End, and the steep buttress immediately beyond is climbed on a distinct path suffering from popularity. This is a shoulder of Bowfell known as The Band and the path rises steadily between the valleys of Mickleden and Oxendale. The ascent is tedious but relieved by fine views on either side – the Langdale Pikes arrayed above Mickleden and Pike o' Blisco overlooking Oxendale. The serrated top of Crinkle Crags, ahead to the left, demands increasing attention as height is gained.

Crinkle Crags from the Band
Below *The Band and Stool End*

Great Langdale

Below *One of the Three Tarns*

The path up The Band was formed for the ascent of Bowfell, and is the usual route to the summit of that noble mountain. When the ground steepens into the final rugged pyramid, it trends to the left to find an easy way to the top, arriving there ascending a stony and badly eroded breach in the rough ground above the depression occupied by the Three Tarns. The path is left when the tarns come into sight and an easy walk leads to them. From higher ground nearby, there is a retrospective view of Great Langdale.

The dominating feature of the Three Tarns depression is the extraordinary line of cliffs high on the side of Bowfell, deeply furrowed by a dozen steep and stony parallel gullies known as the Links and looking as though they were scratched out of the rocks by a giant comb; a formation unique in the district. I once descended one of these boulder-filled cracks and it was not a happy experience.

The tarns are unattractive, giving no cause to linger, and the route continues on a thin track south-west in the direction of Eskdale.

The track goes down along the base of the steeply rising buttresses of Crinkle Crags, its course amply cairned through a desert of loose stones and fallen boulders. When I first came along here, a very long time ago, there was little semblance of a path, the way being indicated by a series of very small cairns, simply one stone placed on another, and it was fun looking for the next. One stone balanced on another is all that is necessary in clear weather; too many Lakeland cairns have grown into immense piles, encouraging in mist or snow, but are today obsolete as paths have been trodden wider and more obvious during the growth of fellwalking since the last war. Too many cairns can be more misleading than too few especially when they have been erected off-route to mark a viewpoint or a dangerous cliff or a rockclimbers' track, all leading into difficult situations. But on the whole cairns are a great comfort when walkers are uncertain of their next move, and even the most experienced have often been glad to see one marking a path in bad weather conditions. During my early explorations in uncharted wastes, I was often mightily relieved to see a cairn that led me to a path. I love mountain cairns but not too many of them.

During the descent, a great rift appears in the side of Crinkle Crags: this is Rest Gill, offering a pathless and scrambling route direct to the top of the highest Crinkle; this is for adventurers only, while walkers bound for Eskdale continue down the stony track, reaching easier ground when Lingcove Beck comes alongside after crossing the grassy hollow of Green Hole. Looking back, Bowfell appears as a gigantic heap of stones, an untrodden wilderness. Bowfell's many attractions are all on the Langdale side.

Lingcove Beck and the path now go down into Eskdale side by side. Soon the cliffs of Crinkle Crags recede to give place to a wide grassy opening with a descending stream: this is another Mosedale, as dreary as the others of its kin but a pass in its own right, the crossing of its low watershed giving an easy route to Cockley Beck in the Duddon Valley.

Bowfell from Lingcove Beck

Mosedale

Lingcove Beck enlivens the continuing descent with waterfalls as the path comes down to the rustic arch of Lingcove Bridge and Eskdale is seen ahead.

Without crossing the bridge, the path goes down to greet the River Esk issuing from a spectacular gorge on the right, and then continues pleasantly along to the farmstead of Brotherilkeld and the Eskdale Valley road. The village of Boot, two miles further, may be reached by the road passing thc Youth Hostel and the Woolpack Inn or, if these establishments are not of immediate interest, the village may be reached by a pleasant riverside path. Either way, the beauties of the valley will be seen and appreciated.

Eskdale with Lingcove Bridge

44 THRESHTHWAITE MOUTH, 1920′
Troutbeck – Patterdale

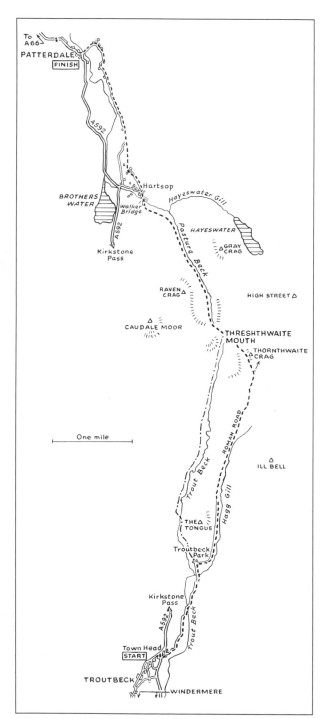

TRAVELLERS BETWEEN Troutbeck and Patterdale, whether on foot or on wheels, invariably make the journey by way of the popular A592 over the Kirkstone Pass. Walkers, however, can avoid the crowds of tourists and the hazards of the pathless tarmac by using a little-known route, roughly parallel, and proceed in blissful silence, out of sight and sound of traffic, over a pass in a wild setting between Caudale Moor and Thornthwaite Crag. This is a watershed named Threshthwaite Mouth and, although lacking the guidance of a distinct path, it is well defined by descending streams, and there need be no fear of straying.

Opposite *The view north from Threshthwaite Mouth*
Hagg Gill

THE A592 IS LEFT at Troutbeck village by a side road at Town Head that heads north along the valley floor amongst pleasant pastures and copses, and crosses the tree-fringed Trout Beck to reach its terminus at the remote farmstead of Troutbeck Park in a lovely situation at the foot of a wooded hill that appears to bar further progress. This hill is The Tongue and may be bypassed on either side, preferably on the right where a good track originated by the Romans goes upstream alongside Hagg Gill.

Hagg Gill is deeply enclosed; The Tongue rises steeply on the left and a lofty mountain range of which Ill Bell, scarred by old quarries, is the dominant height forms the skyline on the right.

At the head of this defile, the path most in use starts to rise in grassy grooves up the fellside on the right to the ridge high above. This is the line of the Roman road over High Street and is here known as Scot Rake, the reputed scene of a skirmish where the native Britons routed a band of Scottish invaders.

Troutbeck Park

Ullswater from Threshthwaite Mouth

Departing from the Roman road, the way to Threshthwaite Mouth goes forward alongside a wall until it turns away left as the declining slopes of The Tongue come down to eye level. Here the valley is again wide and the way ahead clear, although nothing better than a thin track need be expected on the final rise to the gap ahead over rough ground littered by boulders. Caudale Moor is a fine object half-left, rising in craggy tiers to a shapely summit; opposite is the steep downfall of Thornthwaite Crag, fans of scree dropping from a rim of cliffs overtopped by a tall obelisk. Trout Beck is rejoined, here in infancy, and in mist is useful as a sure pointer to the watershed at the head of the valley. This is Threshthwaite Mouth, crossed by a tumbled wall, and suddenly revealing an inspiring view to the north, a tangle of fells and a glimpse of Ullswater: a thrilling revelation.

The Tongue from Threshwaite Mouth
Raven Crag

Retrospectively, too, the view is pleasing, the Troutbeck valley being seen winding down to Windermere in the far distance and The Tongue dwarfed to insignificance by the greater heights around. It is always gratifying to look back aerially over a line of approach.

Threshthwaite Mouth is a lonely place, and in many visits I have yet to see another walker there.

The route continues over descending grassland towards a deep valley ahead and then drops more steeply to the formative waters of Pasture Beck which is followed downstream, a path forming on the left bank, along a narrow glen deeply enclosed by fellsides rimmed with crags. The path passes below the black precipice of Raven Crag, a haunt for rockclimbers, and across the beck slopes rise sharply to the long ridge of Grey Crag. A more friendly and open landscape with trees is entered as the pleasant environs of Low Hartsop are reached and the confines of the fell are left behind. Grass succeeds stones.

Pasture Beck from Walker Bridge

Below *Low Hartsop*

The path leaves Pasture Beck as it joins Hayeswater Gill in an area of former mining activity and goes on to cross the combined waters at Walker Bridge, an old one-arch span in a charming setting.

Low Hartsop is an old settlement and a few buildings preserve features that belong to the distant past. It is a living museum of seventeenth-century Lakeland. Regrettably it is now defaced by an incongruous modern car park alien to its surroundings. It is surely wrong to invite motorists to disturb this tranquil backwater; horses and carts would suit the environment better.

On tarmac again, the short lane through the hamlet joins the busy A592 coming down from the Kirkstone Pass and the illusion fades: we're back in the twentieth century. At the junction, a quiet by-road leads into Patterdale village two miles further and is greatly to be preferred to walking along the busy main road.

45 WALNA SCAR, 1990'
Coniston – Duddon Valley

FOR PEDESTRIANS, cyclists and horses the only easy passage between Coniston and the Duddon Valley is an ancient way that skirts the high mass of the Coniston Fells on their south side. This has long been known as the Walna Scar Road and in days gone by was maintained sufficiently to accommodate wheeled traffic, being much used for the conveyance of slate from the quarries alongsides. Both ends of the road are still accessible by vehicles. In its vicinity are identifiable remains of an early civilisation and, spanning the ages, this is where a local youth in 1954 took the first-ever photograph of a flying saucer (?).

It is a straightforward walk on a clear track made obvious by centuries of use, not in itself exciting but affording extensive panoramas of Coniston Water and the coastline of Morecambe Bay and over the watershed a glorious view over Duddon to the distant heights of the Scafell Range. The highlight, seen only by a short detour off-route, is provided by Dow Crag and Goat's Water, together forming one of the grandest scenes in the district.

Opposite *Sunrise: view south from the Walna Scar Road*
Right *Looking back from the summit of the Walna Scar Pass*

CONISTON IS LEFT along a tarmac road rising sharply to the site of the former railway station which, in its heyday, was the terminus of a branch line from Foxfield Junction. This rural line, provided for the benefit of visitors approaching the district from the Furness area, and for commercial freight, was a casualty of the growth of motorised traffic, the passenger service being withdrawn in 1958. Above the buildings, the road climbs steeply, enclosed by walls and hedges, for a short mile further. At this point, a quarry road serving Coniston's main source of the handsome and durable slate that has won international renown, branches to the right and is commonly used for the ascent of Coniston Old Man. The Walna Scar track goes forward, having been improved in recent years since the reopening of another quarry ahead. Still rising, a small reedy pool, Boo Tarn, is passed and the reopened quarry is seen up the fell side on the right. Deprived now of its new surface but still very distinct, the track continues along the base of the Old Man with a wide moorland gradually declining on the left: this is the desolate terrain upon which important relics of the Bronze Age were discovered. After passing through a natural rock gateway, a branch path leaves on the right, this leading across a green hollow, The Cove, to a most impressive scene. The precipitous cliffs of Dow Crag are poised high above the bouldery shore of Goat's Water; if time permits, this short detour should be made.

Coniston Old Man   *Dow Crag from Goat's Water*

The Scafell range from Walna Scar

The main track continues, crossing the primitive Cove Bridge and then rising steadily with improving views of Coniston Water and the distant coastline. A small slate shelter with very limited accommodation is passed as the ground steepens on the final rise to the highest point of the walk, a watershed between Brown Pike on the right and the long level top of Walna Scar easily attained on the left. But, on a clear day, it is the superb view ahead that compels attention.

After the austere surroundings so far, the prospect from the top of the pass is as refreshing as springtime following a hard winter. Below is the valley of the River Duddon in a wealth of lovely woodlands and the green fields and scattered farmsteads of a contented husbandry. Standing sentinel above this realm of beauty is its guardian angel, Harter Fell, sprouting conifers instead of wings, and in the blue haze of distance, overtopping all, the Scafell range and the other heights of upper Eskdale.

The descent starts at once. The huge ramifications of the disused Walna Scar Quarry appear on the left and the track becomes a walled lane; it reaches the valley road a mile north of Seathwaite and its friendly inn. This last mile is delightful. Tarn Beck, a tributary of the River Duddon and often mistaken for it, races and dances alongside, embowered in trees. The main river in this part of the valley is hidden in a spectacular gorge.

The Duddon Valley is also known as Dunnerdale, this now appearing on Ordnance maps. It is a name I don't like and have never used. The Duddon Valley seems to me a sweeter name and more appropriate to this lovely environment.

46 WHINLATTER PASS, 1043'
Braithwaite – Lorton

WHINLATTER PASS has long been the recognised way from the Vale of Keswick to the Vale of Lorton and the Loweswater area, having had a road across it since early times. A century ago it was in commission by wagonettes on a popular sightseeing tour from Keswick, later becoming used for a bus service: today it is a fast highway for all forms of wheeled traffic. It is less accommodating to walkers who cannot conveniently escape the footpaths and must have recourse to the grass verges or forest roads wherever possible. It is an easy pass with few steep gradients and is sheltered by large plantations bordering the tarmac which unfortunately conceal nearby mountains from view. The plantations on the Braithwaite side are old, being indicated on maps 150 years ago; however they have been greatly extended and are continuous for many miles to the top of the pass and beyond.

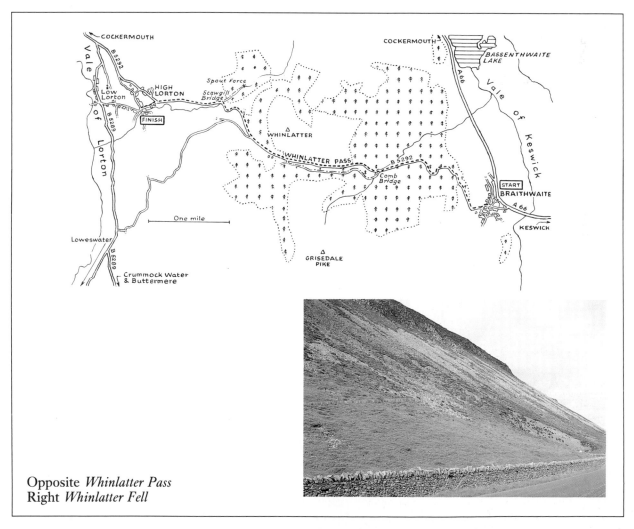

Opposite *Whinlatter Pass*
Right *Whinlatter Fell*

THE ROAD CLIMBS immediately out of Braithwaite, rising steadily with many curves, and soon becomes an avenue of trees which relent at one point to permit a lovely view of Bassenthwaite Lake and Skiddaw; this is a favourite halting place for both motorists and pedestrians.

Then follows a straight mile, passing a solitary building that was formerly an isolation hospital. Beyond, at Comb Bridge, walkers can pass into the silence of the trees on a forest road, from which branches another that runs parallel to the motor road and joins it beyond the highest part of the pass. Or the more adventurous may continue along the road from Comb Bridge and leave it to climb the heathery slopes of Whinlatter, which has escaped plantings. Walkers on this route first attain the ridge and then traverse this to the wind shelter on the summit, there enjoying a splendid view denied to those who pursue the road closely; Grisedale Pike, in particular, soars majestically from its skirt of conifers. It should be mentioned, however, that the direct descent to rejoin the road is both rough and steep.

Over the pass, there is a break in the plantations on the left and the lane branches away: this was the route adopted by the horse-drawn coaches on the Grand Tour in Victorian times. It is still, for walkers, the most direct way to the delights of Loweswater and Crummock.

The present road descends more steeply to Scawgill Bridge.

Bassenthwaite Lake

Scawgill Bridge

Spout Force

A halt should be made at Scawgill Bridge. Not long ago a peep over the parapet would have given a view of the diminutive bridge Scawgill replaced but this has now disappeared. Scawgill Bridge is the point of departure for a walk upstream to locate the handsome yet little-known waterfall of Spout Force. My first visit here entailed a desperate struggle through a new plantation, the forestry workers having completely disregarded the public footpath – a fault since remedied.

From the bridge, the road gradually descends to Lorton, a village in two parts, High and Low, which achieved a measure of fame when Wordsworth was moved to write a poem about a venerable yew he found there. Roads go south to Loweswater and Buttermere and north to Cockermouth through a lovely countryside that also deserves poems of praise.

High Lorton

47
WIND GAP, 2600'
Ennerdale – Wasdale Head

ALTHOUGH NOT CLASSED as a pass in guidebooks and not often used as such, the sharp col at the top of Windgap Cove between Pillar and Scoat Fell has all the characteristics of a true pass and indeed is one of the best defined in Lakeland. The ridge connecting the two mountains is short, a matter of yards only, and the crest is so narrow that ascent to it becomes descent from it in a few paces. The situation of the col is exceedingly grand; like an eyrie, the col overlooks a savage untamed landscape of crags and rivers of scree where solitude is absolute and silence unbroken. This is Wind Gap, attained from below only by rough and steep scrambling, and in terms of effort a poor alternative to the much easier Black Sail Pass. Wind Gap is for the adventurous and the lover of grim mountain scenery.

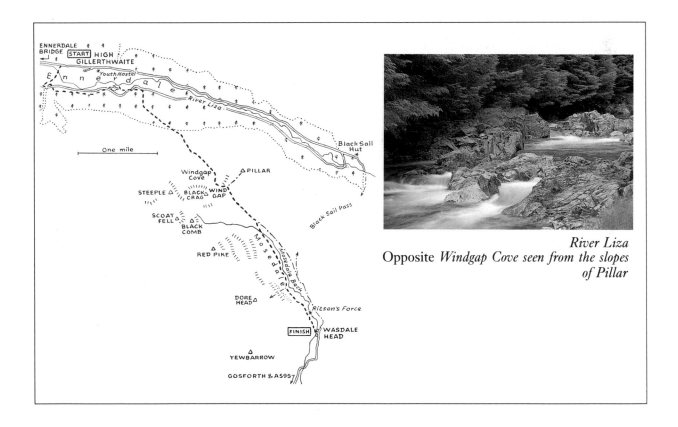

River Liza
Opposite *Windgap Cove seen from the slopes of Pillar*

APPROACHING FROM ENNERDALE, the first problem is to find a breach in the plantations to give access to the open fellside ahead, and this is provided as a footbridge over the River Liza near the Gillerthwaite Youth Hostel; this indicates a forest ride or firebreak that points the way to a stile in the upper enclosing fence. Clear of the trees, an exciting view of Windgap Cove is disclosed ahead.

Windgap Cove

Pillar rises as a ridge on the left, Steeple is the tremendous declivity on the right, and the skyline directly in front is formed by the Black Crag of Scoat Fell. Wind Gap appears as the walk proceeds into the wild hollow of Windgap Cove littered with debris fallen from the heights around. The path is sketchy but the direction obvious as altitude is gained on steepening ground and, with Steeple becoming more imposing and intimidating with every step, the col is at length attained.

The summit of Pillar can quickly be reached from this point on a rough track rising on the left and it would be a pity to miss its extensive view at the cost of so little extra effort.

The path crossing the gap continues on the other side over the top of Black Crag to Scoat Fell. Ahead is a new landscape.

The valley seen far below and continuing towards the majestic mountains encircling Wasdale Head is the best known of the many Mosedales, and the path down into it is both steep and stony; much care should be taken. A long and tedious descent ends when the valley floor is reached and Mosedale Beck is alongside, its main flow issuing from the craggy recesses of Blackem (Back Comb) Head on the right. This is a natural sanctuary where few people ever go and the starry saxifrage grows profusely among the wet rocks and in moist crevices without fear of human disturbance.

Either side of the beck may be followed down the valley, the Ordnance Survey preferring the left bank and I the right, where a narrow trod leads below the beetling crags of Red Pike and passes a large split boulder known to the climbing fraternity as the Y Boulder; this provides a short climb that experts can accomplish feet first. The path improves when joined by the scree run from Dore Head, beyond which, with the beck now tree-fringed and deserving a deviation to Ritson's Force, it descends gradually through green fields along the base of Yewbarrow to the bridge and buildings of Wasdale Head.

Mosedale

48 WINDY GAP, 2450′
Sty Head – Ennerdale

WINDY GAP IS almost a twin, even in name, to Wind Gap, having the same features: a narrow col linking two mountains reached in ascent over very rough ground, and rarely used as a pass. It is, in fact, only of use as a pass for travellers coming from the east by Sprinkling Tarn and seeking a direct course for Ennerdale or Buttermere or vice versa in which case the long descent to Wasdale Head is avoided.

Like Wind Gap, it calls for arduous efforts and rewards those who do it with scenes of mountain grandeur.

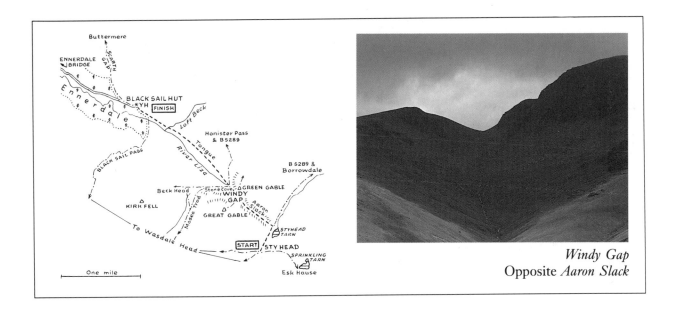

Windy Gap
Opposite *Aaron Slack*

THE FELLSIDE WEST of Styhead Tarn is cleft by a great ravine, given the name of Aaron Slack by pioneer adventurers who had a liking for biblical names. A track, often obscured by loose stones, goes up this defile, soon becoming deeply confined by the enclosing slopes that shut out all distant views. The effect is claustrophobic. Although not excessively steep, progress is slow and tedious, over tumbled stones and unremitting with no couches of greenery inviting halts. This strange cutting, between Great Gable and Green Gable, leads directly to Windy Gap.

After the arid and dusty recesses of Aaron Slack, arrival at Windy Gap is a relief; here too the awesome loneliness of the ascent is often dispelled by the sight and sound of walkers crossing the gap on a popular route to the summit of Great Gable. From this point, the top of Great Gable's summit is a tough proposition, its ascent and return to Windy Gap taking an hour, and longer if the superlative views from the top are to be studied at leisure. Apart from this tempting detour, the next stage of the journey, the descent into Ennerdale, can be prospected from the crest of Windy Gap, this valley being seen framed by Pillar and the High Stile range and identifiable by a dark covering of conifers.

[439]

Windy Gap

The descent starts unpromisingly amongst the boulders of Stone Cove without the help of a clear path, a way having to be threaded through a maze of rock debris, difficult to negotiate and needing care. Some recompense is provided as the cliffs of Green Gable come into sight, seen intimately at close range nearby. But the eyes turn quickly as the great arc of Gable Crag is fully revealed high above on the left, a formidable precipice split by intimidating gullies and cracks.

Green Gable crags   *Stone Cove*

Ennerdale from Windy Gap

The infant River Liza trickles from the desert of boulders in Stone Cove, soon becoming a defiant watercourse heading directly for Ennerdale and a perfect guide in mist. When welcome grass comes underfoot, the best stage to easy progress is provided on the right bank of the stream, where a thin track will be found on the long descending spur of Green Gable called the Tongue. This is crossed by Moses Trod on its way from Honister to Beck Head and Wasdale.

During the descent, the depression of Beck Head succeeds Gable Crag with Kirk Fell rising steeply from it. Beck Head also qualifies as a pass between Wasdale Head and Ennerdale, but few people will have used it as such since Moses made his regular journeys with his cargo of slate and whisky, the usual route from one valley to the other being the much easier and more direct crossing of Black Sail Pass.

At the foot of the Tongue, a tributary of the Liza, Loft Beck, is forded and a simple path continues forward to Black Sail Youth Hostel, passing a field of drumlins like giant molehills. At the hostel are the only beds for miles around; to find others in the valley a trip of several miles on forest roads is necessary – an anticlimax to the excitement of Windy Gap.

49 WRYNOSE PASS, 1270'
Little Langdale – Duddon Valley

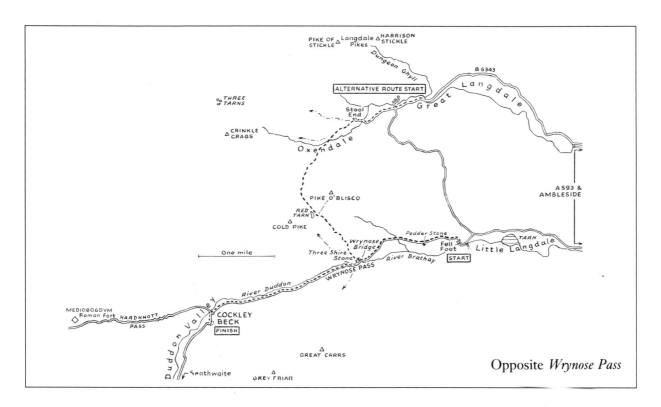

Opposite *Wrynose Pass*

WHEN THE ROMAN surveyors were planning a network of roads to link their forts in the north-west, they were faced with difficulties in finding easy passages for the movement of men and supplies in the mountainous terrain of Lakeland. Ease of passage, however, was secondary to directness of route; here, as elsewhere, a straight course from A to B was preferred. Their High Street is the best example of their fixation for directness, climbing to 2700 feet although simple but more circuitous routes were available. Another example is the road they made between their forts at Galava (Ambleside) and Glannaventa (Ravenglass). In this case, however, by placing a ruler on their maps they found that advantage could be taken of two passes through the mountain barrier. Little Langdale pointed the direction to a gap in the skyline beyond, now known as Wrynose Pass (Wrayene in twelfth-century records = path of the stallion); this was succeeded a few miles further by Hardknott Pass. From here it was an easy march to the west coast.

The Romans adopted this route and their primitive road can still be traced in parts although it is mostly overlaid by a modern surface: a narrow strip of tarmac winds unenclosed in a wild and untamed landscape and gives motorists the thrill of mountaineering without leaving their cars. During the last war, the road was requisitioned for military training and badly cut up by tanks and other heavy vehicles, but it was repaired and restored after the cessation of hostilities. It has remained narrow and unenclosed over the pass, calling for care and negotiation, in an atmosphere which, on a busy day, is charged with the expletives of frustrated motorists.

Fell Foot

THE CLIMB TO Wrynose Pass starts at Fell Foot, once an inn, at the head of Little Langdale; here the farm children used to man a gate giving access to the road beyond, but the gate and the children have long gone, as has so much of the Lakeland I knew fifty years ago. The road rises at once, giving a view of the Langdale Pikes and becoming unenclosed beyond the intake walls. A flat-topped boulder at the side of the long incline has the name of Pedder Stone, being a resting place for the pedlars who in olden days carried their wares in backpacks and found it a convenient height for taking the weight off their shoulders.

The road to Wrynose Pass

The stream coursing down the valley on the left is the Brathay, formerly a boundary between Westmorland and Lancashire. The incline halts briefly at Wrynose Bridge, crossing a tributary from Pike o' Blisco, and then continues at a steeper gradient with the Roman road in evidence alongside; it levels out towards the top.

On flat ground usually occupied by parked cars near the highest point of the pass stands a simple monolith, the Three Shire Stone, erected in 1816 to mark the meeting of three counties, Westmorland, Cumberland and Lancashire. All became Cumbria at midnight on 31 March 1974, and Lancashire lost its proud claim to own a part of the Lake District.

A path leaves here for Crinkle Crags and Pike o' Blisco and further, on the left, another path trends off for the ridge of Great Carrs and the Coniston fells.

Over the pass, the road descends sharply into the Duddon Valley below the steep slopes of Grey Friar, becoming level as the infant Duddon forms alongside on the two miles to Cockley Beck Bridge where Highland cattle may be seen grazing and the first habitation since Fell Foot is reached.

The road goes on down the valley but a branch crosses the bridge bound for Hardknott Pass. This is the way the Romans went.

The Duddon Valley   Above *The Three Shires Stone*

Wrynose Pass is not kind to pedestrians, who can only escape from the hard surface of the road and its traffic, in the absence of a footpath, by tramping along the rough verges. Nevertheless, it is a fine walk, best enjoyed in winter when all is quiet.

Walkers starting from Dungeon Ghyll in Great Langdale, however, can avoid much of the road and arrive at the summit of Wrynose by an alternative route along the Oxendale path from Stool End, climbing steeply out of this valley on a track that crosses a minor pass at Red Tarn and descends to the Three Shire Stone at the top of Wrynose Pass. This alternative route requires more effort than walking on the road but is infinitely to be preferred; the ascent to the tarn and its vicinity affords scenes of mountain splendour not seen from the road.

Red Tarn

INDEX

Bold type indicates the passes and their main entries; *italic* type indicates illustrations.